European Police and Criminal Law Co-operation

This volume in the series Swedish Studies in European Law, produced by the Swedish Network for European Legal Studies, focuses on EU criminal law and transnational police cooperation.

Against the background of the most important changes introduced by the Lisbon Treaty in the area of criminal law and police cooperation, this volume is divided into four main sections. Each section analyses some specific challenges. The first section includes a critical analysis of the boundaries of the new criminal law competencies, as well as some more general challenges for EU criminal law. Specific focus is set on the lawmaking process. The second section deals with EU criminal law and fundamental rights, in particular the protection of personal data and individual privacy. In this section, focus is on the implementation of EU law into national legal orders and the challenges that this process brings with it. The third section maps out specific challenges in transnational police cooperation, in particular, the important issue of sharing of information between law enforcement agencies and its potential impact on the protection of fundamental rights. In the fourth section, focus is shifted toward networks, horizontal agency and multi-level cooperation in a wider sense within the area of freedom, security and justice.

European Police and Criminal Law Co-operation

Swedish Studies in European Law
Volume 5

Edited by

Maria Bergström
and
Anna Jonsson Cornell

·HART·
PUBLISHING

OXFORD AND PORTLAND, OREGON
2014

Hart Publishing, 16C Worcester Place, Oxford, OX1 2JW
Telephone: +44 (0)1865 517530 Fax: +44 (0)1865 510710
Email: mail@hartpub.co.uk
Website: http://www.hartpub.co.uk

Published in North America (US and Canada) by
Hart Publishing
c/o International Specialized Book Services
920 NE 58th Avenue, Suite 300
Portland, OR 97213-3786
USA
Tel: +1 503 287 3093 or toll-free: (1) 800 944 6190
Fax: +1 503 280 8832
Email: orders@isbs.com
Website: www.isbs.com

Hart Publishing is an imprint of Bloomsbury Publishing plc.

British Library Cataloguing in Publication Data

Data Available

ISBN: 978-1-84946-350-8

Typeset by Criteria International
Printed and bound in Great Britain by
Lightning Source UK Ltd

Foreword

HANS G NILSSON, JUR DR H.C.[1]

The area of Justice and Home Affairs (JHA) has undergone almost sensational development in the past 20 years. No one, except the most Orwellian soothsayer, would have believed that in the area of criminal justice and police cooperation, sovereign states would accept that decisions were taken by qualified majority voting, accept that the European Parliament, and not national parliaments, would decide together with the Council as full co-legislator on criminal law and accept a supra-national control over interpretation, application and implementation of international instruments by the European Commission and the Court of Justice.

This development, which has taken nearly twenty years, has not been devoid of friction (this is a polite understatement for outright resistance, at least in some Member States), and has largely contributed to the *gradual* evolution of police and judicial cooperation both from an institutional perspective and from a perspective of substance.

You could speculate as to the reasons why the Member States have, finally, accepted that these changes in the institutional set up have taken place. There are probably many reasons for this; increased criminality and a necessity also for criminal justice and law enforcement to be able to move across borders, for example. Then there is the free movement of persons across borders, and also the free movement of crime with criminals using the open borders for their illicit ends. There are also events that have shaken the European Union such as the London and Madrid bombings, the Dutroux affair in Belgium and the 57 dead Chinese immigrants in a container in Dover.

The one single event that clearly contributed in a comprehensive manner to the development of police and judicial cooperation in criminal matters was no doubt the 9/11 tragedy in Washington and New York which also had a profound impact on the relationship of both the European Union and the Member States with the USA. Instruments such as the European Arrest Warrant, Eurojust, the Framework Decisions on terrorism and the setting up of Joint Investigative Teams would not have been the same without those tragic events and there would not have been any agreements on mutual legal assistance and extradition at all without 9/11.

[1] The opinions expressed are the author's own, and not necessarily those of the Council of the EU, which is the Institution for which he works.

The Treaty of Maastricht, which entered into force on 1.11.1993, incorporated the JHA area into the remit of the European Union for the first time. Police and judicial cooperation in criminal matters were matters of 'common interest' and the Commission was not even allowed to take initiatives in the area. The European Parliament was 'consulted' and immediately forgotten. The Court of Justice had no powers unless the adopted instrument (in some cases a Protocol to a Convention that had not been ratified) expressly gave that power. Intergovernmental cooperation used the Community institutions and took decisions by unanimity by adopting instruments that had an uncertain legal value. Only Member States could take initiatives.

The Treaty of Amsterdam, which entered into force on 1.5.1999, was the beginning of a revolution that lasted ten years. Suddenly the JHA had an objective – the creation of a high level of safety in an Area of Freedom, Security and Justice (AFSJ) – and the new instruments, Decisions and Framework Decisions, were binding according to the Treaty, although they did not have direct effect (the Court of Justice later clarified in its landmark judgment in the Maria Pupino case that they had 'indirect effect' – there was an obligation for national judicial and other authorities to interpret national legislation in conformity with adopted Framework Decisions and the principle of loyal/sincere cooperation also applied in the former Third Pillar). The Commission gained the right of initiative but the Member States still retained theirs. In fact, more than half of the initiatives in police and judicial cooperation during Amsterdam were taken by Member States. The European Parliament was again only consulted, and the Court of Justice could only be seised if the Member States had accepted preliminary references. At the end of Amsterdam, 18 Member States had done so. The Commission had enforcement powers in relation to conventions (but never used them) but not in relation to Framework Decisions or Decisions.

The Nice Treaty did not change much of the institutional structure, but inserted Eurojust and the European Judicial Network in the Treaty in spite of the fact that these bodies already existed, or at least their establishment had been agreed on. The setting up of Eurojust had already been decided by the Tampere European Council and the EJN was set up by a Joint Action in 1998.

The Lisbon Treaty, which entered into force on 1.12.2009, was a second-generation revolution for police and judicial cooperation in JHA. It is still too early to be able to have a complete overview of all its potential, but the changes have been radical. After a transitional period ending on 1 December 2014, the Commission and the Court of Justice will have full powers of enforcement in relation to adopted Framework Decisions, and this may even come about earlier if a Framework Decision or a Decision is amended by only one paragraph. The Member States can now only take initiatives if 25% of them (currently 7) join forces and the European Parliament has now in most cases become a full co-legislator in the so-called ordinary legislative procedure. The EU will now be able to use Directives and Regulations (mostly for instruments on mutual recognition) and this will have the potential to revolutionise the JHA area even further if you accept that the case law relating to the direct effect of Directives will also be applicable in this area. There is nothing in previous case law or preparatory documentation that says that this will not happen; it is rather the contrary.

This has been counterbalanced by an increased right of scrutiny by national parliaments, both as regards their scrutiny over the principle of subsidiarity and their involvement, for instance, in Europol and Eurojust under the Treaty. At the same time, transparency has further been increased in relation to public deliberations in the Council and access to documents held by the bodies and agencies of the European Union.

This development shows that the policy area of police and judicial cooperation has become an important policy-making area for the European Union that cannot be neglected. It is in addition one of the areas where citizens are immediately concerned as shown by numerous Eurobarometer polls. Its sensitiveness makes it also vulnerable in that it includes the habitual tension of every lawmaker in the field: the quest for efficiency while at all times safeguarding fundamental rights. The new technologies, Facebook and Google, DNA exchange and possibilities to use databases make it possible for law enforcement to work more efficiently but also to infringe the right to privacy of individuals more readily.

It is against this background that you can state that a book like the present one comes at the right moment. Already nearly three years after the entry into force of the Lisbon Treaty a discussion has begun on the necessity for the EU to develop its own criminal policy and stop with the piecemeal approach that has characterised the area before. The new possibilities offered by the Lisbon Treaty, as noted in the Stockholm Programme, should be used to their full potential. At the same time the Lisbon Treaty will also pose challenges as there will be limits on the powers that have been conferred on the European institutions by the Member States. The entire AFSJ is now an area of shared competence between the EU and the Member States.

A key element in the possible development in the future will be the impact of the Charter, where it appears that already more than 30 requests for preliminary rulings on the interpretation of the Charter have been made to the Court of Justice. The inclusion of data protection in the Charter and the new legal basis provided under Article 16 TFEU will no doubt have an impact in the future, where the Commission already has proposed a legislative package with a general data protection Regulation and a Directive on police and judicial cooperation.

Another important area of development may in the future be mutual recognition where the EU has already adopted a Directive on a European Protection Order and negotiations are underway with regard to a European Investigation Order, where no doubt sensitive issues like proportionality and fundamental rights protection will be raised. In the current political climate, where you may ask whether the necessary mutual trust exists, this will become a Litmus test in the negotiations between the Council and the European Parliament.

At the same time, police cooperation needs to be developed further. Europol has been turned into a fully-fledged European Agency with a EU funded budget of € 85 Million. The Member States are getting increasingly used to cooperating with the agency (finally after nearly twenty years of existence), and the Internal Security Committee COSI finds its ways in the Council of the EU with a view to taking strategic operational perspectives. At the same time, Eurojust is being assessed through the practical and operational impact it has made in the Member States in the sixth round of mutual peer evaluations, and this will no doubt have an impact when it comes to new legislative initiatives in the area, including the setting up of a European Public Prosecutors Office.

All these topics and many more are dealt with in this book, edited by Maria Bergström and Anna Jonsson Cornell. They are both congratulated for their unflagging effort in bringing together so many knowledgeable scholars who will no doubt shed light on this complex and sensitive area for the reader and the citizen.

Preface

MARIA BERGSTRÖM AND ANNA JONSSON CORNELL

This edited volume has been made possible with the generous support and funding from the Swedish Network for European Legal Studies and the Faculty of Law at Uppsala University. Several of the chapters in this volume were presented at the conference 'Interests and Actors in European Police and Criminal Justice Cooperation: Legal and Practical Challenges' hosted by the Swedish Network for European Legal Studies in collaboration with the Faculty of Law at Uppsala University in Uppsala April 18–19, 2011. The main purpose of the conference was to bring together practitioners and researchers to discuss recent developments concerning European Police and Criminal Justice Cooperation within the Area of Freedom, Security and Justice, and to identify challenges and opportunities as a result of the Lisbon Treaty entering into force. At the conference some of the most prominent actors in Sweden in this field, inter alia the Swedish General Prosecutor Anders Perklev, gave key speeches. These speeches are published in Uppsala Faculty of Law Working Paper Series 2011:6c.

The editors would like to extend their great appreciation and gratefulness to Eddie Exelin and Louise Ratford who have assisted in the editing process. We would also like to thank Professor Antonina Bakardjieva Engelbrekt, chair of the Swedish Network for European Legal Studies, for her support and patience throughout this process.

Table of Contents

Journal Abbreviations

AJIL (Am J Int'l L)	American Journal of International Law
Brit Y B Int'l L	British Year Book of International Law
Cal W Int'l LJ	California Western International Law Journal
CML Rev	Common Market Law Review
EPA	European Policy Analysis, Published by the Swedish Institute for European Policy Studies (SIEPS)
ERA Forum	ERA Forum, Published by the Academy of European Law (ERA)
EuConst	European Constitutional Law Review
Eur J Crime Cr L Cr J	European Journal of Crime, Criminal Law and Criminal Justice
ICLQ	International & Comparative Law Quarterly
Int Law: Rev Colomb Derecho Int	International Law: Revista Colombiana de Derecho Internacional
RIDP	International Review of Penal Law, *Revue internationale de droit penal*
SvJT	Svensk Juristtidning
Wash U L Rev	Washington University Law Review
YEL	Yearbook of European Law
ZIS	Zeitschrift für Internationale Strafrechtsdogmatik

Table of Cases

European Court of Justice

European Commission of Human Rights

European Court of Human Rights

International Court of Justice

International Criminal Tribunal for Rwanda

International Criminal Tribunal for the former Yugoslavia

National Courts

Germany

Greece

Ireland

Romania

Sweden

United States

Table Legislation

European Union

Treaties, Agreements, Charters and Conventions

Regulations

National

International

1
Introduction

MARIA BERGSTRÖM AND ANNA JONSSON CORNELL

EU criminal law and police cooperation is one of the fastest growing areas of EU law, and the evolution of the European Union into an Area of Freedom, Security and Justice (AFSJ) has been one of the most far-reaching constitutional developments in the EU. EU legislative action in the field poses significant challenges to the legal orders of the Member States and is one of the most contested fields of EU action. There are two main reasons for this: First, the development of EU criminal law has a significant impact on the protection of fundamental rights and the relationship between the individual and the state. Second, the development of EU criminal law poses challenges to state sovereignty and the relationship between the EU and its Member States.[1] There is thus a necessity for further legal analysis of this rapidly evolving field,[2] both from a constitutional law perspective, and a more general EU law perspective.[3]

The same is true for European police cooperation and its regulatory framework. Transnational police cooperation in general and European police cooperation in particular pose challenges to our understanding of traditional concepts such as national sovereignty, and national security and order. Upholding national security, protecting law and order, and guaranteeing the safety and rights of its citizens are some of the core tasks of the state. Thus, the delegation of legislative powers, the development of common strategies and operational measures, and the creation of EU bodies within the field should be considered an enormous and complicated, although sometimes necessary, step to take. The increase of transnational police cooperation and the regulation thereof can be subscribed to two developments: the political decision to establish an

[1] V Mitsilegas, *EU Criminal Law* (Oxford, Hart Publishing, 2009).

[2] Important volumes include C Eckes and T Konstadinides (eds) *Crime within the Area of Freedom, Security and Justice – A New Public Order* (Cambridge, Cambridge University Press, 2011), E Herlin-Karnell, *The Constitutional Dimension of European Criminal Law* (Oxford, Hart Publishing, 2012), A Klip (ed) *Substantive Criminal Law of the European Union* (Antwerpen, Maklu, 2011), V Mitsilegas, *EU Criminal Law* (Oxford, Hart Publishing, 2009) and S Peers, *EU Justice and Home Affairs Law*, 3rd edn (Oxford, Oxford University Press, 2011).

[3] These perspectives were also analysed by M Bergström, 'EU som lagstiftare inom straffrätten och reglerna mot penningtvätt' (2011) *Svensk Juristtidning* 357.

AFSJ within the European Union, which brings with it the erosion of internal borders, and the increase of transnational crime globally. The EU regulation of police cooperation entered a new phase subsequent to the entry into force of the Lisbon Treaty in December 2009, which will be further elaborated below.

The most recent and substantial developments leading up to the changes introduced by the Lisbon Treaty, as well as the changes themselves, can be analysed from a number of different perspectives. The focus chosen in this volume is the broader European constitutional law perspective, albeit supplemented with a more general EU law perspective. Moreover, national constitutional law aspects are important for an analysis of the overall impact of recent developments on constitutional law. Hence, this perspective is also discussed in the various chapters with examples from Sweden and the Nordic countries. Although intertwined, any legal analysis of the changes must include all three perspectives in order to explain the dynamic evolution of the policy areas studied in this volume. The EU- and national constitutional law perspectives will thereby embrace the major constitutional changes introduced by the Lisbon Treaty, where the focus is on changes in competence between the EU Institutions on the one hand, and between the EU and its Member States on the other. In order to gain a proper understanding of these changes, a brief overview of the evolution of European police and criminal law cooperation will follow.

1. THE EVOLUTION OF EUROPEAN POLICE AND CRIMINAL LAW COOPERATION

1.1 The Early Days

In 1993, the Maastricht Treaty introduced the provisions on police and judicial cooperation in criminal matters. Thus, the development of the area of Justice and Home Affairs (JHA) dates back some twenty years now, and as Hans G Nilsson points out in his foreword to this volume, this development has been sensational. Nevertheless, EU police and criminal law cooperation predates the Maastricht Treaty albeit at a more intergovernmental level outside the then existing European Community's legal framework. At that point in time focus was on the exchange of information and best practice in certain specific fields. The 1967 Naples Convention on cooperation and mutual assistance between customs administrations provided the first framework for exchanges between Member States.[4] Thereafter, from the mid-seventies onwards, informal arrangements for sharing and exchanging information and expertise were established dealing with immigration, asylum, and police and judicial

[4] Later replaced by Naples II, Council Act 98/C 24/01 of 18 December 1997 drawing up, on the basis of Article K3 of the Treaty on European Union, the Convention on mutual assistance and cooperation between customs administrations, OJ 1998, C 24/1.

cooperation.[5] The setting up of networks to facilitate contact between Member States was important and working parties like the TREVI Group on terrorism, radicalism, extremism and political violence were set up and their scope extended at a later stage to also cover illegal immigration and organised crime.[6]

With the Single European Act in 1986, the internal market and the free movement of persons demanded compensatory measures such as anti-money laundering (AML) regulations, the strengthening of external border controls and the definition of European asylum and immigration policies. However, since progress on the free movement of persons and on cooperation in the field of justice and home affairs failed to appear within the then existing Community framework, the Schengen Agreement was concluded by France, Germany and the Benelux countries in 1985, and an implementing convention was signed in 1990.[7] Although still outside the Community framework, the aim was to abolish internal border checks, improve control at external borders and to harmonise certain provisions on visas, asylum, and police and judicial cooperation.

This intergovernmental approach led to problems of coordination where different groups deliberated separately and reported to different groups of ministers.[8] Hence, the Maastricht Treaty introduced provisions on police and judicial cooperation in criminal matters in Title VI of the Treaty on European Union. The areas covered were asylum policy, external border controls, immigration, combating drug addiction and international fraud, judicial cooperation in civil and criminal matters, customs and police cooperation. Three types of legal instruments were introduced which all required unanimity in the Council. The Court of Justice had only limited jurisdiction, and was only permitted to interpret legal instruments and resolve disputes between Member States when expressly provided for in the adopted instrument. The Commission's right of initiative was limited and shared with the Member States. The role of the European Parliament was limited to the right of being consulted by the Council, and thereby often informed only after the event.[9]

[5] See further, E Baker and C Harding, 'From Past Imperfect to Future Perfect? A Longitudinal Study of the Third Pillar' (2009) 34 *European Law Review* 25. One of their main arguments is that 'police and judicial cooperation in criminal matters' is in fact not a new policy area but that the cooperation between the Member States dates back several decades.

[6] The TREVI group set up in 1975 to counter terrorism and to coordinate policing in the EC. It was an intergovernmental network of national officials structured on three levels. See further above n 5 at 28; T Bunyan, 'Trevi, Europol and the European State' in *Statewatching the New Europe: A Handbook on the European State* (Statewatch, 1993), available at http://www.statewatch.org/news/handbook-trevi.pdf; and HG Nilsson, 'The Justice and Home Affairs Council' in M Westake and D Galloway (eds) *The Council of the European Union* (London, John Harper Publishing, 2004).

[7] The Schengen acquis – Convention implementing the Schengen Agreement of 14 June 1985 between the Governments of the States of the Benelux Economic Union, the Federal Republic of Germany and the French Republic on the gradual abolition of checks at their common borders, OJ 2000, L 239/19.

[8] Summaries of legislation, previously available http://europa.eu.int/scadplus/leg/en/lvb/l33022.htm.

[9] As Hans G Nilsson puts it in the foreword to this volume: 'The European Parliament was "consulted" and immediately forgotten.'

1.2 Introducing an Area of Freedom, Security and Justice

The Area of Freedom, Security and Justice (AFSJ) was introduced and defined with the Amsterdam Treaty in 1999. The measures concerning external border controls, asylum, immigration and judicial cooperation in civil matters were moved to the first pillar and thereby 'communitarised', whereas police and judicial cooperation still fell under the third pillar. EU measures used under the third pillar were common positions, framework decisions, decisions and conventions. Framework decisions resembled directives under the first pillar but had explicitly no direct effect.[10] The Schengen Agreement was included in Union cooperation through an implementing convention.[11] The UK, Ireland and Denmark were allowed to opt out of certain measures under the AFSJ through a protocol to the Amsterdam Treaty. However, the UK and Ireland were later allowed to participate in certain Schengen provisions according to Council Decisions in 2000 and 2001.[12] The Amsterdam Treaty also introduced formal rules of closer cooperation into the Treaty thus allowing certain Member States to work together more intensively within the framework of the Treaties. Thereby these Member States could make use of the institutions, procedures and mechanisms provided in the Treaties. Closer cooperation had to be established by the Council through a qualified majority vote at the request of the Member States following a Commission opinion and the transmission of the request to the European Parliament.[13] The conditions governing closer cooperation between police forces and judicial authorities on crime and the related procedures were derived from the relevant articles in the treaties.[14] The European Parliament was still only consulted and the Court of Justice only had jurisdiction if the Member States had accepted preliminary references. As pointed out by Hans G Nilsson in his foreword, 18 had done so by the end of Amsterdam.

Some smaller adjustments were made by the Nice Treaty in 2003. Eurojust and the European Judicial Network (EJN) were brought into the Treaty on European Union.[15] A Commission proposal for a European Public Prosecutor

[10] This is the only time the term 'direct effect' has made it into the Treaty (Article 34 Union Treaty/Treaty on European Union).

[11] The Schengen acquis – Convention implementing the Schengen Agreement of 14 June 1985 between the Governments of the States of the Benelux Economic Union, the Federal Republic of Germany and the French Republic on the gradual abolition of checks at their common borders, OJ 2000, L 239/19.

[12] See further M Fletcher (2009) 'Schengen, the European Court of Justice and Flexibility Under the Lisbon Treaty: Balancing the United Kingdom's "Ins" and "Outs"' 5 *European Constitutional Law Review* 71.

[13] See further Article 11 EC Treaty/Treaty on establishing the European Community and Articles 40 and 43 Treaty on European Union.

[14] Article 11 of the EC Treaty/Treaty establishing the European Community, read in conjunction with Articles 40, 43, 44 and 45 of the Treaty on European Union.

[15] Article 31 of the Treaty on European Union. As pointed out by Hans G Nilsson, the setting up of Eurojust was decided by the Tampere Council and the European Judicial Network was set up by a Joint Action in 1998.

did not, however, make its way into the Treaty.[16] Co-decision eventually became the rule for most of the subject matters that were previously brought under the first pillar by the Amsterdam Treaty.[17] The Nice Treaty further developed the provisions on closer cooperation.[18] The Council and the Commission were responsible for ensuring the coherence of actions undertaken but they were no longer required to inform the European Parliament.[19]

1.3 Political Priorities Embracing Freedom and Security

In July 1998 the European Commission published a Communication on the AFSJ setting out the basis, form and main objectives.[20] The main political priorities were subsequently determined at consecutive meetings of the European Council and set down in a number of different documents. In 1999, the Cologne European Council decided to draw up a Charter of Fundamental Rights of the European Union (the Charter) by December 2000. Closer instructions on how to draw up the Charter were approved at the Tampere European Council in 1999, which was devoted to the creation of an AFSJ.[21] Although legally binding as of the entry into force of the Lisbon Treaty in 2009, the Presidents of the European Parliament, the Council and the Commission signed and proclaimed the Charter on behalf of the three institutions already during the Nice intergovernmental meeting.[22] Moreover, the Tampere European Council adopted the Tampere Programme, which was the first multiannual programme to set priorities for an AFSJ.

In the post-Cold War era, the fight against non-military threats such as drug trafficking, organised crime and terrorism has become a top political priority globally. While referring to some basic connotations from international relations theory, contemporary security studies and the notion of securitisation, it can be argued that the securitisation of transnational

[16] According to Article 86 TFEU, there is now a possibility to establish a European Public Prosecutor's office 'from Eurojust' through a unanimous decision in the Council after the European Parliament has given its consent.

[17] Title IV of the EC Treaty on visas, asylum and immigration.

[18] Article 43 of the Treaty on European Union on enhanced cooperation consolidated all the relevant conditions, which were previously divided between Article 11 of the Treaty on establishing the European Community and the former Article 43 of the Treaty on European Union on closer cooperation.

[19] Compare Article 45 of the Treaty on European Union (Nice) on enhanced cooperation and former Article 45 of the Treaty on European Union (Amsterdam) on closer cooperation. See further M Bergström, 'What happened/is happening with the constitutional crisis in the EU?' in *Swedish Institute for European Policy Studies,* 2006:6.

[20] Communication from the Commission, Towards an Area of Freedom, Security and Justice, COM(1998) 459 final.

[21] Tampere European Council 15 and 16 October 1999 Presidency Conclusions, the site of the European Parliament, available at http://www.europarl.europa.eu/summits/tam_en.htm.

[22] The Charter of Fundamental Rights of the European Union, the Charter site of the European Parliament, available at http://www.europarl.europa.eu/charter/default_en.htm.

organised crime and terrorism financing has been used to increase, or has at least led to an increase in EU competencies. This is most evident in the area of EU criminal law and police cooperation, where the handling of organised, serious crime and terrorism, arguably has been used to securitise single issues as well as entire policy areas.[23] Most notably, the terrorist attacks of 11th September 2001 accelerated the decision-making process in the European Union. At the extraordinary JHA Council on 20th September 2001, and the extraordinary meeting of the European Council on 21st September 2001, the Member States undertook to take decisive action against increasingly transnational organised crime and terrorism. For example, intensified AML regulations are the result of the securitisation of transnational criminality, and more recently, securitisation of terrorism as such. Both these threats demand action at the global, as well as the EU and regional levels. AML and financial freezing measures thereby exemplify the shift towards securitisation of threats to the financial sector in general.[24]

Subsequently, the prevalence of the security rationale was directly reflected in the nature and priorities structuring the second multiannual programme on an AFSJ – The Hague Programme adopted by the Dutch presidency in November 2004.[25] The Hague Programme gave preference to the security of the Union and its member states, and

> understood the EU's AFSJ as primarily driven by security (urgency-led) considerations and concerns. The Hague Programme also invented the metaphor of a 'balance' between freedom and security, calling for the need to strike the right balance between law enforcement purposes and safeguarding the fundamental rights of individuals. Overall, the political elements of the EU's AFSJ agenda have been vulnerable to political demands for more 'security cooperation' within and outside Europe, perhaps without paying due consideration to the effects on and ethical implications of these very security policies for the liberal democratic principles, fundamental rights and liberties at the heart of the EU.[26]

The 2004 Hague Programme was the successor of the 1999 Tampere Programme and was followed by the Stockholm Programme in 2009. In contrast to its predecessor, the Stockholm Programme did not speak of a 'balance' to be struck between liberty and security. With the Stockholm Programme – An open

[23] M Bergström, 'The Place of Sanctions in the EU System for Combating the Financing of Terrorism' in I Cameron (ed) *EU Sanctions: Law and Policy Issues Concerning Restrictive Measures* (Cambridge, Intersentia, 2013).

[24] Ibid. See also K Svedberg Helgesson and U Mörth (eds) *Securitization, Accountability and Risk Management – Transforming the Public Security Domain* (London, Routledge, 2012).

[25] Communication from the Commission to the Council and the European Parliament of 10 May 2005 – The Hague Programme: ten priorities for the next five years. The Partnership for European renewal in the field of Freedom, Security and Justice COM(2005) 184 final.

[26] E Guild and S Carrera, 'The European Union's Area of Freedom, Security and Justice Ten Years on' in E Guild, S Carrera and A Eggenschwiler (eds), *The Area of Freedom, Security and Justice Ten Years on Successes and Future Challenges under the Stockholm Programme* (The Centre for European Policy Studies (CEPS), 2010) 10.

and secure Europe serving and protecting citizens,[27] focus was shifted towards the interests and needs of the citizens. According to the European Council, the challenge was to 'ensure respect for fundamental rights and freedoms and integrity of the person while guaranteeing security in Europe.' Thus, it was 'of paramount importance that law enforcement measures, on the one hand, and measures to safeguard individual rights, the rule of law and international protection rules, on the other, go hand in hand in the same direction and are mutually reinforced'.[28] The Stockholm Programme was adopted in December 2009 during the Swedish Presidency and coincided with the entry into force of the Lisbon Treaty.

After briefly touching upon the historical development of EU criminal law and European police cooperation in order to place current policies in a wider historical context, the developments towards transforming EU criminal and police cooperation into a policy area of its own, will now be discussed.

2. THE STRUCTURE OF THE LISBON TREATY

According to Article 3(2) TEU: 'The Union shall offer its citizens an area of freedom, security and justice without internal frontiers, in which the free movement of persons is ensured in conjunction with appropriate measures with respect to external border controls, asylum, immigration and the prevention and combating of crime.' Article 67(3) TFEU further states that the Union shall 'endeavour to ensure a high level of security through measures to prevent and combat crime, racism and xenophobia, and through measures for coordination and cooperation between police and judicial authorities and other competent authorities, as well as through the mutual recognition of judgements in criminal matters and, if necessary, through the approximation of criminal laws.' After the changes made by the Lisbon Treaty in 2009, the provisions on EU criminal law and police cooperation can be found in Part three, Title V of the TFEU, an Area of Freedom, Security and Justice. The more general provisions can be found in Chapter 1, whereas the provisions on judicial cooperation in criminal matters are found in Chapter 4, and the provisions on Police cooperation are inserted in Chapter 5. These provisions are again brought together with the provisions on policies on border checks, asylum and immigration that can now be found in Chapter 2. Finally, the provisions on judicial cooperation in civil matters have a chapter of their own under the same Title (Chapter 3). Thus interestingly, the overarching principle of mutual recognition of judgments and judicial decisions can be found both in Chapter 3 and Chapter 4 thereby emphasising its importance in both civil and criminal law matters.

[27] The Stockholm Programme – an open and secure Europe serving and protecting citizens, OJ 2010, C 115/1.

[28] Ibid at 4.

3. CHANGES AND CHALLENGES

The main changes introduced by the Lisbon Treaty relevant to EU criminal law and police cooperation concerns the introduction of a competence catalogue in Articles 2 to 6 TFEU, where Article 4(2) states that the Union shall share competence with the Member States in the Area of Freedom, Security and Justice (j). Further, the Lisbon Treaty's introduction of new legislative power within this field with reference to the ordinary legislative procedure (Article 294 TFEU) for provisions on judicial cooperation in criminal matters are of great importance thereby involving the European Parliament to its full legislative power. The Member States have lost their veto due to the introduction of qualified majority voting in the Council. The compensation available through Articles 82(3) and 83(3) TFEU for a Member State to raise an issue affecting fundamental aspects of its criminal justice system in the European Council is in contrast a mere possibility without much limiting effect. In practice this simplified procedure towards enhanced cooperation (Articles 82(3) and 83(3) TFEU) may well have a triggering effect rather than becoming a breaking mechanism. Interesting in this respect, are also the various possibilities of opting out that have so far been used with diverse effects.[29]

This law-making competence is still shared with the Member States and the principle of subsidiarity needs to be respected. National parliaments have a Treaty-specific competence and a duty to review EU legislative proposals and their compatibility with the principle of subsidiarity within this field, Article 5(3) TEU. According to Article 12 TEU, national parliaments are supposed to contribute actively to the good functioning of the European Union, shall be informed by the Union institutions, and draft Union legislative acts shall be forwarded to them in accordance with the Protocol on the role of national parliaments in the European Union.[30] The national parliaments thereby conduct a subsidiarity control.[31]

The national parliaments also participate in the evaluation mechanism for the implementation of the policies within the AFSJ in accordance with Articles 12 TEU and 70 TFEU. Finally, national parliaments are involved in the political monitoring of Europol and the evaluation of Eurojust's activities together with the European Parliament in accordance with Articles 88 and 85 TFEU. This is of increasing importance since these bodies have been granted more powers after Lisbon. The main purpose of Europol and Eurojust is to facilitate mutual aid and cooperation. Europol's main mission is to assist and strengthen the national police authorities of the Member States in preventing serious crime affecting

[29] Opt outs by the UK, Ireland and Denmark. Protocols 21 and 22.

[30] Protocol 1 on the Role of National Parliaments in the European Union.

[31] This new mechanism has been used eg by the Swedish Parliament, Riksdagen. See further, CF Bergström, 'Subsidiaritetsprövningen: Riksdagen hittar en ny roll i EU:s lagstiftningsprocess' (2010) *ERT* s 423, and A Jonsson, 'EU:s lagstiftningsprocess och subsidiaritetsprövningen: Nya möjligheter för nationellt inflytande?' (2011) 4 *SvJT* 413–429.

two or more Member States, terrorism, and crime which affects a common interest covered by a Union policy (Article 88 TFEU). Europol can, for example, participate in joint criminal investigations, collect data and provide analysis on transnational crime, and request national law enforcement agencies to open a criminal investigation.[32] The task of Eurojust is to support and reinforce coordination and cooperation between national investigating and prosecuting authorities in relation to serious crime affecting two or more Member States or requiring a prosecution on a common platform, on the basis of operations conducted and information supplied by the Member States' authorities and by Europol (Article 85 TFEU).[33] The role of national parliaments as well as the European Parliament is thereby of utmost importance, although due to the limited space, not analysed further in this volume.

It was only with the entry into force of the Lisbon Treaty on 1 December 2009, that it was possible to speak about EU Criminal Law and EU police co-operation as a policy area of its own. For the first time, the EU was provided with a criminal law competence to legislate, not only as a form of compensation when other policy areas were being developed which is a typical feature of EU law exemplified by Maria Bergström in this volume, but as a policy area in its own right. The EU has now been granted some, although still limited, competence to decide on definitions of criminal offences and sanctions in the area of particularly serious crime with a cross-border dimension (Article 83(1) TFEU). The EU may further adopt directives with minimum rules with regard to the definition of criminal offences and sanctions if deemed essential to ensure the effective implementation of a Union policy in an area which has been subject to harmonising measures (Article 83(2) TFEU).

The fact that the CJEU has almost full jurisdiction within this field further strengthens the notion of a policy field of its own. There is no limit concerning preliminary references. Instead, the CJEU shall act with the minimum of delay when a preliminary reference is raised in a case concerning a person in custody (Article 267(4) TFEU).[34] Only a few narrow limits remain concerning the CJEU's jurisdiction, which is in stark contrast to the pre-Lisbon situation. In relation to the AFSJ and more specifically Chapters 4 and 5 on judicial cooperation in criminal matters and police cooperation, the court has no jurisdiction to review the validity or proportionality of operations carried out by the police and other law enforcement services of a Member State, or the exercise of the responsibilities incumbent upon Member States with regard

[32] The European Parliament and the Council may now adopt regulations determining Europol's tasks, including collecting, storing, processing, analysing and exchanging information (Article 88 TFEU).

[33] The European Parliament and the Council may now adopt regulations determining, Eurojust's tasks, including initiating criminal investigations and proposing the initiation of prosecutions by national authorities (Article 85 TFEU).

[34] See also the rules on expedited and urgent preliminary ruling procedure, Title III, Chapter 2 and 3 respectively of the Rules of Procedure of the European Court of Justice, OJ 2012, L 265/1.

to the maintenance of law and order and the safeguarding of internal security (Article 276 TFEU). Anna Jonsson Cornell will further elaborate on these aspects in her contribution to this volume. These very specific limitations in the CJEU's jurisdiction are to some degree compensated for by the Commission's general possibility to use its infringement procedure within the entire area, at least as from 1 December 2014 when all remaining Framework Decisions will be given full legal effect and the Commission and the CJEU will have full powers of enforcement.[35]

The area of police cooperation in the EU has been constitutionalized in the sense that important questions of inter alia competences, legal basis and legislative processes are dealt with in for example Title V, Chapter five TEU. Historically, international regulations on transnational police cooperation have focused on facilitating cooperation as well as the sharing of information. This was also the case in the EU pre-Lisbon, which both the Treaties and secondary legislation such as the Framework Decision on Joint Investigation Teams are testimony to. However, ambitions are now more far-reaching and include legislative measures adopted through both the ordinary and special legislative procedure (depending on whether the measure is non-operational or operational) concerning, for example, the collection, storing, analysis and sharing of data, training and exchange of personnel and techniques, and finally the creation of common investigative techniques. This, together with the existence of EU agencies such as Europol and Eurojust, changes the preconditions for police cooperation in the EU. Moreover, from a strategy point of view it will be interesting to see what changes COSI can bring with it and the impact EU strategies will have on national strategies. This issue will be further discussed by Anna Jonsson Cornell in Chapter 8. Several of the chapters in this book deal with important aspects of this overall development. As will be shown, there are still several challenges that have to be met. Some of these are subscribed to the continuing fragmentation of the regulative framework, large discrepancies between national legislation, differences in how law enforcement bodies are organized nationally, and finally the will and ability of national law enforcement bodies to play a constructive part in EU police cooperation.

When a constitutional law perspective is adopted it usually leads to the emphases of state power per se, the distribution and control thereof, and the protection of the individuals and their fundamental rights. Constitutional safeguards, including the protection of fundamental rights, take a central role in the analysis of the legislative framework and the challenges that the implementation of the AFSJ is likely to bring. However, the constitutional law perspective needs to be put in relation to other principles guiding the exercise of state power, be it by the Member States at large, the EU or individual Member States. In contrast to the constitutional law perspective which is focusing on limiting competences, ensuring control, upholding safeguards and requirements

[35] Protocol 36 on Transitional Provisions, Article 10.

of due process; an EU integrationist perspective is introduced. The development within the AFSJ is subsequently analysed also from an EU integrationist perspective emphasising notions such as effectiveness, integration, legal effect and harmonisation. By highlighting both the constitutional law and the EU integrationist perspective more nuanced conclusions embracing the EU law development of constitutional principles and rights protected by the ECHR and the Charter including due process rights and the wider reference to the rule of law can be reached.

4. OUTLINE

Against the background of the most important changes introduced by the Lisbon Treaty in the area of criminal law and police cooperation, this volume is divided into four main sections. Each section analyses some specific challenges.

The *first section* includes a critical analysis of the boundaries of the new criminal law competencies, as well as some more general challenges for EU criminal law. Specific focus is set on the lawmaking process. In Chapter 2, Ester Herlin-Karnell charts recent case law by the CJEU in the field of European criminal law and the AFSJ more broadly. This chapter addresses the question of the extent to which this case law has changed the EU's course of navigation in EU criminal law – or if the compass is still the same – and the legal impact of the entry into force of the Lisbon Treaty in this area. Herlin-Karnell further investigates some recent legislative initiatives introduced by the EU institutions, particularly with regard to the EU's security agenda. In doing so, this chapter considers which EU institutions, if any, are the main drivers in EU criminal law. Moreover, the chapter considers to what extent the Member States are themselves responsible for reinforcing integration in the AFSJ. The chapter concludes by offering a general outlook of the prospect of EU criminal law.

In Chapter 3, Anna Wetter reviews the legislative procedure that led to the adoption of Directive 2009/52/EC that provides for minimum standards on sanctions and measures against employers of illegally staying third-country nationals. The Directive was adopted before the Lisbon Treaty entered into force and provided the EU with an explicit legal basis to adopt criminal sanctions. Prior to the adoption of the Lisbon Treaty it was still uncertain whether the EU could adopt criminal sanctions under the then Community pillar, and some Member States disputed the legal basis that was chosen for the Directive which makes it a particularly interesting case study. A broader purpose of the chapter is to shed light on how general EU law principles and guidelines were taken into account during the legislative procedure. The chapter also looks beyond the Lisbon Treaty and discusses whether the new provisions suffice to encounter the argued democratic deficit that permeated the former Treaty in the area of criminal law.

In Chapter 4, Petter Asp focuses on the explicit criminal law competences the EU was provided with through the Lisbon Treaty. Article 82 TFEU (on mutual recognition and criminal procedural harmonisation), Article 83 TFEU (on harmonisation of substantive criminal law), Article 86 (on the European Public Prosecutor) and Article 325 (on the protection of the financial interests of the union) are particularly important. According to Asp, these new competences – as well as the transformation of criminal law cooperation from a 'third pillar issue' to one area of cooperation among others – show that we are heading towards something that can be described as EU criminal law. This chapter focuses on the challenges that we are facing in this process.

The *second section* deals with EU criminal law and fundamental rights, in particular the protection of personal data and individual privacy. In this section, focus is on the implementation of EU law into national legal orders and the challenges that this process brings with it. This section embraces Chapters 5, 6 and 7 which each provide an analysis of a specific issue and the general challenge of combining EU criminal law development with a high level of fundamental rights protection. In particular the harmonisation of data retention in the European Union through the Data Retention Directive (2006/24/EC) has been controversial. Chapter 5 by Theodore Konstadinides delves into the constitutional and human rights implications arising out of the retention of traffic data for the purpose of law enforcement. First, the chapter provides a critical account of the main challenges met by Member States during the transposition of the Data Retention Directive, which is of particular interest in Sweden due to the difficulties met when transposing the directive. Second, the chapter discusses the basis of justification of EU data retention legislation vis-à-vis the interference by a public authority with a person's right to privacy under the ECHR and the Charter. The analysis conducted leads to the conclusion that blanket harmonisation of the length of time that telecom operators and internet providers must retain data has proven to be superfluous for the investigation and prosecution of serious crime. It is argued that both the Directive's uneven implementation in the Member States as well as the Commission's delayed evaluation report fail to prove that the strict criteria for justifying non-consensual, blanket and indiscriminate retention and therefore interference with a person's right to privacy have been met. Equally, this chapter concludes that the smooth functioning of the internal market and maintenance of internal security should not compromise the fundamental right to privacy and the rule of law – ie the values on which the EU is founded.

In Chapter 6, Alexandros Ioannis Kargopoulos describes and analyses the ne bis in idem principle established in EU law. This chapter contains a short introduction of the ne bis in idem principle including a presentation of the main legal texts where it is enshrined. The introduction is followed by the ratio legis of the European ne bis in idem, with due consideration of the principle of mutual recognition with which ne bis in idem has been associated by the CJEU. Next, focus is shifted to the actual interpretation and implementation of the principle in the case law of the CJEU: the scope of the application of the principle is analysed, followed by a thorough analysis of the 'idem' element and subsequently the 'bis' element. Thereafter, focus is again shifted to the application of the ne bis in idem in cases of concurring crimes arising out of the same material acts where only one or some have been assessed by the first court, the lis pedens etc. The most important of these is the issue touched upon in recent judgements (C-489/10 *Bonda*, C-617/10 *Åkerberg Fransson*) that concern the application of the ne bis in idem in other than criminal proceedings. The chapter further considers the case law of the ECtHR in the light of the 'conformity' clause, Article 52(3) of the Charter, which obliges the CJEU to interpret any corresponding rights in line with Strasbourg jurisprudence. Finally, the chapter concludes with a short epilogue on the function of the ne bis in idem in the integration process.

In Chapter 7, Per Ole Träskman analyses the European Arrest Warrant (EAW) and its implementation in three of the Nordic countries in the light of the Nordic Arrest Warrant (NAW) that was introduced through a Convention in 2005. Träskman analyses the new legislation that has been passed in Denmark, Finland and Sweden as result of the EAW and the NAW. The intention of this chapter is to follow up the development of both the EAW and the NAW in order to establish their impact in the Nordic countries. Träskman notes, inter alia, that the EAW has quickly become an important and frequently used measure, which the authorities hail as a significant part of a modern and efficient European crime prevention scheme. Träskman also concludes that there is no Nordic cooperation and coordination as the implementation of the EAW into national law and that this potentially is detrimental to the longstanding history of Nordic cooperation within criminal law. Viewed from the legal rights perspective, the implementation of the EAW can be seen as just one more sign of the ongoing shift in the EU towards a new paradigmatic model for adjudication and criminal proceedings.

The *third section* maps out specific challenges in EU police cooperation, in particular, the important issue of the sharing of information between law enforcement agencies and its potential impact on the protection of fundamental rights. In Chapter 8, Anna Jonsson Cornell provides a constitutional analysis of the development of EU police cooperation after the entry into force of the Lisbon Treaty. She describes the Lisbon provisions on police cooperation with their focus on competence issues, the legislative process, different types of control of police cooperation, and definitions which focus on operative and non-operative police cooperation. She also provides an analysis of different challenges concerning the sharing of police information, in particular in relation to the problems with defining operational and non-operational police cooperation, as well as the unclear boundaries between police cooperation on the one hand and criminal law cooperation on the other.

The particular issues concerning the sharing of police data are followed up in Chapter 9 by Iain Cameron, who outlines the European legislative framework regulating the collecting and sharing of information. He argues that the need for effective police cooperation between EU states requires a degree of EU regulation of these national systems with regard to the storing and sharing of intelligence. The existing, and future, EU regulations involve both an application of the mutual recognition principle as well as a degree of harmonization. This takes into account and builds on the variety of 'soft' standards of data protection produced within the Council of Europe, particularly the standards emerging as a result of the case law of the European Court of Human Rights (ECtHR). This Chapter aims to give an overview of these standards. Previously, the transfer of police data was for a given purpose; a specific criminal investigation, a specific intelligence gathering exercise etc. However, at least in the future, the transfer of data between police forces in Member States is expected to be much more extensive and more 'routine', even automated. When players act together in a network, securing accountability for the individual actions of each player can become much more difficult. Cameron analyses this particular issue from the perspective of ECtHR case law.

In the *fourth and final section*, focus is shifted toward networks, horizontal agency and multi-level cooperation within the AFSJ. The specific challenges arising when players act together in networks is further analysed in Chapter 10 by Bo Wennström who thus widens the perspective towards multi-agency cooperation. As a starting point, he notes that fighting crime is a concern for several players at different levels – from the local to the international level, while nation states are still modelled around vertical thinking. This 'new order' has been caused by an internal diffusion of power due to privatisation and deregulation, and by globalisation. The need for multi-agency cooperation is evident and the call for horizontal cooperation has become a co-occurring phenomenon in every debate on government, governance and public service. Especially in the field of security and fighting crime, the call for horizontal cooperation is now ever-present. Wennström argues that a kind of naïve 'horizontal ideology' exists, which presupposes that what is done in the name of horizontal collaboration is always good in itself, because it is done with a good purpose in mind: to increase safety and reduce violence. But multi-agency cooperation creates complex hierarchies in which the players tend to demonstrate a high degree of independence. The aim of this chapter is to offer a broader understanding of horizontal agency cooperation in the field of crime and security. A special focus will be on the shift from cooperation to coordination in the AFSJ in EU.

Finally, Chapter 11, by Maria Bergström connects some of the themes in this volume by contrasting and emphasising a two-dimensional analysis of the multi-level cooperation previously discussed. First, drawing on the constitutional analysis presented in this introductory chapter including the main changes introduced by the Lisbon Treaty and their broader constitutional implications that holds together several of the issues discussed in the previous chapters. Second, the EU law perspective is eventually added, where focus is on the development of EU criminal law in context, including both a broader historical and integration perspective. As a result she will be able to draw some general conclusions about the constitutional developments of EU law in general and EU criminal law in particular.

5. CONCLUSIONS

The most recent and substantial developments leading up to the changes introduced by the Lisbon Treaty as well as the changes themselves, can be analysed from a number of different perspectives. The focus chosen in this volume is a broader European constitutional law perspective that is supplemented by a more general EU law perspective,[36] as well as some national constitutional law aspects with particular examples from Sweden and the Nordic countries. Although intertwined, any legal analysis of the changes must include all three perspectives, at least to some extent, in order to explain the dynamic evolution of the policy area.

So far, mainly a broader European constitutional law perspective, and some national constitutional law aspects have been discussed in the various chapters. The European constitutional law perspective embraces the major constitutional changes introduced by the Lisbon Treaty, where focus is on changes in competence between the EU Institutions, and between the EU and its Member States. The role of national parliaments as well as the European Parliament is of utmost importance. However, due to the limited space, this is not subject to further analysis in this volume. Since a constitutional law perspective emphasises state power, and the distribution and control of such power, the protection of individuals and fundamental rights are also of utmost importance. Constitutional safeguards, the protection of fundamental rights and due process take a central role. But also other principles, under which the state power must act, be it the Member States at large, the EU, individual Member States or agents for these interests, have been discussed and analysed further.

In stark contrast to such a restraining perspective where focus is on limiting competence, ensuring control, upholding safeguards and requirements of due process; an EU integrationist perspective is introduced as a contradistinction and further challenge. Underlying and reinforcing these differences, which of course do not exist to this exaggerated extent, the development is viewed wearing EU integrationist spectacles emphasising notions such as effectiveness, integration, legal effect and harmonisation. Well aware of the artificial separation such a constructed division entails, the idea is to emphasise these differences to form a common base for the analysis as well as some more nuanced conclusions embracing also the EU law development of constitutional principles and rights protected by the ECHR and the Charter of Fundamental Rights of the European Union including due process rights and the rule of law. The contributions to this volume show in a multifaceted way the challenges that the EU and its Member States are facing when it comes to defining and implementing policies of relevance for establishing an Area of Freedom, Security and Justice.

[36] These perspectives were also analysed in M Bergström, 'EU som lagstiftare inom straffrätten och reglerna mot penningtvätt' (2011) 4 *SvJT* 357.

The range of questions dealt with is wide; starting with the widened competence for the EU within the area of criminal law and police cooperation, dealing with issues of accountability, control, rights and efficiency, and ending with a discussion on new ways of cooperation and the challenges that they pose. It has become clear that the developments within this particular area, from the EU's point of view, increasingly are considered a harmonization project. Herlin-Karnell interprets this development as an attempt to create a 'common European sense of fairness' when it comes to recent developments within the area of procedural law, especially procedural rights of suspects and accused. This in combination with the development of substantive law of relevance for the protection of victims' rights is symptomatic for the overall trend within the EU to also include the protection of individual rights. Thus, the EU has moved from focusing solely on cooperation between law enforcement agencies and judicial bodies in order to convict criminals and fight serious crime and terrorism, to also include procedural and substantive rights of both criminals and victims. As a result of both developments, the degree of harmonization between Member States is likely to increase, a development which arises high emotions and provokes critical analyses of the competence and role to be played by the EU within the area of criminal law and police cooperation.

A common feature of almost all contributions to this book is that they high light the role of the nation state as the holder of the exclusive right to use violence and force against individuals within its jurisdiction. Certainly, the very fact that the EU does have regulatory powers of direct relevance for national criminal policy and law, and the powers and modus operandi of national law enforcement agencies, does challenge our perceptions of sovereignty, democratic accountability and control, legitimacy, popular rule and representativity. Moreover, new actors such as private organizations and companies have entered the area of criminal law and police cooperation. These actors also have access to the decision making process at the EU level and hence can steer the development in directions that benefit their interests. This adds to the important question of how accountability can be exercised in systems of multilevel governance. Who is, and can be held responsible in complex systems? Or to put it bluntly, who can actually be found, charged and punished, for what and by whom at what level? Nevertheless, the development embraces so much more. Besides harmonisation and implementation, cooperation and mutual assistance are still key concept.

To sum up, EU criminal law and police cooperation is one of the fastest growing areas of EU law, and the evolution of the Union into an Area of Freedom, Security and Justice arguable has been one of the most far-reaching constitutional developments in the Union. Above all, this volume has sought to identify and address some of the Union's main challenges in this respect, where a balance has to be found between state power, Union competence, meaningful cooperation, and the common values that the cooperation builds upon, including the protection of individuals and fundamental rights. Thus, hoping to improve the dynamic evolution of EU criminal law and police cooperation, some of these underlying challenges have been identified, discussed and analysed at the current stage of this process. Accordingly, the aim of this contribution is to take part also in this wider challenge.

Part I

EU Criminal Law

2

Recent Developments in the Field of Substantive and Procedural EU Criminal Law – Challenges and Opportunities

ESTER HERLIN-KARNELL*

1. INTRODUCTION

This short introductory chapter charts recent developments in the field of EU criminal law and more broadly the area of freedom, security and justice (AFSJ). The chapter addresses the question of the extent to which the course of navigation of EU criminal law has changed by considering recent developments in EU criminal law. The chapter looks at the recent Communication issued by the Commission and argues that this Communication, 'Towards an EU Criminal Policy: Ensuring the effective implementation of EU policies through criminal law', offers an example of a more nuanced approach in the EU institutions towards the EU criminal law project.[1] Therefore, the intention is to use it as a starting point, or benchmark, for discussing recent initiatives in this area and the extent to which these initiatives live up to the Commission's promise of more consistency in its approach to criminal law. Consequently this chapter investigates recent legislative initiatives as proposed by the EU institutions by focusing on developments within both substantive and procedural criminal law. In doing so, the chapter discusses recent initiatives in the area of procedural safeguards in criminal law, and substantive criminal law in the area of market abuse and proceeds of crime. The chapter concludes by offering a general outlook of the prospect of EU criminal law.

The chapter begins by briefly outlining the main changes in criminal law introduced by the Lisbon Treaty including the implications of the Stockholm

* Senior in EU Law, VU University of Amsterdam and Co-Director of the VU Centre for European Legal Studies. This chapter was completed in July 2012 and updated in February 2013.

[1] Com(2011) 573 final.

Programme.[2] Hence the chapter charts recent case law in the area of EU criminal law and also looks at recent legislative initiatives in this area. The chapter concludes with a note on the future impact of the EU Charter of Fundamental Rights (the Charter) with regard to criminal law and the AFSJ project.

2. SETTING THE SCENE: EU CRIMINAL LAW A CONSTITUTIONAL CONSTRUCTION SITE

Today it seems natural to speak about EU criminal law as a subject as good as any other EU law topic.[3] The Lisbon Treaty reshuffled the constitutional setting for how to understand EU criminal law by abolishing the Third Pillar. A great deal has been written about this constitutionalization process, and the present chapter will therefore not spend time covering the development of EU criminal law.[4]

In the Lisbon Treaty, the crucial provisions for criminal law are Articles 82 TFEU (procedural criminal law) and 83 TFEU (substantive criminal law). These provisions need, however, to be read in the light of Chapter I of Title V of TFEU, which sets out the general goals to be achieved in this area. More specifically, Article 67 TFEU stipulates, inter alia, that the Union shall constitute an area of freedom, security and justice (AFSJ) with respect for fundamental rights and the different legal systems and traditions of the Member States. So the project of EU criminal law is part of the bigger venture of establishing an AFSJ.

Apart from the abolition of the Third Pillar and also the specific EU competences with regard to criminal law, there are several important novelties that need to be considered. For example, the emergency brakes provisions (where Member States can pull a brake if the proposed legislation is sensitive to the national legal criminal law system) as well as the notion of expedited procedures for persons in custody. Article 267 TFEU provides that if a question is raised in a case pending before a court or tribunal in a Member State with regard to a person in custody, the Court of Justice of the European Union shall act with a minimum of delay. This is obviously an extremely important change and reflects the debate on speedier justice in Europe.[5] However, despite the reformation of the Court of Justice's jurisdiction introduced by the Lisbon Treaty, the Court of Justice does still not have the power to review the validity or proportionality of operations carried out by the police or other law enforcement agencies of

[2] The Stockholm Programme – An open and secure Europe serving and protecting the citizen (OJ C115/1, 02.12.2009).

[3] See eg E Herlin-Karnell, 'What Principles Drive (or Should Drive) European Criminal Law?' (2010) 11 *German Law Journal* 671 and V Mitsilegas, *EU Criminal Law* (Oxford, Hart Publishing, 2009).

[4] Eg V Mitsilegas, 'The Transformation of Criminal Law in the Area of Freedom, Security and Justice' (2007) 26 *YEL* 1 and E Herlin-Karnell, *The Constitutional Dimension of European Criminal Law* (Oxford, Hart Publishing, 2012) ch 2.

[5] The procedure is governed by Article 23a of the Protocol on the Statute of the Court of Justice and Article 104b of its Rules of Procedure.

a Member State, or the exercise of responsibilities incumbent upon Member States with regard to the maintenance of law and order and the safeguarding of internal security (Article 276 TFEU).

Regardless of the changes in EU Law introduced by the Lisbon Treaty there are, however, several unresolved issues concerning the exact implications of these amendments. For example, the full effect of the Court of Justice's jurisdiction in this field is unclear. After all, the Lisbon Treaty Protocol on Transitional Provisions provides a five-year transition period before the existing Third Pillar instruments are, treated in the same way as Community instruments.[6] Therefore, the precise impact of the Court's jurisdiction within the field of EU criminal law remains to be seen.

In addition, it should be noted that we have not seen the 'famous' emergency brake in use yet. Indeed, one of the most interesting, albeit very 'technical', innovations of the Lisbon Treaty is the emergency brake provision. More specifically, both Articles 82(2) and 83(1) and (2) provide in their respective paragraph 3 for the possibility of applying an emergency brake if the law in question would affect fundamental aspects of a Member State's criminal justice system. More specifically, if such an emergency brake scenario arises, a Member State may request that the measure be referred to the European Council. In that case, the ordinary legislative procedure is suspended, and after discussion and 'in case of a consensus, the European Council shall, within four months of this suspension, refer the draft back to the Council, which shall terminate the suspension of the ordinary legislative procedure'. So far, as noted, there has been no such emergency brake procedure in action. The present author would, however, not be surprised if Sweden were one of the first states to pull it, given that this Member State has traditionally been very sceptical with regard to criminal law and EU involvement.[7] Sweden has thus for a long time subscribed to a very Nordic approach to criminal law, which is perhaps distinguished from

[6] Article 10 of this Protocol stipulates that:

1. As a transitional measure, and with respect to acts of the Union in the field of police cooperation and judicial cooperation in criminal matters which have been adopted before the entry into force of the Treaty of Lisbon, the powers of the institutions shall be the following the date of entry into force of that Treaty: the powers of the Commission under Article 258 of the Treaty on the Functioning of the European Union shall not be applicable and the powers of the Court of Justice of the European Union under Title VI of the Treaty on European Union, in the version in force before the entry into force of the Treaty of Lisbon, shall remain the same, including where they have been accepted under Article 35(2) of the said Treaty on European Union.

2. The amendment of an act referred to in paragraph 1 shall entail the applicability of the powers of the institutions referred to in that paragraph as set out in the Treaties with respect to the amended act for those Member States to which that amended act shall apply.

3. In any case, the transitional measure mentioned in paragraph 1 shall cease to have effect five years after the date of entry into force of the Treaty of Lisbon.

[7] In other areas such as the implementation of the Third Money Laundering Directive, Sweden has been extremely cautious to the project of criminal law in the EU. See E Herlin-Karnell, *The Constitutional Dimension of European Criminal Law* (Oxford, Hart publishing, 2012) Ch 6. On Sweden see also M Bergstrom, 'EU Anti-money Laundering Regulation: Multilevel Cooperation of Public and Private Actors' in C Eckes & T Konstadinides (eds) *Crime within the Area of Freedom, Security and Justice* (Cambridge, Cambridge University Press, 2011) 97.

the rest of Europe in that it has represented a more lenient approach to levels of punishment and retribution.[8]

Certainly, much of EU criminal law cooperation has been characterized by a rushed approach to legislation in the aftermath of 9/11. The EU criminal law project is now steadily evolving into a more mature system. As will be discussed in further detail below, the Charter has an important role to play here. With respect to criminal law, Articles 47–50 of the Charter could have a huge influence as they guide the Union's action in this area and draw up an overarching theoretical framework. Most importantly, Article 49 provides for the guarantee of legality and proportionality in a more extensive way than the European Convention on Human Rights (ECHR). Also, Article 47 of the Charter guarantees the right to a fair trial, while Article 48 stipulates the presumption of innocence and the right of defence. The latter provision also makes it clear that the severity of penalties must not be disproportionate to the criminal offence. This is actually a more extensive guarantee than the ECHR framework (and its promise via Article 6 ECHR – of a fair trial – as the only guarantee of proportionality).

The EU's presence on the criminal law scene has been a turbulent one for a long time. As mentioned above, the notion of EU criminal law was considerably speeded up with the events of 9/11. In this ten-year period ending with the entry into force of the Lisbon Treaty at the end of 2009, the phenomenon of EU criminal law has been transferred to the supranational level. Much of the EU's focus in this area has been centred on security.[9] The Communication on EU Counter-Terrorism Policy offers an example of such a focus on security.[10] This Communication is to be read in conjunction with a Commission staff working paper, 'Taking stock of EU Counter-Terrorism Measures'[11] and the Stockholm Programme. The Commission staff working paper includes a table with concrete achievements and future challenges to be achieved by focussing on four prestigious words, 'prevent, protect, pursue and respond'. This Communication points at the success of current instruments, such as the European Arrest Warrant and the Third Money Laundering Directive to name a few examples.[12]

With the Commission's recent Communication for a coherent criminal law system there is perhaps reason to believe that the future will offer a move away from a 'security' focussed approach. Whatever the answer to the question asked the recent Communication is an example of a more sophisticated approach to

[8] See eg K Nuotio, 'The Rationale of the Nordic Penal Policy Compared with the European Approach' in K Nuotio (ed) In Honour of Ramio Lahti, Festschrift (University of Helsinki, 2007) 157, P-O Träskman, 'Strafflagen för Europeiska Unionen – fakta och fiction' (2002) 4 *Svensk juristtidning* 345.

[9] See eg C Murphy, *EU Counter Terrorism Law* (Oxford, Hart Publishing, 2012) 224.

[10] COM (2010) 386 final The EU Counter-Terrorism Policy: main achievements and future challenges. See also COM (2011) 790 final, First report on the implementation of the EU internal security strategy.

[11] SEC (2010) 911 final.

[12] Framework Decision, [2002] OJ L 190/1, on the European Arrest Warrant and the Third Money Laundering Directive 2005/60/EC OJ L309 against money laundering and terrorist financing.

the EU criminal law project. There is still a strong focus on effectiveness concerns but the general tone is more nuanced.

3. THE COMMISSION'S VISION FOR A COHERENT AND CONSISTENT EU CRIMINAL POLICY: A WELCOME IMPROVEMENT

The Commission's recent Communication 'Towards an EU Criminal Policy: Ensuring the effective implementation of EU policies through criminal law' is particularly interesting as it offers a concrete example of a nuanced debate in the EU institutions in the sphere of EU criminal law.[13] This Communication explicitly mentions not only the need to develop a coherent system of EU criminal law policy, but also highlights the concerns of EU citizens. Part of the justification for this Communication is, therefore, the added value of EU criminal law, in line with the wishes of the EU citizens. Indeed, the latest Eurobarometer[14] places the fight against crime high in the EU list of what the citizens want the EU to tackle effectively. As such, it was ranked fourth after concerns about fixing the debt crises, immigration policy and health policy.[15]

The Communication states that while EU criminal law measures can play an important role as a complement to the national criminal law systems, it is clear that criminal law reflects the basic values, customs and choices of any given society. For this reason, the Commission emphasizes that it is particularly important to ensure that EU legislation on criminal law, in order to have a real added value, is consistent and coherent. The question is, however, what does this actually mean? After all, if consistent and coherent are always taken to mean 'more EU legislation' then the added value of the Communication is less impressive if the EU also wishes to recognize diversity as promised in the Communication. In any case, the Commission concludes by stating that there should be a common understanding of the guiding principles underlying EU criminal law legislation, such as the interpretation of basic legal concepts used in EU criminal law; and how criminal law sanctions can provide most added value at the EU level. If this is seriously embraced in practice, it is undoubtedly a very welcome development.

The next section of this chapter will briefly outline some recent developments with regard to procedural and substantive criminal law and discuss the extent to which these initiatives live up to the consistency requirement as promised in the Commission's Communication.

[13] COM (2011) 573 final, Towards an EU Criminal Policy: Ensuring the effective implementation of EU policies through criminal law.

[14] Eurobarometer 75, spring 2011 available at http://ec.europa.eu/public_opinion/archives/eb/eb75/eb75_en.htm (last accessed 1 October 2011).

[15] See E Herlin-Karnell, 'Is the Citizen Driving the EU's Criminal Law Agenda?' in Spaventa & Nic Shuibhne (eds) *Empowerment and Disempowerment of the European Citizen* (Oxford, Hart publishing, 2012) ch 9.

4. RECENT LEGISLATIVE INITIATIVES: PROCEDURAL AND SUBSTANTIVE LAW

The aforementioned Stockholm Programme drew up the guidelines for EU action in criminal law.[16] It was drafted in the run up to the Lisbon Treaty changes and reflects the need to read the Stockholm Programme in the light of these changes. In short, the Stockholm Programme defines strategic guidelines for legislative and operational planning in the area of freedom, security and justice in accordance with Article 68 TFEU. According to the Stockholm Programme, all action taken in the future should be centred on the citizen of the Union and other persons for whom the Union has a responsibility. One of the main priorities of the Stockholm Programme was therefore to create a web of procedural protection at the EU level in cross-border proceedings.

The roadmap for strengthening procedural rights of suspected or accused persons in criminal proceedings forms part of this ambition.[17] The roadmap focuses on certain areas of particular importance and follows the guidelines set out in Article 82 TFEU, which empowers the EU to legislate, inter alia, on the rights of individuals in criminal proceedings and the rights of victims. The areas in question are:

- Translation and interpretation
- Information on rights and information about the charges
- Legal aid and legal advice
- Communication with relatives, employers, and consular authorities
- Special safeguards for suspected or accused persons who are vulnerable.

Moreover, as part of this roadmap, the European Parliament and the Council adopted a Directive on the right to interpretation and translation in criminal proceedings.[18] But it is regrettable that in relation to the measures contained in the Roadmap elaborated by the Stockholm Programme as well as in the Directive, there is no clarification regarding the precise procedural stage at which they should be guaranteed.[19] Moreover, it seems unclear how much the EU framework really differs from existing ECHR case law. ECHR case law means that the right to a fair hearing applies also to pre-trial scenarios.[20] Of course as is so often pointed out, the Member States of the EU are no 'saints' but most of them continue to have cases pending in front of the ECtHR and that it is therefore good to have as much

[16] The Stockholm Programme – An open and secure Europe serving and protecting the citizen (OJ C115/1, 02.12.2009).

[17] Resolution of the Council 30 November 2009, OJ C 295 (2009), see eg M Jimeno-Bulnes, 'The EU roadmap for Strengthening Procedural Rights of Suspected or Accused Persons in Criminal Proceedings' (2009) 4 *Eucrim* 159.

[18] Directive 2010/64/EU OJ L 280 (2010) p 1, for a comment S Cras and L de Matteis, 'The Directive on the Right to Interpretation and Translation in Criminal Proceedings' (2010) 4 *Eucrim* (2010) 153.

[19] S Allegrezza, 'Critical remarks on the Green Paper on Obtaining Evidence in Criminal Matters' (2010) *ZIS* 569.

[20] Ibid.

protection stipulated as possible. At a more sophisticated level, it could, however, be argued that the most important aspect is to create a common European sense of fairness which genuinely cares for the individual. Part of this mission involves pinning down what the shared values of the EU actually are. Article 2 TEU states that the EU respects values founded on human rights, but it is somewhat unclear on what it means in the context of procedural safeguards in criminal law.[21]

Below I will try to discuss certain areas where legislative action appears to be moving particularly fast.

4.1 Directive for Procedural Rights in Criminal Law

The EU is currently very active in the field of procedural protection, which is a welcome development and a result of the extended competences granted by the Lisbon Treaty. The first step in this process is Directive 2010/64EU on the right to interpretation and translation, which has already entered into force (though the implementation deadline is in 2013).[22] A more recent legislative initiative is the Directive on the right to information in criminal proceedings.[23] And the third step is the proposal for a Directive on the right of access to a lawyer in criminal proceedings and on the right to communicate upon arrest.[24] Arguably, the proposed Directive on access to a lawyer is the most far-reaching of any piece of EU criminal law legislation in procedural criminal law thus far.[25] These initiatives follow the Roadmap for the strengthening of procedural rights of suspects and accused persons in criminal law proceedings appended to the Stockholm Programme as discussed above. These instruments aim to promote mutual trust in cross-border cases and represent an example of the EU's emphasis on the procedural rights side of the coin instead of (as previously) having mostly focused on the question of enforcement of coercive measures. The proposed instruments are based on Article 82 (2) in order to facilitate mutual recognition in criminal matters.

In line with the mandate set out in the Roadmap for the strengthening of procedural rights, this Directive lays down minimum requirements at EU level governing the rights of suspected and accused persons and their right to have access to a lawyer. It thus promotes the application of the Charter, and in particular Articles 6, 47 and 48 therein, by building upon Article 6 ECHR and the notion of a fair trial.[26] Interestingly, the Directive points out that 'Any

[21] See also the discussion in Herlin-Karnell (n 14).

[22] Directive 2010/64EU, OJ L 280 of 26.10.2010.

[23] Directive 2012/13/EU, OJ L 142 of 1.6.2012.

[24] Proposal for a Directive on the right of access to a lawyer in criminal proceedings and on the right to communicate upon arrest COM (2001) 326.

[25] See the discussion in House of Lords, 30th Report, The European Union's policy on criminal procedure, 30th report session 2010–2012.

[26] On the notion of a fair trial see eg I Cameron, *An Introduction to the European Convention on Human Rights* (Iustus, Uppsala, 2011) and A Ashworth, Ben Emmerson and Alison Macdonald, *Human Rights and Criminal Justice* (Thomson Sweet & Maxwell, 2007).

derogation must be justified by compelling reasons pertaining to the urgent need to avert danger for the life or physical integrity of one or more people'. In addition, any derogation must comply with the principle of proportionality, which implies that the competent authority must always choose the alternative that least restricts the right of access to a lawyer and must limit the duration of the restriction as much as possible. Furthermore, the proposed Directive states that in accordance with ECtHR case law, no derogation may be based exclusively on the type or seriousness of the offence and any decision to derogate requires a case-by-case assessment by the competent authority. It should be mentioned that also the Charter of Fundamental Rights grants exceptions to the rule of absolute fundamental rights protection.

It is to be hoped that this is how the derogation granted in Article 52 of the Charter of Fundamental Rights is to be interpreted in the future as well. According to this provision, Member States can derogate from Charter obligations on the basis of what is proportionate. Therefore, in criminal law it seems rather obvious that what is needed here is a strict application of proportionality.

However, regarding the proposal for access to a lawyer, and regardless of whether it actually adds much to ECtHR case law, where Article 6 ECHR grants such rights, the UK has decided not to opt into this instrument. The UK considers the proposal as too intrusive with regard to national criminal law.[27] More specifically, in view of the UK stance, the requirement of access to a lawyer at such an early stage could potentially hamper the need to prevent further criminality since it would prevent suspects from providing information at the earliest stage possible. As pointed out by the House of Lords inquiry, this would require a lawyer to be present before a house could be searched for drugs or firearms.[28]

4.2 Protection of the Victim

A welcome development, and as emphasized in the Stockholm Programme, is the need for an adequate European regime for the protection of the individual. It is worth recalling that according to the Stockholm Programme agenda, the main focus of the Union's action in the coming years will be 'advancing a people's Europe', ensuring that citizens can exercise their rights and fully benefit from European integration.[29] Part of this plan is to visualize the victims of crimes instead of only focusing on the offender. The Commission states that a criminal justice strategy, fully respecting subsidiarity and coherence, should guide the EU's policy for the approximation of substantive and procedural criminal law. It

[27] House of Lords, 30th Report, The European Union's policy on criminal procedure, 30th report session 2010–2012.

[28] Ibid at 32.

[29] Commission, 'Delivering an Area of Freedom, Security and Justice for Europe's Citizens Action Plan Implementing the Stockholm Programme' COM (2010) 171 (Communication).

should be pursued in close cooperation with the European Parliament, national parliaments and the Council, and acknowledge that focus will remain primarily on mutual recognition while the harmonization of offences and sanctions will be pursued for selected cases.

The latest step in the direction of establishing a European framework for the protection of the victim is the proposed Directive on the protection of the victim.[30] This proposal aims to ensure that the wide ranging needs of victims of crime, which cut across a number of other EU policies, are respected and met. In particular, the protection of victims' rights is an essential part of a range of EU policies and/or instruments related to human trafficking, sexual abuse and the sexual exploitation of children, violence against women, terrorism, organized crime, and the enforcement of road traffic offences. As pointed out by Fichera, the protection of the victim is, however, far from new on the European stage.[31] It has been on the agenda of the Council of Europe, the Commission and the Parliament since the 1970s. But until recently, until the entry into force of the Lisbon Treaty, there was no legislative competence at the supranational level in this area. Instead the EU produced a Framework Decision partly dealing with the issue.[32] However, the Framework Decision for the protection of victims applies only to witnesses or parties to the process. With regard to the implementation aspect it has furthermore been pointed out that it left too much discretion to the Member States and that it was therefore difficult to assess the exact implications of this Framework Decision.[33] The Stockholm Programme sought to remedy this by linking the need for the protection of the victim with the general wave of increased participation of the citizens. The current 'weak' status of the victim in EU law is perhaps confirmed by the recent cases of *Gueye* and *Criminal proceedings against* X concerning the interpretation of Framework Decision 2001/220/JHA on the protection of the victim.[34] In these cases the Court of Justice stated that not only did this Framework Decision leave a large margin of appreciation to the Member States in their implementation but also that the Framework Decision does not impose any obligation on Member States to ensure that victims will be treated in a manner equivalent to that of a party to proceedings. Thus, the proposed Directive on the protection of the victim would represent an important symbolic gesture of the EU on the global criminal justice stage.

In any case, in its Communication 'Towards an EU Criminal Policy: ensuring the effective implementation of EU policies through criminal law' the Commission emphasizes that a criminal justice strategy, fully respecting subsidiarity and coherence, should guide the EU's policy for the approximation

[30] Proposal for Directive on establishing minimum standards on the rights, support and protection of victims of crime, Com (2011) 275 final.

[31] M Fichera, 'The Status of the Victim in European Union Criminal Law' (2011) 2 *Eucrim*.

[32] Framework Decision 2001/220/JHA on the standing of victims.

[33] Ibid.

[34] Case C-483/09 and C-1/10 *Gueye and Sanchez* judgment of 15 September 2011 nyr and Case C507/10 *criminal proceedings against X* judgment of 21 December 2011 nyr.

of substantive and procedural criminal law. With this promise in mind, the next section aims to look at recent developments within the substantive field of crime and legislation.

4.3 Market Abuse and Proceeds of Crime

Market abuse and insider dealing has been a hot topic in EU law for a long time. The Commission's recent proposal for a Directive on market manipulation is the first attempted use of Article 83 (2) TFEU.[35] As noted above, Article 83 (1) TFEU sets out a list of crimes in respect of which the EU shall have legislative competence such as terrorism, organized crime, and money laundering. It also states that the Council may identify other possible areas of crime that meet the cross-border and seriousness criteria. However, interestingly, Article 83(2) establishes that the possibility exists for approximation if a measure proves essential towards ensuring the effective implementation of a Union policy in an area that has already been subject to harmonization measures. So Article 83 (2) TFEU is interesting as it provides for a more extensive competence than what you may think at first glance. Although Lisbon provides for fairly strictly drafted provisions on criminal law competence, it has equally resulted in slippery provisions that would allow legislation 'when necessary' for the effective implementation of a Union policy which has been the subject of harmonization measures as stipulated in Article 83 TFEU.

As noted, the proposal for a Directive on criminal sanctions for insider dealing and market manipulation is instructive as the first concrete example of the use of Article 83 (2) TFEU. The proposed Directive argues that market integrity is needed for the smooth functioning of the internal market. Also the Commission states that the adoption of administrative sanctions has proved insufficient. This proposal refers to the Commission's Communication on reinforcing regimes in the financial sector.[36] In addition, the Commission points out that its proposal is in line with the Commission's Communication 'Towards an EU Criminal Policy' – ensuring the effective implementation of EU policies through criminal law' as discussed above. Regardless, of such an assertion, it appears less clear why the proposal is based on Article 83 (2) TFEU at all and not Article 114 TFEU governing the internal market. In other words, you could cautiously ask yourself whether the Commission will from now on be able to pass legislation relating to the internal market more easily under Article 83 (2) TFEU compared to Article 114 TFEU. In any case,

[35] Directive 2003/6/EC on insider dealing and market manipulation (market abuse) L 96/16. Proposal for a Directive on criminal sanctions for insider dealing and market manipulation, COM (2011) 654 final. See also Proposal for a Regulation on insider dealing and market manipulation, COM (2011) 651 which regulates the fight against market abuse through administrative sanctions. See E Herlin-Karnell, 'White-collar Crime and European Financial Crises: Getting Tough on EU Market Abuse (2012) 37 *EL Rev* 481.

[36] Commission, Reinforcing regimes in the financial sector COM(2010)716 (Communication).

the proposed Directive claims to be boosting confidence in the market and ensuring investor protection.

What is interesting with this proposal is that it makes the imposition of criminal liability for legal persons mandatory (Article 6 in the proposed Directive). Indeed, this might pose difficulties for states like Sweden, which, in principle, do not recognize criminal liability for legal persons.[37]

The further recent example of activity in the field of substantive criminal law legislation at the EU level is the recent proposal for a Directive on the confiscation of the proceeds of crimes.[38] This is the recent proposal for a Directive on the freezing and confiscation of the proceeds of crime in the EU.[39] The aim of this proposal is to make it easier for Member States' authorities to confiscate and recover the profits which criminals make from serious and organized cross-border crime. Interestingly the proposal is based on both Articles 82(2) and 83(1) of the TFEU. Article 82(2) makes it clear that any legislation adopted under this provision must aim to facilitate mutual recognition. Against this requirement it is perhaps difficult to see how the proposal in question facilitates mutual recognition. The reason as to why the Commission might have chosen this dual approach with regard to legal basis, is perhaps the fact that the confiscation of the proceeds of crime is not listed in Article 83(1). For this reason, the Commission argues that the confiscation of the proceeds of crime should fall under the umbrella labelled 'organized crime' which is listed in Article 83 TFEU. More specifically, the Commission argues that existing provisions of EU rules on confiscation should remain in place in order to maintain a degree of harmonization with regard to activities that fall outside the scope of the proposed Directive.

5. THE CHARTER OF FUNDAMENTAL RIGHTS: CAN IT ADD VALUE?

A further question is of course the impact of the Charter of Fundamental Rights. How much will its legally binding status change the current state of play?

As pointed out by the House of Lords Select Committee, the ECHR is widely considered as providing the benchmark for minimum human rights standards.[40] Thus, some of the rights set out in the Charter correspond directly to those in the ECHR as discussed above. There is a further aspect here regarding judicial review and human rights protection: that of workload and the long waiting times in the European Court of Human Rights in Strasbourg. The accession of the EU to the ECHR is therefore more complicated than a blessing per se.

[37] S Jönsson, 'Criminal Legal Doctrine as a Spanner in the Works? The Swedish Experience' in A Stanislas et al (eds) *Corporate Criminal Liability in Europe* (Brussels, La charte, 2008) ch 14.

[38] Proposal for a Regulation on insider dealing and market manipulation, COM (2011) 651.

[39] Proposal for a Directive on the freezing and confiscation of the proceeds of crime in the EU, COM (2012) 0036.

[40] House of Lords, 30th Report, The European Union's policy on criminal procedure. 30th report session 2010–2012.

Moreover, the question of the workload in the Court of Justice itself will pose a real challenge for the future. This is an ever-increasing burning issue in an EU that wishes to guarantee that an AFSJ actually materializes and brings that sense of 'added value' to EU involvement and guarantees access to justice.

Of course it is true that Article 49 of the Charter provides for the guarantee of legality and proportionality in a more extensive way than the ECHR. Also, Article 47 of the Charter guarantees the right to a fair trial, while Articles 48–49 stipulate the presumption of innocence and the right of defence. The latter provision also makes it clear that the severity of penalties must not be disproportionate to the criminal offence. It is therefore likely that the binding status of the Charter will both hold a significant symbolic importance and have a real substantive impact on criminal law. Moreover, Article 50 of the Charter guarantees the right not to be tried twice for the same offence (ne bis in idem). A recent example of tensions with *ne bis in idem* and national sanctions regimes, is the recent case of Åkerberg Fransson concerning the compatibility with the *ne bis in idem* principle of a national system involving two separate sets of proceedings to penalize the same wrongful conduct.[41] Recently, AG Cruz Villalon stated in his opinion that Article 50 of the Charter did not preclude the Member States from bringing criminal proceedings relating to facts in respect of which a final penalty had already been imposed in administrative proceedings relating to the same conduct, provided that the national criminal court was in a position to take into account the prior existence of an administrative penalty for the purpose of mitigating the situation.[42] Yet it seems as if the AG puts his trust in the hands of a stringent application of proportionality here in the national courts. The Court of Justice in turn, in its recent ruling, did not elaborate on this aspect of proportionality as a mitigating principle.[43] Nonetheless, it is argued that the Court adopted a very broad reading of the Charter despite the limits set by Article 51. Specifically, the Court held that although the national rules in questions did not *stricto sensu* involve any implementation of EU law as such, it was clear from Article 325 TFEU that the Member States are required to fight fraud against the EU. Moreover, such an obligation could be deducted from the general obligations to punish tax fraud as stemming from VAT Directive (2006/112).[44] From this it followed, in the view of the Court, that the Sweden was 'implementing' EU law as it was under an established obligation to supply the same level of penalties for EU fraud and domestic fraud respectively. Besides, the Court observed that EU law precludes a judicial practice which makes the obligation for a national court to disapply any provision contrary to a fundamental right guaranteed by the Charter conditional upon that infringement being clear from the text of the Charter or the case-law relating to it. According to the Court such an interpretation would withhold from the

[41] C-617/10, *Åkerberg Fransson*, judgment of 26th February 2013 nyr.
[42] Opinion of AG Cruz Villalon delivered on 12 June 2012.
[43] Case C617/10, *Akeberg Fransson* judgment of 26th February 2013 nyr.
[44] Paras 27–28 of the judgment.

national court the power to assess fully whether the provision in question is compatible with the Charter.[45]

As noted above though, it remains the case that Article 52 of the Charter grants some important exceptions to the application of the Charter which also apply to EU criminal law.

This provision makes it clear that

> (1) Any limitation on the exercising of the rights and freedoms recognized by this Charter must be provided for by law and respect the essence of those rights and freedoms. Subject to the principle of proportionality, limitations may be made only if they are necessary and genuinely meet objectives of general interest recognized by the Union or the need to protect the rights and freedoms of others.

Although the Charter sets out some important axioms which guide the EU (and the Member States when they are implementing EU law) in its activity in this area, in the context of security, the proportionality test as set out in Article 52 might 'lose' out too easily unless strictly applied. Finally, in the recent case of *Stefano Melloni*,[46] on the validity of the amendments made to the EAW by Framework Decision 2009/299/JHA,[47] the Court of Justice held an interpretation of Article 53 of the Charter would undermine the principle of the primacy of EU law. Particularly, the Court stated that where an EU legal act calls for national implementing measures, national authorities and courts remain free to apply national standards of protection of fundamental rights, provided that the level of protection provided for by the Charter, as interpreted by the Court, and the primacy, unity and effectiveness of EU law are not thereby compromised.[48] Without guessing to wildly, it seems safe to predict that this area is set for important developments in the future.

6. CONCLUSION

This short introductory chapter has sought to chart recent developments in EU criminal law. As the EU is currently searching for the boundaries of a successful regime in EU criminal law, the present chapter aimed to take stock and use the Commission's recent Communication on the effective implementation and consistency of EU law by asking the question: to what extent do recent initiatives adopted by the Commission live up to this promise? The conclusion here is that it will be crucial for the future to demonstrate the exact requirement of the facilitation of mutual recognition legislation under Article 82(2) TFEU, and how

[45] Para 48 of the judgment.

[46] Case C-399/11, Criminal proceedings against *Stefano Melloni*, Opinion of AG Bot delivered on 2 October 2012

[47] 2009 OJ L81/24.

[48] Case C-399/11, Criminal proceedings against *Stefano Melloni*, judgment of 26 February 2013, § 60.

direct or concrete such a link needs to be. There is also reason to believe that procedural criminal law at the EU level will become one of the most expanding areas where the impact of the Charter of Fundamental Rights and the ECHR have an important role to play. The added value of the Charter of Fundamental Rights will largely depend on the willingness of the Court of Justice to interpret the wording 'implementation of EU law' in a liberal fashion. Regardless, it serves as an important benchmark in the discussion on EU criminal law and the development of a consistent regime in this area.

In conclusion, while legal measures for procedural safeguards in EU criminal law as well as the protection of the victim constitute important steps towards a fair system of criminal law, which could rightly be claimed to form part of an AFSJ, the area of substantive criminal law offers a more delicate test case with regard to legitimacy questions. For example, this chapter points at Article 83(2) in the context of the fight against market abuse and insider dealing through the use of criminal law and the open-ended character of this provision. A further delicate testing field in the ever-growing security concerns is that of the confiscation of the proceeds of crime.

Whilst this chapter offers a glimpse of recent developments within the broad field of contemporary EU criminal law integration, the future has only just begun.

3
Conditions for the Legislative Procedure in the Area of Criminal Law – Before and After the Lisbon Treaty

ANNA WETTER*

1. INTRODUCTION

It has taken less than a decade for the EU to gain competence to lay down criminal sanctions for violations of EU law. Actually, it is no more than seven years ago since the Court of Justice ruled for the first time that the EU had competence in this area.[1] Competence prior to this ruling related only to the area of justice and police cooperation – an area within which any legal measure required consensus in the Council and where Framework Decisions were adopted without the involvement of the European Parliament. Seen from a law-making perspective it can be argued that this former arrangement was uncontroversial considering the fact that any Member State could stop a legal proposal that did not please it. It can, however, also be argued that the exclusion of the European Parliament was inappropriate considering the often claimed importance of criminal sanctions being laid down as close to the citizens as possible due to the highly intrusive nature of criminal sanctions on the people. Not all Member States include their national parliaments in the preparations of legal proposals from the EU. The fact that the Member States were in agreement did not necessarily imply that the citizens (represented by their national parliaments) were always so keen on the cooperation. Another disadvantage with the former system was that at the time the Court of Justice had only minimum jurisdiction in the area (Art 35 EU Treaty).

For the sake of this chapter it is important to keep in mind the very basics of EU legislative powers; in other words that the legality of EU action is conditioned by the powers that have been attributed to it through the Treaties. Or put differently, the EU may not adopt legislation unless a legal basis in the

*Anna Wetter is employed as a researcher at the Law Faculty at Uppsala University.
[1] Case C-176/03 *Commission v Council*, judgment of 13 Sept 2005.

EU Treaties can be identified.[2] Sometimes the EU legislative competence belongs to the European Union exclusively, while it in other situations is shared with the Member States. After having established a legal basis, the EU is further limited through the principles of proportionality and subsidiarity.

This chapter will review the legislative procedure that led to the adoption of Directive 2009/52/EC providing for minimum standards on sanctions and measures against employers of illegally staying third-country nationals (the Sanctions Directive).[3] The fact that the Directive was adopted despite disagreement in the Council concerning the reference to the legal basis makes it an interesting case study. This fact is what brought it to my attention. However, the main purpose of this text is not to discuss the disputed legal basis but to highlight the importance of taking criminal law principles seriously in the law-making process at EU level. These principles include the principle of ultima ratio and the principle of proportionality. Towards the end of this chapter, I will discuss the approach, which appears to have been taken by the legislative bodies in this case. My interpretation of the preparatory documents indicates that the institutions seem to have argued that a weak legal basis could be compensated with proper concern for the principle of proportionality.

Considering the fact that the Directive was adopted before the Lisbon Treaty entered into force, the text will refer to the Treaties that were applicable at the time.[4] Prior to the review of the Directive, a few thoughts will be shared regarding the transfer of power within the field of criminal law. Finally, the chapter will make a few suggestions that could contribute to increasing the credibility of the EU legislative process.

2. CONCERNS WITH REGARD TO CRIMINAL LAW IDEALS

The transfer of criminal law competence, which indisputably took a major step forward after the 2005 judgment on environmental protection, has broken new ground by disqualifying the Member States in their former capacity as the exclusive legislators in criminal law.[5] As known to most European law researchers of today, the new order provides a possibility for the EU to adopt legally binding criminal sanctions. Since the ordinary legislative procedure should apply (both prior to the entry into force of the Lisbon Treaty through the 2005 ruling and after) Member States could end up in a position where they are forced to

[2] It should perhaps be noted that under certain conditions the EU may apply the doctrine of implied powers in the absence of a clear legal basis, see for example Cases 281, 283–285, 287/85, *Germany v Commission* [1987] ECR 3203.

[3] Council Dir 2009/52/EC of the European Parliament and of the Council of 18 June 2009 providing for minimum standards on sanctions and measures against employers of illegally staying third-country nationals, [2009] OJ L168/24.

[4] Consolidated versions of the Treaty on European Union and the Treaty on the Functioning of the European Union of 30 March 2010, [2010] C83/53.

[5] See n 1 above.

introduce criminal sanctions in their national laws although it would clearly go against their criminal law traditions. In some EU Member States this has led to an intense debate among criminal law researchers, where the majority seems to argue that criminal law is a field that requires specific concern considering the particularities of the topic. This position has been particularly highlighted by a group of European law scholars through the European Criminal Policy Initiative (ECPI).[6] Their specific concerns relate to some criminal law principles that need to be considered during the legislative procedure and which are always present at the national level in each of the Member State that they represent.

Two leading criminal law principles are the principle of ultima ratio and the principle of proportionality. Compliance with the former principle will ensure that criminalisation is a last resort.[7] Despite the absence of constitutional support for the principle (in for example Sweden), it is evoked in most respectable textbooks and treaties. A well-known Swedish professor of criminal law notes in a journal that the principle is obviously not a constitutional one but rather a principle of legislative ethics, which is evoked in respectable textbooks and treaties.[8] Needless to say, perhaps, the (EU) principle of proportionality exists to ensure that the proposed measure does not go beyond what is necessary in order to achieve a particular objective.

One suggestion, which has been emphasised by the aforementioned ECPI scholars, is that the EU legislator is unsuitable if it cannot ensure that these criminal law principles are seriously taken into account at the EU level.[9] Other debaters add concern with respect to the democratic ideal, arguing that criminal law needs to be adopted as close to the people as possible and that the European law-making model, despite the principle of subsidiarity could never meet this ideal.

At the time of the adoption of the Sanctions Directive, the Lisbon Treaty had not yet entered into force meaning that there were no provisions in the EU Treaties which provided the EU with the necessary legal competence to adopt criminal sanctions.[10] Sweden voted against the adoption, arguing that the choice of legal basis (Article 63 in the Nice EC Treaty) could not be used as a legal basis for introducing criminal sanctions, at least not using the reasoning of the Commission. It should be noted that (often) due to the political disadvantages that may follow when a Member State decides to vote against a legal proposal it is more common that the Member States choose the option of abstaining when

[6] European Criminal Policy Initiative, A Manifesto on European Criminal Policy, *Zeitschrift für Internationale Strafrechtsdogmatik*, 4 Jahrgang, Ausgabe 12/2009, pp 707–716.

[7] It should perhaps be noted that this is the most commonly used definition of the concept of ultima ratio although there are many more interpretations.

[8] N Jareborg, 'Criminalization as Last Resort (Ultima Ratio)' (2005) 2 *Ohio State Journal of Criminal Law* 521, 523.

[9] See n 6, p 707.

[10] As mentioned above, there was, however, a ruling by the Court of Justice, which established that the EU could adopt criminal sanctions if it was necessary to protect Community law, and especially in areas such as environmental law, which forms part of the essential values of the EU, see n 1 above.

they disapprove of a legal proposal. This is normally Sweden's approach, which might indicate that Sweden in this particular case wished to make the point clearly that it disapproved of the choice of legal basis.

With this as a background, the following section will analyse the legislative process, which led to the adoption of the Sanctions Directive. It starts by reviewing the initial steps that were taken by the Council and subsequently by the Commission and goes on to examine the discussions, which took place in the Council working parties. It should be noted that the discussions in the European Parliament will not be emphasised due to reasons of delimitation.

3. THE SANCTIONS DIRECTIVE'S INITIAL STEPS

In 1995, the Council adopted a Council Recommendation, (based on a French initiative) which first introduced the idea that penalties should be harmonised in order to combat illegal immigration in the Member States.[11] The idea was to remove all possible incentives for illegal immigration into the EU in the destination countries.

The Council Recommendation advised that the Member States should ensure that any person who is considered, under the national law of the Member State concerned, to be employing a foreign national who does not have a resident permit should be made subject to appropriate penalties. The Recommendation was put forward on the basis of Article K.3 of the then Maastricht EU Treaty, which stipulated that the Council could adopt joint positions and promote any cooperation contributing to the pursuit of the European Union.[12] Article K.3 further referred to Article K.1, according to which immigration policy and policy regarding nationals of third countries are stipulated as a matter of common interest. The initiatives that were subsequently taken by the Commission took their point of departure in the Council Recommendation.

The Commission applies policy plans to help it fulfil its mission to bring about the objectives of the EU Treaties. In 2006, the Commission noted in a Communication on policy priorities in the fight against illegal immigration of third-country nationals that some Member States had already undertaken measures to enforce the Council Recommendation from 1995.[13] According to the Communication, such measures included criminal sanctions for employers. This noted, the Commission decided that the next step would be to ensure that all Member States would adopt similar measures.[14]

[11] Council Recommendation of 22 December 1995 on harmonizing means of combating illegal immigration and illegal employment and improving the relevant means of control, [1996] OJ C5/1.

[12] Treaty on European Union of 29 July 1992[1992] OJ C191.

[13] Communication from the Commission on Policy priorities in the fight against illegal immigration of third-country nationals, COM(2006) 402 final, 19 July 2006, p 9.

[14] See n 13 above, p 9.

Illegal immigration as such had at this stage already been dealt with in numerous action plans and Communications. For example, according to one Directive, which defined the facilitation of unauthorised entry, transit and residence, any person who intentionally assisted a person who was not a national of a Member State to reside within the territory was to be penalised with appropriate sanctions.[15] This Directive was adopted in November 2002 with reference to Article 61(a) and 63(3)(b) of the then EC Treaty. Article 61(a) EC Treaty provided that the Council should adopt measures to combat crime with reference to Article 31(e) of the EU Treaty. Article 31(e) provided that common action on judicial cooperation in criminal matters included the progressive adoption of measures establishing minimum rules relating to the constituent elements of criminal acts and to penalties in the fields of organised crime, terrorism and illicit drug trafficking. This implies that the sanctions, which were imposed in the 2002 Directive, had their legal support in the general article in the EU Treaty, which was aimed at combating organised crime and terrorism.

However, and importantly, the purpose of the 2002 Directive was not to adopt penalties but only to adopt common definitions of the offences, which were to be punished with harmonised penalties in the Member States. In order to supplement the 2002 Directive with harmonised sanctions the Council adopted Council Framework Decision 2002/946/JHA.[16] The legal basis for the Framework Decision was Articles 29, 31(e) and 34(b) of the EU Treaty, which implies that it was adopted in accordance with Third Pillar procedures requiring consensus in the Council.

4. THE PROPOSAL

As noted above, the Commission circulated a Communication to the other EU institutions in 2006, aiming to make it clear that the employment of illegally staying third country nationals might contribute to illegal immigration. It emphasised the need to adopt measures with regards to illegal immigration and illegal residence, including repatriation of illegal residents with reference to Article 63(3)(b) of the EC Treaty.[17]

The Communication includes a list of threats that the Commission believed were posed by the presence of the identified pull factor. These include losses to public finances, the depression of wages and working conditions, distortion of competition between business and means, and the risk that the undeclared workers will not benefit from health insurance and pension rights that depend on contributions.[18]

[15] Council Dir defining the facilitation of unauthorised entry, transit and residence of 28 Nov 2002, [2002] OJ L328.

[16] Council Framework Decision 2002/946/JHA on the strengthening of the penal Framework to prevent the facilitation of unauthorised entry, transit and residence of 28 November 2002, [2002] OJ L328.

[17] Treaty establishing the European Community of 24 Dec 2002, [2002] OJ C325.

[18] Proposal for a Dir of the European Parliament and of the Council providing for sanctions against employers of illegally staying third-country nationals of 16 May 2007, COM(2007) 249 final, p 2.

In its impact assessment report the Commission examined six possible legislative options.[19] It chose a combination of two of them (options 4 and 6). The first option implied a *status quo*, meaning that nothing would be done to the current situation. The second option implied the introduction of sanctions for employers of illegally staying third-country nationals across the EU with an enforcement obligation for Member States. In the Commission's view, this option would foster a level playing field and reduce the variation in legislation and its enforcement in the Member States. It also believed that an increase in the minimum level of employer sanctions would create a stronger deterrence factor for the offence.

According to the third option, the EU would harmonise preventive measures. Such measures would include the introduction of common requirements across the EU for employers to copy the relevant documentation and to notify the competent national bodies. This option excluded the introduction of criminal penalties. Option four implied the introduction of harmonised employer sanctions and preventive measures. In effect, it was a combination of options two and three. This choice was expected to send a clear message regarding the EU's commitment to the fight against illegal employment. Option five would simply bring awareness to the consequences of the employment of illegally staying third-country nationals through a campaign. Finally, option six implied that Member States should identify and exchange good practices on the implementation of employer sanctions. This option was added to the choice of option four.

By comparing the options, the Commission came to the conclusion that preventive measures had to be harmonised in the Member States in parallel with the introduction of criminal sanctions. The impact assessment report does not reveal how this conclusion was drawn, although it notes that the conclusion was made in the light of the views shared by the Member States and stakeholders.[20]

In the part, which comprised the detailed explanation of the proposal, the Commission provided a further motive for supporting the need for the adoption of criminal sanctions. Here, the Commission noted that administrative fines and other non-criminal sanctions might not be enough to deter certain employers.[21] While addressing the principle of subsidiarity, the Commission emphasised that the objectives of the proposal could never be sufficiently achieved by the Member States.[22] The Commission was of the opinion that, if the Member States were to legislate at the national level, there would be a significant risk that there would be different levels of sanctions and enforcement in the Member States. This, it feared, could in effect lead to a distortion of competition within the Single Market and to secondary movements of illegally staying third-country

[19] Commission Staff Working Document, Accompanying document to the Proposal for a Dir providing for sanctions against employers of illegally staying third-country nationals, Impact Assessment SEC(2007)603, 16 of May 2007.

[20] Ibid, p 3.

[21] See n 18, p 10.

[22] See n 18, p 6.

nationals to Member States with lower levels of sanctions and enforcement. Having confirmed that the proposal complied with the principle of subsidiarity the Commission assessed its compliance with the principle of proportionality. In the Commission's view, the proposal would give the Member States a sufficient degree of flexibility in terms of implementation to conform to the principle of proportionality.

In summary, it is clear from the Commission's proposal that the aim of the Directive was to introduce criminal penalties in order to reduce one of the pull factors which encourages illegal immigration into the EU. The identified pull factor is the possibility for illegal immigrants to find work. Hence, by targeting employers of illegally staying residents the Commission wished to decrease the rate of illegal immigration.

5. PREPARATIONS IN THE COUNCIL

In addressing the Council's review of the Commission's proposal it is perhaps necessary to provide those readers who are not familiar with the legislative procedure in the Council with some background. The following background relates to proposed legislation, which includes references to criminal provisions.

All legislative proposals are addressed to the General Secretariat of the Council of the EU, which is responsible for initiating the legislative process in the Council. The Secretariat refers the proposal to the EU Presidency, which is the body responsible for appointing the Council Working Party that shall have the main responsibility for reviewing a particular proposal from the Commission. Since 2006, an arrangement has been in place, which is meant to ensure that all provisions, which include reference to criminal penalties, must be assessed by a special Working Party.[23] The system has been set up in order to ensure that EU criminal law remains consistent and follows a certain structure. The Council conclusions do not identify any particular Working Party but refer to an *appropriate* body.[24] However, in recent years there has been a clear trend in that the EU Presidencies refer the proposals, which include criminal penalties, to the same group, in other words to the Working Party on Substantive Criminal Law (in internal documents referred to as DROIPEN). It should be noted that the 2006 Presidency conclusions were codified in 2009 when it was also agreed that criminal law provisions should be introduced when they are considered essential in order to protect the interests, and as a rule, should only be used as a last resort.[25] However, at the time of the adoption of the Sanctions Directive these guidelines were not yet in force.

[23] Procedure for future handling of legislative files containing proposals relevant to the development of criminal law policy, Doc 7876/06 of 28 March 2006.

[24] Ibid, p 2.

[25] Council Conclusions on model provisions, guiding the Council's criminal law deliberations, 2979th Justice and Home Affairs meeting of 30 Nov 2009, p 2.

While the 2006 Presidency conclusions were being drafted, it was agreed that the system should be evaluated on a regular basis. The first evaluation for which Coreper bore responsibility was conducted in 2007. Coreper confirmed that the first experiences of the new scrutiny mechanisms were generally positive.[26] It also emphasised that the procedure corresponded well with a real need to ensure the effective scrutiny of legislation on criminal law provisions in EC law by those Council preparatory bodies that have special expertise in substantive criminal law.[27]

The system of referral to the appropriate Working Party had two formats. In a case where the proposed legislation had a predominantly criminal law nature the idea was to refer it to a working group in the Justice and Home Affairs (JHA) area. On the other hand, if the legislative file included criminal law provisions only in part it was to be referred to a working group with particular expertise in the criminal law area.

The 2006 Council conclusions were drafted just after the Commission had communicated its proposal for a Sanctions Directive to the Council; hence these conclusions were not applicable to the proposal. Coreper still made the assessment that the proposal should be referred to the Working Party for Migration and Expulsion in the first place, since it only partly contained criminal law measures. The Presidency was later to agree with Coreper in this regard.

The incoming Portuguese Presidency decided to initially address the Migration and Expulsion Working Party for examination, adding also the need to engage the Working Party on Substantive Criminal Law in the review.[28] Finally, it noted that appropriate arrangements would also be undertaken in order to ensure that the Working Party on Social Questions would be kept informed of developments.

The Working Party for Migration and Expulsion held its initial meeting on 5 June 2007, even before the Presidency had decided to make the Group responsible for the examination of the legislative proposal. Hence, the Working Party based its initial discussion on the presentation made by the Commission. The Working Party agreed with the need to involve other Working Parties since the proposal contained proposed legislation in the criminal law area.[29] The only comment which the Working Party made with reference to the criminal law provisions had to do with Article 10, which it emphasised must not oblige the Member State to provide for criminal sanctions unless it could be proved that an employer was not acting in good faith when he/she employed the illegally staying third-country national.[30]

Coreper presented its initial interpretation of the proposal in September 2007. It is presented in a document submitted by the Presidency but Coreper is the

[26] Review of the procedural consequences of the judgment of the Court of Justice in Case 176/03 of 30 May 2007, Doc 10105/1/07 REV 1, p 5.

[27] Ibid.

[28] Incoming Portuguese Presidency to Coreper, Doc 11035/07 of 29 June 2007.

[29] Outcome of proceedings from Working Party on Migration and Expulsion, Doc 10669/07 of 15 June 2007, p 3.

[30] Ibid, p 10.

body, which is responsible for preparing the communications by the Presidency for which this text will refer to Coreper instead of the Presidency. Its opinion was based on the opinions communicated by the Working Party for Migration and Expulsion. The review started with a presentation of the group's interpretation of the Commission's proposal. It moved on with an analysis of the justification for the legal basis. With reference to the 13 September 2005 judgment by the Court of Justice[31] Coreper drew the conclusion that the EC legislator might provide for criminal sanctions if it deemed it necessary to bring effectiveness to Community legislation.[32] Finally, Coreper's review included a proportionality test (although a very implicit one), of the proposed sanctions. The following will focus on the evaluations concerning the choice of legal basis and the proportionality test.

It is clear from Coreper's Communication that it was not convinced that Article 63(3)(b) provided an adequate legal basis for the adoption of the proposal. Although unsure about the choice of legal basis, the Group concluded that the typical features of the offences in the Directive under the criminal law provisions did not, in general, give rise to difficulties or problems.[33] The reason for this was that Coreper found (with a few exceptions) the offences in the proposed Directive to be objective and couched in terms that afford interested parties a precise understanding of the prohibited conduct. In Coreper's view the article could only support the adoption of criminal penalties if those penalties were directly related to the encouragement or the intentional facilitation of illegal immigration. Due to this, it found that criminalising employment, because employment is a pull factor for illegal immigration would imply going too far.[34] It believed that that the relationship between the proposed measure (the sanction) and the interest it would serve to protect (hinder illegal immigration) would prove insufficient to justify criminalisation at EU level. In other words Coreper seemed to suggest that the pull factor argument did not sufficiently provide the relationship, which was necessary to justify the use of Article 63, with support from the 2005 judgment. If the relationship were to prove insufficient, as suggested by Coreper, it would probably have been the right choice to refrain from adoption with regards to the Court's settled case law.[35] Accordingly, the choice of legal basis for a Community measure must rest on objective factors, which are amenable to judicial review, including in particular the aim and the content of the measure.[36]

So far, it is easy to follow the line of reasoning in Coreper's document. However, despite this conclusion, Coreper still seems to argue in the end that the Directive

[31] See n 1.

[32] Presidency to the Working Party on Substantive Criminal Law, Doc 12776/07 of 12 Sep 2007, p 2.

[33] Ibid, 3.

[34] See n 32, p 2. The exact words of Coreper read: '(.) and to criminalize the employment of illegally-staying residents under this rule of jurisdiction merely because it is a pull factor would be going too far.'

[35] Case C-300/89, *Commission v Council* (1991) ECR I-2867, 'Titanium Dioxide'.

[36] Ibid, para 10.

could be adopted with reference to Article 63(3)(b). The reason for this seems to be that once Coreper had disqualified the direct reference to the suggested legal basis, it found that the proposed measures could be justified based on the fact that the measures paid adequate respect to the principle of proportionality. As mentioned above, the group concluded that the typical features of the offences under the criminal law provisions did not in general give rise to difficulties or problems. It believed that the descriptions of the offences were objective and couched in terms that afforded interested parties a precise understanding of the prohibited conduct.

After having collected written comments from the Member States, the Working Party on Substantive Criminal Law adopted its final opinion.[37] It first noted that since the central element of the measures in the proposal aimed at combating illegal employment by prohibiting employment of third-country nationals it was a correct choice to give the main responsibility for the review to the Working Party for Migration and Expulsion. Hence, it shared this opinion with the Presidency.[38] Furthermore, on 6 November 2007, it had addressed a question to the Presidency, asking about the binding character of its opinions.[39] However, none of the documents at consilium.eu reveal whether or not the group received an answer to this question.

In drafting its opinion, the working group on Substantive Criminal Law considered the comments made by the Member States. Some of the comments by the Member States expressed doubt on the choice of Article 63(3)(b) EC Treaty as the legal basis for the legislation. Other Member States were convinced that a legal basis could be found in Article 63 but opposed the necessity of adopting criminal penalties in this case. A third group of Member States fully supported the Commission's proposal. Having noted the difficulties in reaching an agreement on the question of whether the EU had a legal basis to base its legislation on the group decided to refrain from 'taking a position on the question of the adequacy of the legal basis and of the necessity to take criminal measures to combat illegal immigration'.[40] The group emphasised that it had not been asked to give comments on the choice of legal basis and that it therefore did not have to come to a conclusion in this matter.

It should be added that at times during the preparatory negotiations in the Council, the Article 36 Committee (also referred to as CATS) was asked to comment on the proposal. The Working Party on Substantive Criminal Law had emphasised the fact that this group would take a further look at the proposal when it decided to refrain from taking a stand on the legal basis.[41] Its role involves coordinating activities in the field of police and judicial cooperation in criminal matters. One of its functions is to contribute to the preparation of the Council's

[37] Opinion of the Working Party on Substantive Criminal Law, Doc 6407/08, Feb. 2007.

[38] Ibid, 2.

[39] Outcome of proceedings of the Working Party on Substantive Criminal Law of 6 Nov 2007, Doc 14669/07, p 2.

[40] See n 37, 4.

[41] See n 37, 4.

work. It submits opinions to the Council on request, on legislative proposals, for instance. The idea is that CATS is kept informed about a legislative proposal at an early stage, enabling it to react early if a proposal were to cross the line of EU competence. None of the documents accessible reveal that CATS wished to stop the proposal for the Sanctions Directive.

The Directive was adopted in June of 2009. As already noted, Sweden initially voted against its adoption although the country was in favour of the objectives of the Sanctions Directive. Nevertheless, the Swedish delegation believed that Article 63(3)(b) could not be used as a legal basis, hence agreeing with Coreper's initial view.

Finally, a few words will be said in this section about the Council's legal service. During the preparations in the Council preparatory bodies, the Working Party for Migration and Expulsion referred two questions to the Council's legal service. It first asked whether Article 63(3)(b) would constitute the correct choice of legal basis and secondly it wished to know whether it would be possible to extend the scope of the Commission's proposal to also cover legally staying third-country nationals.

According to information, which is provided at consilium.eu, the Council's legal service gave its Opinion on 6 November 2007.[42] The content of the document was, however, confidential with reference to a Council Regulation from 2001.[43] This Regulation provides, in principle, that all EU documents should be accessible to the public. Exceptions to this main rule include documents with a highly sensitive content, for example, where certain public and private interests must be protected. In addition to this, the Regulation gives the EU institutions the right to protect their internal consultations and deliberations if they must in order to carry out their tasks. This is stipulated in Article 4(3) paragraph 3. The possibility to restrict the access to document remains also after a decision has been made if it is believed that the disclosure of the document could seriously undermine the decision-making process of the institution. The only time when access cannot be refused is when there is an overriding public interest in a disclosure. Arguably, restrictions on the access to the Council's assessment regarding the legal basis could delimit the possibility of making European legislation amenable to judicial review. In the Tobacco Advertising Case from 2000, the Council's legal service had expressed doubt with regards to the legal basis, which leaked to the public.[44] Later the Council (jointly with the Parliament) had to defend itself before the Court of Justice arguing that the chosen legal basis had been the correct one. The fact that the legal service's doubts had been exposed to the public made this a greater challenge as opposed to if it had remained an unofficial document.

[42] Corrigendum to Opinion of the Legal Service, Doc 14655/07 of 6 Nov 2007.

[43] Regulation (EC) No 1049/2001 of the European Parliament and of the Council of 30 May 2001 regarding public access to European Parliament, Council and Commission documents, [2001] OJ L145/43.

[44] M Bergström, 'Spillover or Activist Leapfrogging? Criminal Competence and the Sensitiveness of the European Court of Justice' (2007) 2 *EPA* 5.

6. THOUGHTS ON THE LEGISLATIVE PROCESS

This section discusses the legislative preparations in the Council. Four issues will be highlighted.

First, there is legislation, which is adopted in the absence of a clear legal basis but which is not brought to the Court of Justice of the European Union for examination. Despite the fact that Sweden argued that the EU did not have the legal competence to adopt criminal sanctions in the fight against illegal immigration, it chose not to refer the Directive to the Court of Justice. There is obviously no obligation to refer cases to the Court of Justice but the system of referral is meant to ensure that legislation, which is disputed by one or more parties, is referred to the Court of Justice for examination. The fact that Sweden or any other Member State refrained from taking action perhaps indicates that the mechanisms, which aim to ensure that EU legislation stays within the limits granted through the Treaties, are not functioning as planned. To anyone who has the habit of following the law-making process at EU level in detail this may not come as a great surprise. However, my impression is that few legal scholars follow it at this detailed level, implying possibly that the EU lawmakers may push the limits in more cases than this one. In effect, EU law may become more politicised than necessary. You would perhaps expect the European Parliament to constitute a hurdle but the example of the Sanctions Directive does not support this assumption. In this particular case the European Parliament held the view that criminalising employers of illegal immigrants would decrease the risk of social dumping, which constitutes another goal of the European Parliament.[45]

Second, the procedure for how Working Parties in the Council were appointed in 2006 seems remarkably unclear to anyone who studies it from the outside. Hopefully, it makes more sense from the inside. However, it is important that law-making procedures are comprehensible to the public. As noted above, the proposal was communicated to the Working Party for Substantive Criminal Law on the request of the Working Party for Migration and Expulsion, the latter acting on its own initiative. When the proposal was being circulated in the Council, there were still no clear guidelines on when an expert group had to be consulted. Furthermore, the documents reveal that the Working Party on Substantive Criminal Law was not sure of its role. It finally decided to refrain from giving its opinion on whether or not the Directive could be adopted with reference to Article 63(3)(b) EC Treaty.[46] The German delegation had a different view. In one of its Opinions it expressed that the Working Party for Substantive Criminal Law must consider all of the criminal law aspects.[47] It

[45] Proposal for a Directive of the European Parliament and of the Council providing for sanctions against employers of illegally staying third-country nationals – Outcome of the European Parliament's first reading, 10 Feb 2009, Doc 6039/09.

[46] See n 37, 4.

[47] Opinion by the German delegation to the Working Party on Substantive Criminal Law of 12 Dec. 2007, Doc 16485/07, p 2.

believed that this would include ensuring that the proposal remained loyal to all other criminal law standards, which are created at EU level. This implies that the German delegation believed that the group was responsible not only for ensuring that each particular proposal was in accordance with EU law but also that its adoption did not have an unsuitable impact on the general development of EU criminal law.[48]

In the absence of further instructions from the Presidency on the role of the Working Party on Substantive Criminal Law, it seems that it has developed into a body that replies to the questions referred to it without actually taking into consideration the impact the adoption of the legislative file may have on the general development of EU criminal law. This conclusion is, however, limited to the scenario where the predominant content of the legislative file is not criminal law. When it is, the Working Party on Substantive Criminal Law will have the main responsibility for the assessment of the legislative file, which may result in a more consistent evaluation of EU criminal law as a whole. However, as noted above, this was not the case with the Sanctions Directive.

This said there is not much more to add concerning the decision of the Working Party to refrain from assessing the legal basis. It seems as if the group was freely able to decide the items it will include in an assessment. It is possible that this order may, however, undermine the idea of appointing special groups with the responsibility for examining legal proposals. If the Presidency conclusions from 2006 are to have any relevance, the appointed groups cannot randomly pick their items of assessment from one time to another but instead need clearer instructions on their role. In addition, if a Working Party comes to the conclusion that the proposed legislation cannot be adopted, it needs to be clear what the effect of this conclusion will be.

Which brings me to the third item of discussion in this section. As noted above, there are documents which include decisive information on, for example, the assessment made on the choice of legal basis that are kept confidential. This could undermine the credibility of EU institutions. None of the accessible documents reveal whether in fact the EU had the legal competence to adopt the sanctions. Considering the fact that this matter was discussed openly by the preparatory bodies it seems unreasonable that the final assessment of whether a legal basis could actually be established is not accessible to the public. The conclusion of the legal service of the Council remained confidential. Hence, there is no way of knowing whether Sweden was right in its view that a legal basis was missing. It should be added here that the opinions of the Council's legal service often play an important role for the final decision in the Council. The fact that Sweden chose to vote against the adoption could be an indication that the legal service did not approve with the choice of legal basis. This is of course highly speculative but the fact that it is actually illustrates the need for

[48] It is possible that CATS was the body responsible for confirming that European criminal law remained consistent.

increased openness if the EU institutions wish for their actions to reach a high level of credibility.

Fourth, and finally, this section will discuss the conclusions that Coreper finally reached with regards the legal basis. It is possible that a successful proportionality test at EU level could justify the absence of a proper legal basis in Coreper's view. This theory will now be considered in light of the 2005 ruling.

In its 2005 ruling, the Court of Justice established that whenever the application of effective, proportionate and dissuasive criminal penalties by the national authorities is an essential measure for combating serious environmental offences, the EU has competence to adopt such sanctions.[49] This could be interpreted as meaning that although there was no explicit legal basis in the Treaties, which could justify the adoption of criminal sanctions when the Council's Framework Decision was adopted, the EU could adopt criminal law measures under Community law provided that the criteria in paragraph 48 of C-176/03 were fulfilled. These criteria include the establishment of *the need* to use criminal penalties as necessary instruments for the enactment and full effectiveness of the rules laid down by the Community legislator in exercising its powers. The necessity criteria could be interpreted here as being equal to the necessary relationship between the essential measure and sanction selected. However, as Coreper concluded that the relationship between the sanction and the interest it serves to protect was not clear enough, this cannot be the justification for adoption of the proposal. Had Coreper instead chosen to substitute the *relationship* identified in its assessment with *the need* (which is referred to by the Court of Justice), it might have reached the conclusion that the criteria of effectiveness had been fulfilled. In effect, the Directive could have been adopted despite the absence of a legal basis in the Treaties.

However, as noted above, this was not the option chosen by Coreper. The group seems instead to have foreseen the criteria of effectiveness. Consequently, it chose to support the adoption of criminal sanctions despite both the absence of an explicit Treaty provision or support found in case law.

7. FINAL REMARKS AND THE WAY FORWARD

The Sanctions Directive serves as a good example to illustrate how EU legislation can at times be adopted without a clear legal basis. It also shows how the proportionality test is being used by the EU institutions to compensate for a weak legal basis. These conclusions may provoke few feelings in some while they may annoy others more. Perhaps there are those who are comfortable in the knowledge that the European Treaties may never express the clarity, which is needed in order to ensure that all legislation is passed with reference to a clear legal basis. On the contrary, there may be those who fear that due to this

[49] See n 1, para 48.

fact, EU law may lead its own life, far away from the legal traditions of the Member States. This latter circumstance does not sit well with the democratic ideal, which is shared among all EU Member States, especially as long as the voter turnout in the European Parliament elections remains relatively low in most Member States.

The study also shows that there was a transition period when it was not clear whether the EU would gain competence to lay down criminal sanctions. The Sanctions Directive was adopted in the absence of a clear legal basis but with the support of a Court of Justice ruling which established that the EU could adopt criminal law measures provided certain criteria were met in the field of environmental law. Since the entry into force of the Lisbon Treaty, it is clear that the EU has the legal competence to adopt criminal law measures.[50] Nevertheless, the period between the ruling of the Court of Justice and the entry into force of the Lisbon Treaty arguably opened up a far too big playing field for the EU to adopt criminal law measures considering the importance of clear rules in the area of criminal law.[51] In this respect, the Lisbon Treaty is warmly welcome since it provides the EU with a clear competence. In addition, the Lisbon Treaty has introduced a reinforcement of the principles of subsidiarity and proportionality, which provide interested national parliaments with a stronger role in preparing EU legislation.[52]

Despite these positive improvements it would be wrong to refrain from further investigation of how the new Treaty is actually implemented in the area of criminal law. This is particularly important considering the fact that this study has also shown the dynamic character of the EU Treaties. It seems impossible to lay down all the provisions that are necessary to keep EU cooperation alive. Hence, we can probably expect future judgments by the Court of Justice of the European Union, which will establish new areas of cooperation. As also shown in this study, it is not even necessary to involve the Court of Justice at every turn but legislation may be adopted in the absence of an uncontested legal basis. Knowing this, it is crucial that the criminal law principles, which are shared among all EU Member States, are taken into account during the legislative process at the EU level. If the EU institutions were able to show that these principles were taken seriously during the legislative process, we would perhaps dare to be less obsessed about the legal basis. Today, we look to the choice of legal basis for confirmation that the EU does not go beyond its legislative powers. Whenever the legal basis is disputable we need to wait for a Member State or one of the EU institutions to refer the legislation to the

[50] See n 4, Art 83(2).

[51] See Bergström (n 45) for a slightly different perspective. Although agreeing in principle, Bergström supports the view that there was a unified will in the Member States to amend the Treaty in accordance with the 2005 ruling, a circumstance which the Court of Justice presumably took into account although the Lisbon Treaty was not yet in force.

[52] Protocol (No 2) on the Application of the Principles of Subsidiarity and Proportionality, C 83/206, 30 March 2010.

Court of Justice for examination (unless of course the legislation has direct effect). Such a system does not sufficiently guarantee a transparent legislative process in my view. Transparency is particularly crucial in the case of criminal legislation due to the special concerns that need to be taken into account when legislation can have such an intrusive effect on the individual as is the case with a criminal sanction. This text has shown that the principles of ultima ratio and proportionality were considered first by the Commission and later on by the Council preparatory bodies. However, the reviews, at least those that have been made public, do not expose the detail required to be able to confirm that these assessments paid sufficient respect to these crucial criminal law principles. Some would perhaps meet this argument by emphasising that it is not uncommon to find defective reviews of these principles also at the national level. However, the criminal law systems at the national level have been developed over a long period of time and have therefore been scrutinised by the citizens of the Member States. The situation is very different at the EU level, where criminal sanctions are introduced beyond the knowledge of many EU citizens.

My proposal does not suggest that the process of establishing the adequate legal basis should be paid less attention. I am simply suggesting that there should be an added focus on the legislative principles, particularly in the area of criminal law. Additionally, the assessment of the principles must be accessible to the citizens of the EU. An added focus on these principles would bring about many positive effects.

First of all, as the EU institutions would be required to be more explicit about the reasons behind and effects of legislation that is proposed, EU criminal law would be brought closer to the citizens. As of today, the EU legislator is able to hide behind the legal basis that it chooses for the legislation. Second, added transparency could lead to more cases being referred to the Court of Justice. This would be useful in the area of EU criminal law, especially during the initial phase, before the new EU competence has become clear to the EU institutions and the Member States.

In summary, my suggestion is not so ground-breaking after all. I am not suggesting a revision of the current assessment for EU competence. As pointed out at the beginning of this chapter this method includes the establishment of the legal basis as a first step. As a second step, there is the assessment of the principles of proportionality and subsidiarity. During this second step, I propose that the EU institutions take better notice of the other legislative principles that are of particular importance in the area of criminal law. Ultima ratio and the principle of proportionality play important roles in all of the criminal law systems of the EU Member States and need therefore to be considered in depth during the EU legislative process.

This said Coreper's view on the proposal for the Sanctions Directive might not be so bad after all. The group seems to have taken a wider perspective on the legislative proposal when it assessed the legal proposal and the legislative proposals than usual. It argued that a weak legal basis could be compensated by the fact that the proposed measures were proportionate to the interest they aimed to protect. Again, it is not my intention to suggest that the legal basis should be granted less attention. Without a legal basis, the EU institutions cannot proceed with the legislation. However, whenever the legal basis is disputed, it would be ideal if the EU institutions engaged in the evaluation of how the proposal in question complied with the legislative principles. This conclusion, however, demands a great deal more from the EU legislator than what was achieved in the case of the Sanctions Directive. Furthermore, the assessments need to be conducted in a systematic way and be based on some established guidelines. The assessments must also be made public.

In addition to this, there are certain additional aspects that need to be dealt with in order to adapt the EU's legislative process to the criminal law reality of a united Europe. The Court of Justice must continue to develop its case law on the principle of proportionality. Finally, all European researchers must take a joint responsibility for fine-tooth combing the EU legislative procedure. This would eventually force the EU institutions to make more preparatory legislative documents open to the public, which would in turn be likely to encourage national discussions on EU criminalisation. Hopefully, this would also bring European citizens closer to the EU criminalisation process.

4
European Criminal Law – Challenges for the Future

PETTER ASP*

1. INTRODUCTION

The entering into force of the Lisbon Treaty has brought about a new situation for criminal law cooperation within the European Union. Before 1st December 2009, criminal law was an area that was mainly supposed to be dealt with under the Third Pillar – the most important exception was that in 2005 the European Court of Justice surprisingly established that the EU had criminal law competence in (at least) the environmental area under the First Pillar.[1] Cooperation under the Third Pillar was in principle characterized by a form of interstate cooperation where decisions required unanimity (thus each Member State had a 'veto') – but it was institutionalized to such an extent that it was hardly comparable to the cooperation taking place in other international fora (eg within the Council of Europe). The Commission, for example, had a right to initiative, the European Court of Justice had jurisdiction to give preliminary rulings as regards the interpretation of conventions and Framework Decisions (on the condition that the Member States had given a declaration to this effect) and to try the validity of such instruments.

With the Lisbon Treaty, the three former pillars were merged into one. As regards criminal law cooperation this meant that criminal law issues were *transferred from the former Third Pillar to the 'First'* (or rather the one and only remaining) Pillar. The most important consequence of this is, of course, that decisions are no longer made unanimously but with a qualified majority. Thus,

* Professor of criminal law and holder of the Torsten and Ragnar Söderberg chair in legal science.

[1] C-176/03. In addition to the competence that exists/ed according to the judgement of the European Court of Justice, EU law under the First Pillar also had and has several other implications for criminal law (for example (i) EU law could (and can) hinder the application of national criminal law rules that are in conflict with EU law which is directly effective, (ii) there is a general obligation to assimilate EU interests with national interests as regards protection in the Member States, etc).

the Member States can, under the Lisbon Treaty, be bound by decisions which they have not supported or which they have even voted against (in approximately the same way as people represented by a minority in a national parliament becomes bound by decisions by the majority).

This consequence, in other words that the EU as such has the ability to adopt instruments 'on its own accord' (which are binding on others) is normally the *consequence that we refer to when we say that the European Union 'has competence'* in a certain area: through acts adopted by the Council and the European Parliament it is possible for the European Union to issue instruments that are binding on the Member States (without all the Member States supporting the decision).

You can, of course, object to this description by saying that the European Union had a kind of competence as regards criminal law also under the former Third Pillar in the sense that it actually had the right to create criminal law instruments in the form of conventions and Framework Decisions. That competence was, however, *autonomous* (to borrow a term from the field of legal theory[2]) in character in the sense that the EU was not able to bind Member States that did not accept the instrument in question, ie as a matter of principle the former Third Pillar competence only meant that the collective of Member States (acting as the European Union) *could bind themselves*.

Under the Lisbon Treaty the Union can bind the Member States without the participation of all of them, ie the competence is in this sense *heteronomous*. Moreover, it is this heteronomous competence that is the real novelty as regards criminal law decision-making, since it means that ultimately the decisions on the design of the criminal law systems have been formally transferred from the Member States, or (to put it more generally) from the nation states, to the EU as a supranational entity. (The situation can be compared to (i) a society in which all the citizens together, and only as long as they all agree, set new rules for themselves and (ii) a society in which the citizens, performing as 'the state', are able to adopt new rules through majority decisions. It seems clear that it is only in the latter case that we find an entity, beside the citizens, that has a competence of its own.)

The transfer of criminal law from the Third Pillar to the 'First' and the transfer of competence from the Member States to the EU has brought about a new situation in which the EU and the Member States are facing many and different challenges. In this short text I will try to outline what I see as the main questions for the future. The text is divided into two main parts – the first focuses on new legal questions and the second on the challenges as regards criminal policy questions – which are followed by a short concluding section.

[2] See eg T Spaak, Explicating the Concept of Legal Competence, available at: http://papers.ssrn.com/sol3/papers.cfm?abstract_id=1014402.

2. NEW LEGAL QUESTIONS

The new treaty will, in itself, provide us with a major challenge since it creates several problems and raises many *legal questions* which we either have not met before or which we have met before, but in a different shape. Let us start by taking a look at the most important of these legal challenges.

One first and fairly obvious consequence of the Lisbon Treaty is that the transfer of competence that it entails (see *supra*) automatically means that it will be much *more important than before to actually delimit the areas concerned.*

When cooperation in this field was under the Third Pillar and the adoption of new instruments required unanimity, the limits of the competence rarely gave rise to much concern unless, of course, the competence was exercised in such a way that it intruded on the competences under the First Pillar (see Article 47 EU pre-Lisbon).[3] The adoption of an instrument presupposed that all Member States were in agreement and if they were, ie if a number of sovereign states unanimously decided to cooperate and bind themselves, it was normally difficult to argue that there were any hindrances. Thus, the fact that the area which could be subject to harmonization was depicted in a rather ambiguous way in the old Treaty on the European Union – it was, for example, most uncertain whether harmonization was limited to the three areas mentioned in Article 31(1)(e) or not – was actually not that problematic in practice. Perhaps you could argue that the fact that the Third Pillar entailed more than ordinary interstate cooperation (see above about the institutionalized character of the form of cooperation) implied that the limits of the competence did matter, ie it could be argued that the Member States could not even through unanimous decisions do anything they wanted to within the Third Pillar framework. It seems quite clear, however, that the question whether the cooperation was limited to the areas mentioned in Article 31(1)(e) EU, or whether it also covered other areas of criminal law was not discussed or debated in the way that it would have been if the Third Pillar had entailed a real transfer of competence to the EU.

Thus, it is probably no coincidence that the competences under the Lisbon Treaty are described in greater detail than the competences were under the old Third Pillar (cf. the wording of Article 83 TFEU with, on the one hand, the rules in the Maastricht Treaty which merely mentions criminal law as an area of common interest and, on the other, the ambiguous wording in the Amsterdam Treaty). Still there is reason to believe that one important question for the future will be to decide what the competence under Article 83 TFEU (and, when it comes to criminal law cooperation, Article 82 TFEU) actually entails.[4] For example:

[3] Article 47 read as follows: 'Subject to the provisions amending the Treaty establishing the European Economic Community with a view to establishing the European Community, the Treaty establishing the European Coal and Steel Community and the Treaty establishing the European Atomic Energy Community, and to these final provisions, nothing in this Treaty shall affect the Treaties establishing the European Communities or the subsequent Treaties and Acts modifying or supplementing them.'

[4] See, for analysis of some of the most important questions, Petter Asp, *The Substantive Criminal Law Competence of the EU* (Stockholm, Stiftelsen Skrifter utgivna av Juridiska fakulteten vid Stockholms universitet, 2012).

What does the reference to organized crime (and the other areas referred to in Article 83(1) TFEU) cover?

Is it enough that a certain type of offence is covered by the list in Article 83(1) TFEU or does competence also require that the offence in question fulfils the requirement of being particularly serious and that it includes a cross-border dimension?

Does the wording of Article 83(2) TFEU mean that it is only possible to exercise criminal law competence if the area in question *has already been* subject to harmonization measures, ie does it exclude that criminal law is introduced in the same instrument that provides for the harmonization of the area in question?

What is the meaning of the competence as regards harmonization of substantive criminal law in Article 83 TFEU being limited to 'criminal offences and sanctions'. (Does it, for example, exclude all harmonization of the general part of the criminal law? To what extent is it possible to harmonize general rules on confiscation and criminal law jurisdiction? etc)

What does the reference to minimum rules mean? Does it mean that the EU can require the Member States to criminalize up to a certain level, but cannot (under Article 83 TFEU) require them to abstain from criminalization? Or is this way of looking at minimum rules too simplified?[5]

A second equally important question concerns *the relationship between Title V Chapter 4 (especially Article 83 TFEU) and the rest of the TFEU*. Even if the three-pillar structure was abolished with the Lisbon Treaty, there are still certain special features connected to criminal law cooperation under Title V Chapter 4.

The most obvious one is the so-called *emergency brake* which a Member State is entitled to apply if it considers that a certain Directive (that either concerns the harmonization of substantive criminal law under Article 83 TFEU, or the harmonization of national procedural law under Article 82 TFEU) would 'affect fundamental aspects of its criminal justice system'. As regards the harmonization of substantive criminal law under Article 83 and of national procedural law under Article 82(2) the competence is further *limited to being exercised by means of Directives*. You could even argue that these 'particularities' mean that the *former First-Third Pillar structure continues to exist in a soft version* in the new Treaty.

Be that as it may, the fact that there are special rules applicable to the cooperation under Title V Chapter 4 leads to a situation where you can argue either:

1. that Title V contains all of the criminal law competences attributed to the EU, or
2. that there are competences 'outside' Title V Chapter 4 to which the constraints of Title V Chapter 4 do not apply.

[5] See eg Klip, *European Criminal Law*, 2nd edition (2012, Intersentia) 33 ff and 166 f and Nilsson, 'How to Combine Minimum Rules with Maximum Legal Certainty?' (2011) *Europarättslig Tidskrift* 665 ff.

At first glance it may seem that this question only has to do with the actual structure of the Treaty.

For example, one obvious argument in favour of the first line of reasoning (1.) is that the limitations of Title V Chapter 4 would be of little value if there were other competences outside the Chapter where the limitations do not apply. Further, Article 83(2) refers to competences in areas outside Title V Chapter 4, which means that these other areas are 'drawn into' Article 83(2) TFEU. Thus, there is a great deal in favour of the first line of reasoning: If it were true that EU competence in different areas (such as competition, agriculture, transport etc.) already included a general criminal law competence, Article 83(2) TFEU would seem to be more or less superfluous.

The problem is, however, that these quite convincing arguments are met by other arguments which are also quite convincing.

For example, it is definitely possible to argue that Article 325 TFEU (and possibly also Article 79 TFEU) provides the EU with criminal law competence which is not limited in the same way *as* the competence under Title V Chapter 4. As regards Article 325 TFEU it is, above all, the history of the Article that speaks in this direction. In its older version (in Article 280 EC) it contained what was mostly understood as an exception for criminal law. In Article 280(4) EC it was stated that measures taken under the Article should:

> not concern the application of national criminal law or the national administration of justice.

This sentence was abolished in the Lisbon Treaty and this change does, of course, make it quite reasonable, or at least possible, to argue that Article 325 on its own provides the EU with criminal law competence and that this competence is independent of the limitations of Title V Chapter 4. (Cf. the Commission's proposal for a Directive on the fight against fraud to the Union's financial interests by means of criminal law which is based on Article 325.)[6]

In this context it should also be noted that the Lisbon Treaty has arguably and at least according to its wording brought about several limitations that (arguably) did not accompany the competences that the EU had according to the judgement in the environmental case (C-176/03). For example, it could be argued that the annex competence under the old Treaty (as found by the European Court of Justice in the environmental case) was not limited to Directives: the European Court of Justice found that the EU had criminal law competence in the area of environmental protection and if such competence existed it could, arguably, be exercised not only through Directives but also through Regulations. Now, bearing in mind the wording of the Treaty, it is difficult to justify the conclusion that the EU has the competence to issue Regulations containing criminal law rules in the area of the protection of the environment.

[6] COM(2012) 363 final.

A third group of questions concerns the use *of general 'First Pillar' principles as regards the new criminal law competences*. What will the fact that criminal law cooperation is from now on part of a larger setting entail? A setting which is known to be inventive and dynamic to say the least. Will the transfer of criminal law cooperation mean that principles such as direct effect and indirect effect, the precedence of EU law and the principle of sincere cooperation become more important also in the criminal law area? Even if the Pupino case (C-105/03) showed that the cooperation under the Third Pillar was to at least some extent part of this legal environment, it could be argued that the Lisbon Treaty means that criminal law is now fully incorporated in the general EU law context. At least one important reason for 'separate treatment', ie the Third Pillar status of criminal law cooperation, has vanished.

At the same time, there are reasons to believe that criminal law will continue to be a special creature to some extent.

The fact that criminal law cooperation has been merged with the former First Pillar areas in one pillar does not, of course, relieve criminal law of all of its special characteristics. One obvious example is that the principle of legality, which is recognized not only by the Member States but also by EU law and by the European Court of Justice, limits the ways in which EU law can be used as a basis for imposing criminal liability. For example, it is clear that an EU Directive cannot as such form the basis of criminal liability and the principle of legality also means that there are limits to the obligations of courts and authorities in the Member States to interpret national law in the light of relevant EU law.

A fourth and very important question concerns *the relationship between the criminal law competence that now exists and the competence of the EU to issue rules on other types of sanctions* (first and foremost different types of administrative sanctions).

This question can be discussed in (radically) different ways. You can try to answer the question on a general and philosophical level (what is criminal in criminal law?), but you can also discuss it in a rather pragmatic way by trying to find a way to deal with the fact that most states (i) have different types of sanctions which are divided into different categories (criminal law sanctions, administrative sanctions etc) and (ii) have (slightly) different ways of distinguishing between these different types of sanctions.

Before the Lisbon Treaty (or at least before the judgement of the European Court of Justice in the environmental case) the dividing line between administrative sanctions and criminal law sanctions reflected the division between competence (administrative sanctions) and non-competence (criminal law sanctions). You might have thought that the importance of this distinction should have decreased after the Lisbon Treaty, but it has only been transformed: the dividing line between administrative sanctions and criminal law sanctions now reflects the division between general competence (administrative sanctions) and specific competence (mainly) situated under Title V Chapter 4 (criminal law sanctions). The distinction may also be of importance when deciding what the Member States must do with regard to a Directive that requires criminalization.

The question of how to distinguish administrative sanctions from criminal law sanctions is difficult in general, but it becomes, as has already been implied, even harder in a setting where 27 states, which all have slightly different ways of making the distinction, cooperate. You can, of course, make the distinction by using an autonomous EU concept of criminal law (sanctions), but this will inevitably cause problems when it is confronted with the different systems of the Member States (in which EU instruments should be implemented).

In this context it could also be emphasized that the relationship between the criminal law system and the system of administrative sanctions is an important question for the future. The existence of administrative sanctions in a certain area often affects the way criminal law is applied. The existence of administrative sanctions might, for example, under certain conditions exclude the application of criminal law (cf. the principle of ne bis in idem) or affect the way it is applied (the administrative sanctions being taken into account when sentencing an offence). It is, therefore, necessary to include them in the picture if you really wish to achieve harmonization in practice (not only on paper).

You could continue to add further questions that arise out of the new constitutional setting, but I think the ones presented above are the most important ones, or at least some of the most important ones.

3. CRIMINAL POLICY QUESTIONS

The Lisbon Treaty does not only bring about new legal questions and challenges. It also underlines the need to find a way of 'establishing criminal policy' within the European Union.

In the legal debate about the development of EU Criminal Law, it has for a long time been argued that *criminal law cooperation within the EU is one-sided and mainly focuses on increased repression* ('more' criminalization and 'more' punishment) and on facilitating cooperation by removing traditional obstructions to international legal assistance (fewer obstructions and more safeguards when it comes to cooperation).

In my view this criticism is mainly justified.

This is not to say that the EU has got it all wrong or that the EU has done unacceptable things. The point of discussing this one-sidedness has rather been to draw attention to the fact that the general direction of the cooperation is problematic, that there is a general tendency to give priority to the interests of the state rather than to the interests of the individual. Moreover, the Lisbon Treaty has underlined the need for such a discussion: it becomes much more important to deal with these problems if you intend to cooperate continuously and intensively. In short: when the EU is provided with criminal law competence, it means that the need for an all-out criminal law policy becomes increasingly more acute than before.

Having said this, it should immediately be admitted that it is not very surprising that it is difficult to find a proper balance in criminal law cooperation.

One factor that explains this one-sided focus of the form of cooperation is that criminal law cooperation started as an *interstate form of cooperation*, and that such cooperation, if I may generalize slightly, is not characterized by criminal policy thinking, but rather by an ad hoc approach where the cooperating states focus on things which seem important at the time. Thus, you might argue that cooperation within the EU has until now taken the expected path.

Further, criminal law cooperation at an interstate level is characterized by the fact that it is cooperation that is taking place on the basis of, or in addition to, already existing national systems. In other words, it is built on the understanding that *the criminal law systems*, and thus the main responsibility for criminal policy questions, are situated at the national level. Due to this, interstate cooperation obtains a 'complementary' character, which might help to explain why little effort has been made to actually shape a coherent criminal policy.

Thus, I would argue, when we are taking the step *from* a situation where EU criminal law cooperation could basically be described as a type of (boosted) interstate cooperation, to a situation where criminal law is merged into the ordinary EU system, we really need *to rethink our approach to EU criminal law* and find a way of actually forming an EU criminal policy. With new competences and increased ambitions come new and increased responsibilities.

This need for a more well-considered criminal policy has been emphasized by several debaters over the years. One attempt to put criminal policy questions on the agenda was made by the European Criminal Policy Initiative. This is a group of fourteen criminal law professors from different Member States (the author of this article is one of the members of the group) who published a *Manifesto on European Criminal Policy*[7] explicitly calling for a criminal law policy based on fundamental principles. The following is taken from the preamble to the Manifesto:

> The undersigned criminal law scholars from ten European countries would like to present their proposal for European criminal policy.
> This manifesto is based on the principles rooted in the common European Enlightenment tradition, namely:
> – in recognition of the fact that the spirit of Enlightenment is the major contributor to and the motor of European civilisation and current integration, and that it should guide us in the preservation of European culture and future cooperation between European countries; and
> – being convinced that criminal law legislation must adhere to the highest standard of democratic legitimacy and the rule of law (*Rechtsstaatlichkeit*) and that the future of European security can only be safeguarded within a system based on the concepts of democracy, freedom and fundamental legal principles.
> This manifesto reflects the dynamics of European integration, calling attention to the fact that substantive criminal law and criminal procedure law are increasingly becoming the focus of European legislation. At present, European legal instruments used for the

[7] The Manifesto is published (in different languages) in Zeitschrift für internationale Strafrechtsdogmatik 12/2009 (available at www.zis-online.com).

harmonisation of criminal legislation already exert influence on the existing national legal frameworks of substantive criminal law and criminal procedure law. Due to the amendments brought about by the Lisbon Treaty this tendency will be even stronger in future. The European institutions making criminal policy decisions on a large scale have failed to acknowledge criminal policy as an autonomous European policy. As a consequence they do not follow a coherent concept of criminal policy.

The Manifesto Group is convinced that Europe needs a balanced and coherent concept of criminal policy based on a number of fundamental principles (as listed below). These principles should be recognised as a basis for every single legal instrument which deals with or which could influence criminal law. The European legislator has to justify the relevance of its proposals in relation to the principles and standards of good governance. The criminal law principles constitute an integral part of the shared European criminal law tradition and can be derived from the normative structure of the European Union.

In the manifesto six fundamental principles of criminal law are highlighted:

1. The requirement of a legitimate purpose

The legislative powers of the EU in relation to criminal law issues should only be exercised in order to protect fundamental interests if: 1) These interests can be derived from the primary legislation of the EU; 2) The Constitutions of the Member States and the fundamental principles of the EU Charter of Fundamentals Rights are not violated, and 3) The activities in question could cause significant damage to society or individuals.

2. The ultima ratio principle

The European legislator may only demand that an act be criminalised if it is necessary in order to protect a fundamental interest, and if all other measures have proved insufficient to safeguard that interest. Only if this condition has been satisfied can criminal law be regarded as 'necessary' and in conformance with the European principle of proportionality.

3. The principle of guilt

European legislation requiring the Member States to criminalise certain acts must be based, without exception, on the principle of individual guilt (the principle of *nulla poena sine culpa*).

4. The principle of legality

In order to respect the fundamental rule of law requirements a criminal law system must adhere to the principle of legality. This principle, including its different sub-principles, is regarded as a general principle of law, as codified in Art. 6 (3) of the (new) Treaty on European Union or in Art. 7 (1) of the European Convention on Human Rights. For the purposes of criminal policy three central requirements which should be respected by the European legislator can be derived from this principle. [ie The lex certa requirement, the requirements of non-retroactivity and lex mitior and nulla poena sine lege parlamentaria]

5. The principle of subsidiarity

Instruments which are relevant for criminal law and which are enacted on the basis of shared competences in accordance with the general rules of EU law must meet the requirement of subsidiarity. According to this principle the EU legislator may take action only on the condition that the goal pursued (1) cannot be reached more effectively by measures taken at national level and (2) due to its nature or scope can be better achieved at Community level. Accordingly, the national legislator will be given priority in relation to the European legislator to the extent that the Member state is capable of dealing with a given issue. In this way the citizens will be brought closer to decision making in criminal legislation.

6. The principle of coherence

The invasive character of criminal law makes it especially important to ensure that every criminal law system is a coherent system. Such inherent coherence is a necessary condition if criminal law is to be able to reflect the values held to be important by society collectively and by individuals and their understanding of justice. Inner coherence is, furthermore, necessary in order to ensure acceptance of criminal law.

In this respect it was emphasised that it is essential both that the EU has respect for the coherence of the national criminal law systems and that EU instruments are in themselves constructed in a coherent way.)

You may, of course, say that these principles by and large form part of the common legal heritage of the Member States and also that they form part of the basic legal principles of EU law (in the Manifesto it is shown that each of these principles can be derived directly from EU law) and that it, consequently, is not very inventive to argue that they should be respected.

This is, of course, true.

To emphasize the importance of principles such as the principle of legality, the principle of guilt or the principle of subsidiarity is not very inventive.

However, the point of drawing up the manifesto was not to be inventive; as I see it, and as the European Criminal Policy Initiative sees it, the non-inventiveness is not a weakness of the Manifesto but rather one of its real strengths. The fact that the EU does not fully respect the listed principles is problematic precisely due to the fact that the principles are recognized by the EU and form part of the fundamental normative framework of the union.

In later years we have also seen official initiatives intended as contributions to the development. For example, Vice-President Reding has on several occasions outlined the 'the need for a balanced and coherent approach to criminal law policy' and the question is also in focus in the Commission Communication 'Towards an EU Criminal Policy: Ensuring the effective implementation of EU policies through criminal law'.[8] During the spring of 2012 the Commission also set up an expert group on EU criminal policy, the task of which is described in the following way in the Commission Decision:

[8] http://europa.eu/rapid/pressReleasesAction.do?reference=SPEECH/10/89&type=HTML

> Article 2
> Tasks
> The group's tasks shall be to advise the Commission on substantive criminal law in the context of the development of an EU criminal policy. This shall include in particular advice on any legal question that can arise in this context and shall also refer to the gathering of factual evidence for the assessment whether EU criminal law measures are essential to ensure the effective implementation of a Union policy, in consultation with existing expert groups in the policy fields concerned.
>
> Article 3
> Consultation
> The Commission may consult the group on any matter relating to the development of an EU criminal policy.

The expert group (ten academics and ten practitioners from different Member States) held its first meeting in June 2012 and is supposed to hold two meetings every year.[9]

An awareness of the one-sidedness of cooperation also characterized the discussions that preceded the Stockholm Programme. Of importance are also the Council conclusions from late 2009 that were intended as guidelines for the Council's criminal law deliberations (emphasizing, inter alia, the principles of subsidiarity and proportionality, the need for coherence, etc.).[10]

It should be emphasized, however, that the possibility to form a coherent criminal policy is not only a question of ambition on part of the EU institutions and the Member States. You should not forget that we face several challenges in this process.

One challenge is to handle, or rather rethink, *the focus on minimum rules* (cf. the wording of Articles 82(2) and 83 TFEU) which logically presupposes that EU cooperation is all about increased repression: if minimum rules are going to be of any value, it is logically necessary that the minimum level must be set above the existing level in the European Union. In other words, it is presupposed, or taken for granted, that it is the states that are the least repressive in the area which is supposed to be regulated that are the problem (they are the ones that should be brought in line with the others rather than the other way round). This type of minimum instrument is, of course, fully normal in international interstate cooperation. It is if you like the normal way of doing things. However, you could surely question whether it is wise to build the development of EU criminal law on minimum-level thinking.[11] Once again: when we have taken the step from interstate cooperation to EU criminal law competence, we might have to do things in a slightly different way than before.

[9] See Commission Decision of 21 February 2012 on setting up the expert group on EU criminal policy (2012/C 53/05). The author of this article is one of the members of the group.

[10] Council conclusions on model provisions, guiding the Council's criminal law deliberations.

[11] If you compare the minimum-level thinking with the thinking behind the principle of proportionality, you find yourself in a topsy turvy world: you do not (as you do according to the principle of proportionality) have to justify that a more intrusive measure is needed. Rather this idea is built into the very structure of this form of cooperation.

Another more general challenge is to handle the fact that *the legislative process within the EU is not set up in a way which makes it easy to 'steer' developments*. In a nation state there is (normally) a fairly stable situation in the parliament between elections which (normally) puts the government in a position where it can decide on which policy to set and pursue for a certain area. Within the EU the situation is more complex. Legislative acts are adopted by the Council (ie by a collective of Member States which change governments at different points in time and in addition you have the ever shifting Presidencies) and the European Parliament in a co-decision procedure. This is not a process in which you can put someone at the steering wheel. Figuratively speaking we are all on a train which keeps on moving, but where there is really no one who has the power to determine the route. In this perspective, things have become slightly better with the Lisbon Treaty (which provides for decision making with qualified majority voting), but the situation is still different from the one on Member State level.

A further challenge in this area is to handle the fact that all (or most) EU instruments should be implemented in all the different Member States, which all have their own criminal law systems with their own characteristics and peculiarities. This means that it will, for obvious reasons, be difficult to construct rules and regulations which fit well in all of the criminal law systems of the European Union. This is a general problem connected to the fact that European Criminal Law still is based on the different national criminal law systems, but at the same time is developing as an area of its own and is aiming to reshape the criminal law system of the Member States. This is where the principle of coherence comes into play: the EU must find a way of balancing the interest of harmonization and the interest of the respect for the inner coherence of the criminal law systems of the Member States.

4. CONCLUDING REMARKS

The Lisbon Treaty is yet another step in the development of European Criminal Law. It provides the EU with criminal law competence and it definitely creates new possibilities for the future.

At the moment we do not really know what the cooperation will entail at the end of the day. Will it in the end be a matter of continued cooperation based on the partly harmonized criminal law systems of the Member States?, Or will it lead to a situation where there are regional criminal law systems combined with a certain number of 'federal offences'? Or will there be a truly common European Criminal Law system? However, one thing is clear: the time is ripe to take legal policy questions seriously and the discussion on how to use the possibilities provided by the Lisbon Treaty should preferably precede the actual use of these possibilities.

In this text I have mainly asked or pointed at questions and problems. I have not provided many answers. I would, however, like to end the text by advocating that we need to let things take their time.

When the development of European Criminal Law is discussed, it is often said that cooperation is inefficient, that things take time and that it has been difficult to obtain quick results. I have great difficulties in understanding this line of argument. Of course the negotiations on new instruments have, at times, been troublesome and time-consuming. That is only natural when a number of states are to come to an agreement on difficult legal questions (decisions which will be very hard to revoke later on). The problem is, however, not that things take time, but rather that too much is done with too little preparation and too little discussion. When discussing these issues you should bear in mind that quantity is a positive thing only on the condition that the decisions made are good (and that quantity is negative if what is quantified is of a poor quality).

Part II
EU Criminal Law and Fundamental Rights

5
Mass Surveillance and Data Protection in EU Law – The Data Retention Directive Saga

THEODORE KONSTADINIDES*

1. INTRODUCTION

Mass surveillance in the European Union (EU) through the so-called Data Retention Directive (2006/24/EC) has been subject to intense controversy in the Member States. This chapter examines the contribution of the CJEU in unpacking the constitutional and human rights implications arising out of the retention of private data for the purpose of law enforcement. In spite of intense litigation, this chapter argues that the CJEU has not yet had the opportunity to rule on a number of essential constitutional and human rights questions related to the disproportionate invasion of the Directive on the right to privacy. The chapter commences with an account of how the Directive came into being as well as the main challenges met by the EU legislature in the process of adopting it. It then moves on to consider how the CJEU has defended the Directive in relevant cases regarding its interpretation or validity. The CJEU has so far dealt with the legal basis/competence aspect of the Directive. Although unconvincing, the CJEU's rationale for far-reaching supranational action in the field of criminal justice has been endorsed by the Treaty of Lisbon.

To use a colloquialism often employed by EU lawyers, the Communitarisation of what used to be the Third EU Pillar seems to have washed away any hanging questions with regard to the criminal justice spillover effect of internal market legislation. In light of this change, the main argument against Directive 2006/24/EC remains that the smooth functioning of the internal market and maintenance of internal security cannot compromise the fundamental right to privacy and the rule of law – ie the values on which the EU is founded. However, the CJEU has not yet had the opportunity to rule on the encroaching impact of

* School of Law, University of Surrey. The author would like to thank Maria Bergström for her helpful suggestions. All errors are obviously entirely mine.

EU harmonisation legislation on digital civil liberties. The uniform retention of communication and location data throughout the EU has further raised questions on the dubious limits of EU regulation upon the conduct of public enforcement authorities and private market actors through a mandatory data retention law. Hence, it is argued that the above questions exposed in recent litigation have not yet been properly addressed by the CJEU. It is further suggested that the CJEU's jurisprudence does not imply that a set of strict criteria for justifying non-consensual, blanket and indiscriminate retention and therefore interference with a person's right to privacy have been established.

2. THE ADOPTION OF DIRECTIVE 2006/24/EC

The Data Retention Directive (2006/24/EC), which provides for *a priori* mandatory storage by a state and/or exchange between Member States of telecommunications traffic and location data (ie data generated in the ordinary course of service - excluding content),[1] has been in force since 2007. The Directive requires telephone and Internet service providers to retain details of Internet and call data for not less than six months and not more than two years, in order to ensure that the data is available for the purpose of the investigation, detection and prosecution of serious crime. The overall implementation of the Directive in the Member States has been well overdue. Although all Member States have either formally implemented the Directive or have made a start at doing so, effective transposition across the EU is far from reality. The Commission has initiated infringement proceedings under Article 258 TFEU against a number of Member States including those, such as Germany and Romania, that originally transposed the Directive into national law, but whose constitutional courts later ruled that such legislation was unconstitutional.[2] The Commission has also handed down an Article 260 TFEU judgment against Sweden (examined later in this chapter)[3] and is expected to do the same against Germany.[4] Ineffective transposition of the Directive owes to the diversity of practice and difference of

[1] This is taken to mean the source of a communication as well as its destination. It includes the telephone number and the subscriber's name and address as well as the number(s) called (telecommunications) and the user's ID and name and address of the subscriber or registered user (Internet). The duration of the communication and geographical location of the equipment used is also included in the retained data.

[2] See for instance the German Data Retention Judgment, BVerfG, 2 BvE 2/08 of 30.06.2009, Absatz-Nr. (1-421) and the Romanian Data Retention Judgment, Decision no.1258 of 8.10.2009, Official Gazette no.798 of 3.11.2009. See also for more details on national implementation: European Commission, 'Evaluation report on the Data Retention Directive (Directive 2006/24/EC)', 18.4.2011, COM (2011) 225 final. What is more, an up-to-date table of the infringement actions taken by the Commission against the Member States for failure to implement the Directive is available at: http://ec.europa.eu/home-affairs/news/infringements/infringements_by_policy_police_co-operation_and_access_to_information_en.htm.

[3] Case C-270/11, *Commission v Sweden* [2011] OJ C 226/33.

[4] See Reuters, 'EU to Take Hard Line on German Resistance to Data Storage', 29 May 2012. Available at http://www.reuters.com/article/2012/05/29/eu-dataprivacy-idUSL5E8GTE4C20120529.

opinion between Member States on issues such as the duration and purpose of data retention, the procedures regulating access to personal data; and the cost of data retention for economic operators. The purpose of this section is to reveal the legal uncertainties that were somewhat disregarded during the drafting process of the Directive. This analysis will serve to explain why the Directive has been the subject of intense litigation before the CJEU.

The Data Retention Directive is the misshapen child of the aftermath of the London terrorist attacks in 2005, where it was commonly agreed between Member States that increased control over telecommunications is essential in order to investigate and prosecute terrorism and organised crime. Despite the strong political will of the governments of the Member States in favour of the establishment of EU surveillance tools, there was a significant gap in both national and EU legislation vis-à-vis data retention. Traffic data were either not stored systematically in the Member States or merely stored for billing purposes and in order to settle customer disputes. In some Member States, however, such data were not stored at all. As such, traffic data were not always available for public enforcement authorities to use against criminals for anti-terrorism purposes. Hence, following the Brussels EU Summit of 25 and 26 March 2004,[5] a group of four Member States[6] presented a Draft Framework Decision to be adopted under the former Third Pillar as a criminal law measure. It is noteworthy that Sweden was one of the states that helped put forward the proposal and made an argument about extending the scope of data retention beyond judicial cooperation to all kinds of police cooperation. The Draft Framework Decision proposed a retention period between twelve to thirty-six months depending on the value of the data in relation to countering crime and the cost of retention.[7] Finally, the Commission decided that in tune with ex Article 47 TEU (now Article 40 TEU)[8] the harmonisation of retention periods across the EU and exchange of traffic data by law enforcement authorities should be adopted under the former First Pillar. A Directive was thus considered as the most appropriate EU legislative instrument to regulate the obligation

[5] See the Declaration on Combating Terrorism adopted by the European Council on 25 March 2004, Presidency Conclusions available at: www.consilium.europa.eu/ueDocs/cms_Data/docs/pressData/en/ec/79696.pdf.

[6] The proposal was presented by France, Ireland, Sweden and the UK.

[7] Council of the European Union, Draft Framework Decision on the retention of data processed and stored in connection with the provision of publicly available electronic communications services or data on public communications networks for the purpose of prevention, investigation, detection and prosecution of crime and criminal offences, including terrorism, Brussels, 2 April 2004. Available at http://register.consilium.eu.int/pdf/en/04/st08/st08958.en04.pdf.

The Draft mentioned that under Article 15 of Directive 2002/58/EC the EU could adopt secondary legislation on data retention for the purposes of the prevention, investigation, detection or prosecution of crime. The Framework Decision, however, was not designed to achieve other Article 15 objectives – such as provide for data retention rules in order to safeguard national security, defence and public security.

[8] Former Article 47 TEU regulated the relationship between the Treaty on European Union (TEU) and the EC Treaty stipulating that no legal instruments adopted under the TEU may affect the legislative framework adopted under the EC Treaty.

on providers of electronic communication services to retain their subscribers' telephone and Internet data. Indeed, a Directive is less stringent compared to a Regulation and it allows considerable room for implementation manoeuvre to national governments vis-à-vis the appropriate public authorities to have access to the retained data.[9] According to Recital 5 of the Preamble to Directive 2006/24/EC, different requirements and technical differences between national provisions concerning data retention presented obstacles to the internal market and were to be harmonised. Moreover, the Commission set the time limit for the cross availability of data to a period between six months and two years from the date of communication.

The inception and adoption of the Data Retention Directive constitutes a pre-Lisbon example of cross-EU pillar interaction. In this case, a proposal for a Framework Decision by certain Member States inspired the Commission to put forward a proposal for a Directive. This is reminiscent of pre-Lisbon examples which demonstrate temporary synergy between the former EU pillars. For instance, with reference to the ship-source solution, while Directive 2005/35/EC ensured that polluters would be liable to criminal penalties in order to improve maritime safety, Framework Decision 2005/667/JHA contained the nature, types and levels of such penalties as a means of supplementing the Directive. The Framework Decision was, however, annulled by the CJEU which held that Articles 1 to 7 had as their main purpose the protection of the environment and, as such, they could have been properly adopted by using a former First Pillar legal basis (ex Article 175 EC – now Article 192 TFEU). Thus, similar to the Data Retention Directive, in the case of ship source pollution, a Directive was proposed on 13 March 2001 for the protection of the environment through criminal law. This is now Directive 2008/99/EC adopted on 19 November 2008.[10]

To return to our analysis on data retention, it needs to be stressed that had Directive 2006/24/EC been adopted now, the Commission would have most likely resorted to Article 83 TFEU as its legal basis. One should also note that the Treaty of Lisbon provides for a separate legal basis in the form of Article 16(2) TFEU, which is specific for the adoption of rules relating to the protection of individuals with regard to the processing of personal data by EU institutions, bodies, offices and agencies, and by the Member States when carrying out activities which fall within the scope of EU law, and the rules relating to the free movement of such data.[11] Back in 2005, however, the Commission had to justify the appropriateness of using a Directive (a First Pillar instrument) as a means of

[9] Commission Proposal for a Directive on the retention of data processed in connection with the provision of public electronic communication services and amending Directive 2002/58/EC, Brussels, 21.09.2005, COM (2005) 438 final.

[10] Directive 2008/99/EC on the protection of the environment through criminal law [2008] OJ L 328/28.

[11] See the Commission's Proposal for a Directive on the protection of individuals with regard to the processing of personal data by competent authorities for the purpose of prevention, investigation, detection or prosecution of criminal offences or the execution of criminal penalties, and the free movement of such data, Brussels, 25.01.2012, COM (2012) 10 final.

obliging Member States to establish a system for retaining communications data in order to tackle serious crime (a Third Pillar objective). In other words, the Commission had to find a 'market' angle. Hence, the argument was that diverse regulatory and technical national provisions concerning the retention of traffic data subjected service providers to different requirements regarding the types of data to be retained and the conditions of retention. In light of this argument, a Directive on Data Retention was regarded necessary in order to bring down the internal market obstacles caused by such legal diversity in the Member States. It was, therefore, adopted under the legal basis of current Article 114 TFEU, the basis for harmonisation measures for the internal market. To avoid criticism, the Commission noted that data retention had constituted the subject matter of previous legislative instruments based on the former First Pillar, in particular Directives 2002/58/EC and 95/46/EC.[12]

With reference to the protection of fundamental rights, the Commission recognised the Directive's impact upon the privacy right of citizens as guaranteed under Articles 7 (private and family life) and 8 (protection of personal data) of the EU Charter of Fundamental Rights proclaimed and signed in 2000.[13] According to Article 6 (1) TEU, the Charter is legally binding and can be invoked as a guarantee of justice and constitutional recognition of the right to data protection. This is all the more important since the right to protection of personal data included in Article 8 of the Charter is unique and has no equivalent in the ECHR. Yet, the rights guaranteed by the Charter are not unconditional. Article 52 of the Charter provides justification for interference with the right to privacy and protection of personal data. According to Article 52 (1) of the Charter, '[s]ubject to the principle of proportionality, limitations may be made only if they are necessary and genuinely meet objectives of general interest recognised by the Union or the need to protect the rights and freedoms of others'. Article 52 of the Charter, therefore, sets the (limited) scope of the right to respect private and family life and the right to the protection of personal data.

Indeed, the cross-border nature of organised crime and terrorism and the fact that Directive 2006/24/EC only deals with the processing of traffic data by service providers and not their content was considered enough evidence by the EU legislature that the principles of subsidiarity and proportionality had been complied with.[14] The Commission stressed that limitations to privacy and the protection of personal data are proportionate and necessary to meet the objectives of countering serious crime and terrorism. As a result, no general provisions were

[12] Directive 2002/58/EC of the European Parliament and of the Council of 12 July 2002 concerning the processing of personal data and the protection of privacy in the electronic communications sector (Directive on privacy and electronic communications) [2002] OJ L 201/37; Directive 95/46/EC of the European Parliament and of the Council of 24 October 1995 on the protection of individuals with regard to the processing of personal data and on the free movement of such data [1995] OJ L 281/31.

[13] The text of the Charter was not given full legal effect until 1 December 2009, as part of the Lisbon Treaty.

[14] This was stressed in the Preamble of the Directive (para 21).

proposed or adopted by the EU legislature vis-à-vis the safeguarding of the retention of communications data from potential abuses. This was the case especially since, according to the EU legislature, relevant data protection provisions were inherent in previous EU Directives.[15] Despite criticism by the European Data Protection Supervisor (EDPS) and the European Economic and Social Committee (EESC) that a mere reference to the existing legal framework on data protection was insufficient to satisfy the intrusive character of the Directive,[16] the EU legislature adopted a rather 'flimsy' and 'flawed' human rights test to ensure full compliance with citizens' fundamental rights as enshrined in Articles 7 and 8 of the Charter.[17] Directive 2006/24/EC was therefore adopted on 15 March 2006 and entered into force on 4 May 2006[18] with only two Member States voting against it in the Council (Ireland and the Slovak Republic).

3. THE CJEU'S RESPONSE TO CHALLENGES AGAINST THE DIRECTIVE

As the above discussion illustrates, the Data Retention Directive appeared irreconcilable with both EU and national law. First, in the pre-Lisbon pillarised system, it was hard to see how the Directive's central focus addressed the functioning of the internal market and not public safety and crime prevention. Second, the Directive raised concerns with regard to the extent of the interference with individual privacy rights protected by EU law, the ECHR and national constitutions. This section will look into the two challenges that have taken place against the Directive: a direct challenge on the correctness of its legal basis and an indirect one on its compatibility with fundamental rights. The CJEU has, so far, only dealt with the procedural/ legal basis aspect of the Directive in *Ireland v Parliament and Council*.[19] In this case, Ireland brought an action under Article 263 TFEU before the CJEU seeking the Directive's annulment. With reference to the validity of Directive 2006/24/EC vis-à-vis its fundamental rights compatibility, in an action brought by the civil rights advocacy group Digital Rights Ireland (DRI) against the relevant Minister for Communications, the Irish High Court decided to request under Article 267 TFEU a preliminary ruling from the CJEU. Both challenges will be considered in turn hereafter.

[15] See Directives 95/46/EC and 2002/58/EC (see above).

[16] Opinion of the European Data Protection Supervisor on the proposal for a Directive of the European Parliament and of the Council on the retention of data processed in connection with the provision of public electronic communication services and amending Directive 2002/58/EC, 26.09.2005, COM (2005) 438 final.

[17] Opinion of the European Economic and Social Committee on the Proposal for a Directive of the European Parliament and of the Council on the retention of data processed in connection with the provision of public electronic communication services and amending Directive 2002/58/EC, COM (2005) 438 final – 2005/0182 (COD).

[18] Directive 2006/24/EC on the retention of data generated or processed in connection with the provision of publicly available electronic communications services or of public communications networks and amending Directive 2002/58/EC [2006] OJ L 105/54.

[19] Case C-301/06, *Ireland v European Parliament and European Council* [2009] ECR I-593.

Looking back at the first challenge against the Directive in *Ireland v Parliament and Council* one may conclude that it was a wasted opportunity. This is because Ireland that brought action against the EU legislature based its case solely on the grounds that the Directive had not been adopted on an appropriate legal basis – ie that it should have been adopted under a legal basis stemming from the 'Third' rather than the 'First' Pillar (ie not the internal market provision of Article 114 TFEU).[20] Staying faithful to its *tobacco saga* judgments, in particular, its *BAT dicta*[21] the CJEU held once again in favour of Article 114 TFEU. The CJEU also resorted to the 'preference clause' of former Article 47 TEU (current Article 40 TEU) as a means of determining the threshold for connecting a particular measure with the internal market.[22] It was rather revealing at the time that the CJEU approved the indirect approximation of criminal law through internal market legislation. Yet, this aspect of the judgment has evaporated post-Lisbon given that the EC-EU dichotomy has ceased to exist and the field of judicial cooperation in criminal matters has become a fully-fledged EU policy. Indeed, under the current Title V of the TFEU, future measures in the area of police and judicial cooperation in criminal matters will take the form of Regulations and Directives adopted under the ordinary legislative procedure.

The CJEU's decision in *Ireland v Parliament and Council* contains elements of both fundamental rights enhancement and human rights restraint. On the one hand, Ireland's defeat before the CJEU meant that the Irish government could no longer afford to maintain a three-year retention period for telephone data under section 63(1) of the Criminal Justice (Terrorist Offences) Act 2005, which was significantly longer to the one suggested by Article 6 of the Directive (six months and two years respectively). On the other hand, however, the Communications (Retention of Data) Act 2011 – which transposed Directive 2006/24/EC into national legislation – requires Internet service providers to retain Internet data, previously not required by Irish law to be monitored or retained. This brings us to the second challenge against the Directive on fundamental rights grounds. The seeds to this challenge against the Directive before the CJEU were planted in 2009, almost at the same time that the Irish government sought to annul the Data Retention Directive on procedural grounds. It is also worth noting that there was a parallel legal universe behind these challenges as in November 2009

[20] The legal grounds for the choice of Article 114 TFEU as the legal basis for Directive 2006/24/EC had also been disputed in 2006 by the Land of Schleswig-Holstein (Germany) which successfully requested full access to internal Commission documents related to using Article 114 TFEU as the legal basis for the Directive. See Case C-406/06, *Landtag Schleswig-Holstein v Commission of the European Communities* [2006] OJ L 105/54.

[21] Case C-491/01, *R v Secretary of State ex p BAT and Imperial Tobacco* [2002] ECR I-11453. See especially para 62: '… provided that the conditions for recourse to Article 95 EC as a legal basis are fulfilled, the Community legislature cannot be prevented from relying on that legal basis on the grounds that public health protection is a decisive factor in the choices to be made…'.

[22] See for further analysis T Konstadinides, 'Wavering between Centres of Gravity: Comment on *Ireland v Parliament and Council*' (2010) 35 *European Law Review* 88; E Herlin-Karnell, 'Annotation of *Ireland v Parliament and Council*' (2009) 46 *Common Market Law Review* 1667.

the CJEU delivered a judgment against Ireland following an Article 258 TFEU action taken by the Commission for failure to transpose the Directive within the prescribed period.[23]

As mentioned earlier, in the second (human rights) challenge against the Directive, Digital Rights Ireland (DRI) brought a case before the High Court of Ireland against the Minister for Communications.[24] DRI challenged the Communications (Retention of Data) Act 2011, in particular the extent to which the State can require telecommunications providers to retain and to provide to the State, data on how customers use their services. In May 2010, the High Court held that DRI had sufficient standing to challenge the Communications (Retention of Data) Act 2011 and agreed to make a preliminary reference to the CJEU on the validity of Directive 2006/24/EC vis-à-vis its compatibility with the right to privacy.[25] At the request of the Irish Human Rights Commission (IHRC),[26] the High Court also sought guidance from the CJEU on whether national transposition legislation of an EU Directive must be in compliance with the human rights standards set out in the EU Charter of Fundamental Rights in order to be compatible with EU law. In August 2012, the High Court made a reference for a preliminary ruling seeking interpretation of Articles 3,4, and 6 of Directive 2006/24/EC vis-à-vis their compatibility with Articles 7, 8, 11 and 41 of the EU Charter of Fundamental Rights[27]

Let us now make some speculations about how the CJEU may approach the *DRI* case. One would agree that the first High Court's question regarding the compatibility of the Directive with the right to privacy was a matter of balancing necessity with proportionality. The CJEU may probably avoid engaging in a human rights discussion. Similar to *Ireland v Parliament and Council* the CJEU may point out that Directive 2006/24 only goes as far as harmonising the obligations of providers of publicly available electronic communications to retain individual data for the purpose of the investigation, detection and prosecution of serious crime, as defined by each Member State in its national law. As such, the retained data shall be disclosed to the relevant public enforcement authorities in accordance with the national laws of each Member State. One could argue that this would not be the first time the CJEU adopted far-reaching legislation and subsequently left it to the Member States to determine the practicalities vis-à-vis the level of intrusiveness with regard to fundamental rights. The CJEU took a similar stance in *Advocaten voor de Wereld* on the

[23] Case C-202/09, *Commission v Ireland* [2009] OJ C 167.

[24] *DRI v Minister for Communications et al*, Irish High Court, 5 May 2010, [2010] IEHC 221. Available at http://www.bailii.org/ie/cases/IEHC/2010/H221.html.

[25] At the time of writing (May 2012) there is no numerical reference or evidence on the CJEU's website that a preliminary reference has been made and that there is currently a ruling pending by the CJEU.

[26] The IHRC appeared as *amicus curiae* in the DRI case before the High Court.

[27] Case C-293/12, *DRI v Minister for Communications et al*. The preliminary reference was made on 10/08/2012. See http://eur-lex.europa.eu/LexUriServ/LexUriServ.do?uri=OJ:C:2012:258:0011:0011:EN:PDF.

definitions of the extraditable offences listed in the Framework Decision on the European Arrest Warrant (EAW).[28] It merely left the formulation of definitions of all-encompassing crimes such as terrorism and computer crime, to name but a few, to the competent authorities of the Member States. Of course the same could happen with reference to Article 1 of the Data Retention Directive in relation to 'serious crime' which is not defined at EU level.[29]

Advocaten voor de Wereld consists of the first national challenge against the Framework Decision on the European Arrest Warrant (EAW). The case explored the practical consequences stemming from the application of the principle of mutual recognition in criminal matters vis-à-vis the conformity of the abolition of the principle of double criminality with the principle of legality. The CJEU stressed that because harmonisation of national criminal law is not a precondition for the application of the EAW, the absence of definitions for the thirty-two listed offences in Article 2 (2) of the Framework Decision does not imply an inconsistency with the principles of equality and legality in criminal proceedings. The CJEU emphasised that whilst the EAW determines the scope of a procedural rule (the condition for surrendering criminals), it leaves it to the Member States to both define the extraditable offences listed in the EAW and provide for the appropriate penalties. As such, the CJEU held that the EAW is compatible with fundamental rights. The aftermath of *Advocaten* suggested a certain inconsistency deriving from the hesitation on the part of the EU institutions to address issues that are not raised in secondary legislation. It also unveiled the national courts' disinclination to question the protection of fundamental rights in EU law beyond a selfish critique related to the constitutional safeguards against the application of EU legislation upon their own nationals.

The case of data retention is different to extradition. The hesitation of the EU institutions to address the right to privacy owes to the fact that the Directive does not contain any rules governing the activities of public authorities for law enforcement purposes.[30] Perhaps the CJEU had a point in *Ireland v Parliament and Council* not to delve into a human rights discussion. Had the Directive contained a detailed system of data access and safeguards it would have been encroaching into the activities of the State in areas of criminal law and it would have had to be struck down as *ultra vires*. The *Passenger Name Records (PNR)* dicta is indicative of the thin red line that lies between EU legislation on data processing for a supply of services (*intra vires*) and data processing for safeguarding public security (*ultra vires*).[31] In the *PNR* case, a Decision adopted

[28] Case C-303/05, *Advocaten voor de Wereld* [2007] ECR I-03633. See also a case note by F Geyer (2008) 4 *European Constitutional Law Review* 149.

[29] See Joint Statement by the Council and the Commission in relation to Art. 12 Evaluation of the Draft Directive, 5888/06 ADD1, 10.02.2006.

[30] Case C-301/06, *Ireland v Parliament and Council*, paras 86-92.

[31] Joined cases C-317/04 and C-318/04, *European Parliament v Council and Commission* [2006] ECR I-04721.

under Article 114 TFEU enabling the transfer of air passenger name records from the EU to the US Bureau of Customs and Border Protection was annulled. The CJEU held that the internal market measure of Article 114 TFEU could not justify EU competence to conclude an agreement with the United States on data processing for law enforcement purposes. Setting the *PNR* case aside, following the coming into force of the Treaty of Lisbon, a new proposal for a Directive was put forward under Title V of the TFEU for establishing an EU-wide framework governing the collection, retention and use of PNR data – allowing Member States to collect PNR data from intra-EU flights in order to counter terrorism and serious crime.[32] What is more, in April 2012, the European Parliament approved a new EU-US PNR deal which allows US authorities to retain PNR data for up to five years.[33] It is argued that these developments will generate further litigation with reference to the scope of privacy rights in EU law.

As the present author has explored in a different paper, the Data Retention Directive was further fuelled during 2008-2010 by a number of constitutionality claims before the courts of the Member States.[34] The transposition saga of Directive 2006/24/EC reveals that national courts have been reticent to question the protection of fundamental rights in EU law. They have merely resorted to an esoteric criticism of the constitutional safeguards against the right to privacy available in the national constitutions they defend and uphold. In light of these developments one may ask whether the EU Charter of Fundamental Rights is likely to raise the threshold of human rights in EU law and help enhance the external scrutiny of EU legislation. Indeed, as pointed out earlier, post-2009 the Charter has become a formal source of EU law and comprises a standard of review for the validity of EU acts (Article 6 TEU). The case of *Schecke* forms an early example where the Charter was employed as a standard of review of the legality of EU secondary legislation on transparency laws in the management of Common Agricultural Policy (CAP) funding.[35] The judgment is relevant to the question of the legality of the Data Retention Directive since the main provisions invoked in *Schecke* were those on the protection of private life and personal data under Articles 7 and 8 of the Charter, as well as Article 8 of the ECHR.

[32] Proposal for a Directive of the Council and the European Parliament on the use of Passenger Name Record data for the prevention, detection, investigation and prosecution of terrorist offences and serious crime, 23 April 2012. Available at http://register.consilium.europa.eu/pdf/en/12/st08/st08916.en12.pdf.

[33] Council of the EU, 'Council adopts new EU-US agreement on Passenger Name Records (PNR)', Luxembourg, 26 April 2012, 9186/12 PRESSE 173.

[34] See for transposition problems related to Directive 2006/24/EC: T Konstadinides, 'Destroying democracy on the ground of defending it? The Data Retention Directive, the surveillance state and our constitutional ecosystem' (2011) 36 (5) *European Law Review* 722-736.

[35] Joined Cases C-92/09 and C-93/09, *Volker und Markus Schecke GbR and Hartmut Eifert v Land Hessen* [2010] OJ C 13/6. See for detail A-S Lind & M Strand, 'A New Proportionality Test for Fundamental Rights? The Joined Cases C-92/09 and C-93/09 *Volker und Markus Schecke GbR* (C-92/09) and *Hartmut Eifert* (C-93/09) *v Land Hessen* – SIEPS European Policy Analysis' (2011) 7 *EPA*. Available at www.sieps.se/sites/default/files/2011_7epa.pdf.

The CJEU's decision in *Schecke* suggests that despite the limitations to the right to privacy vis-à-vis Article 52 (1) of the Charter, the threshold for allowing data retention in EU law is high. The role of the principle of proportionality is ever crucial. The CJEU interpreted the 'necessary' requirement in the challenged Directive to mean 'strictly necessary' in the context of disclosure of personal data. In light of *Schecke*, the Data Retention Directive may have to be weighed against its alleged impact on privacy, and its overall design regarding its necessity and proportionality. The CJEU's case law may further inform the second question addressed to the CJEU by the Irish High Court in the *DRI* case – ie whether national implementation legislation of an EU Directive must be in compliance with the human rights standards set out in the Charter in order to be compatible with EU law. It is accepted that the Charter only binds EU institutions and Member States when they are implementing EU law. As such, the CJEU's reply will most likely be positive: Whilst EU institutions can be reviewed for compliance with the Charter, national governments may only be reviewed when they act within the scope of EU law or when they transpose EU legislation into domestic law. It follows that the Charter applies not only when Member States directly implement a Directive, but also when they choose to derogate from it. The CJEU will soon be called to determine the external boundaries of the Charter's application in light of two Austrian preliminary references made in 2013 to the CJEU on the compatibility of Directive 2006/24/EC with Articles 7, 8 and 11 of the Charter.[36]

4. LETTERS FROM SWEDEN

One would agree that the much-loathed Data Retention Directive constitutes a radical step in fighting crime in the EU. At the same time, it is hard to dispute that the Directive endorses state interference with the right to private life. Whilst waiting for the CJEU's *DRI* preliminary ruling on the Directive's legality, this final section will attempt to review current litigation before the CJEU and demonstrate the legal problems that Sweden has been called to resolve with reference to the transposition and interpretation of the scope of Directive 2006/24/EC. The section begins by considering the relevant infringement proceedings against Sweden, the first Member State so far to have received a hefty fine for failing to implement the Directive within the prescribed period. It then moves on to discuss the recent case of *Bonnier Audio AB*, which arose from a preliminary reference made by the Swedish Supreme Court. The CJEU's judgment is most controversial in terms of 'floodgates opening' given that the

[36] See Case C-594/12, *Seitlinger*, Preliminary reference made by Austrian Federal Constitutional Court on 1 March 2013l Case C-46/13, *H*, Preliminary reference made by the Austrian Data Commission (*Datenschutzkommission*) on 28 January 2013. See for a critique of the Charter F Fontanelli, The European Union's Charter of Fundamental Rights: Two Years Later' (2011) 3(3) *Perspectives on Federalism*, Available at www.on-federalism.eu/attachments/104_download.pdf.

Luxembourg Court did not exclude the extended use of Directive 2006/24/EC by Member States for any offence committed using telecom networks, including copyright infringements.

The EU adopted the Data Retention Directive in March 2006 and Member States were required to transpose it before 15 September 2007, with the option of postponing until 15 March 2009 the implementation of retention obligations relating to Internet data. Although most Member States have for some time operated a voluntary system of data retention of communications traffic data, they faced infringement proceedings by the Commission and were forced to adopt new legislation in light of the threat of further action.[37] In Sweden, the implementation of the Data Retention Directive has been delayed due to fundamental rights concerns. Sweden, which as mentioned earlier was initially in favour of Data Retention legislation, had a change of government in 2006, which resulted in minimal implementation of the Directive. The consequence of this was that in 2010, the Commission started infringement proceedings against Sweden under Article 258 TFEU and held that the government had failed to fulfil its obligations under the Directive.[38] This action was followed by further Commission proceedings against Sweden in May 2011 under Article 260 TFEU. This time the Commission claimed that under Article 260 (2) TFEU, Sweden should pay financial penalties due to its failure to comply with the CJEU's earlier judgment.[39] In particular, the Commission proposed that the CJEU imposes on Sweden a daily penalty payment of EUR 40,947.20 and a fixed daily amount of EUR 9,597 for each day that the necessary measures were not taken to implement the Directive. Almost a year later, the CJEU is still expected to rule on the case against Sweden. However, on 31 May 2012, in light of Sweden's full implementation of Directive 2006/24/EC, the Commission made a partial withdrawal of the case.[40] This effectively means that although the Commission decided to withdraw the daily penalty payment, it has maintained the request to the Swedish government to pay the lump sum. The aim of the lump sum in this case is to penalise the continuation of Sweden's infringement between the initial Article 258 TFEU judgment and the subsequent Article 260 TFEU judgment.

On top of the Commission's infringement proceedings related to the Directive's delayed implementation, Sweden has been confronted with yet another value judgment related to the interpretation of the Directive's scope with regard to who can have access to the retained data and the purpose for which such data can be used. The uncertainty related to the scope of Directive 2006/24/EC stems

[37] During 2009-2010 only there are a number of public enforcement actions by the Commission: Case C-394/10, *Commission v Luxembourg* [2010] OJ C 274/26; Case C-189/09, *Commission v Austria* [2010] OJ C 246/12; Case C-192/09, *Commission v the Netherlands* [2009] OJ C 180/58; Case C-211/09, *Commission v Greece* [2009] OJ C 193/17; Case C-202/09, *Commission v Ireland* [2010] OJ C 24/26.

[38] Case C-185/09, *Commission v Sweden* [2010] OJ C 80/10.

[39] Case C-270/11, *Commission v Sweden* [2011] OJ C 226/33.

[40] European Commission Press Release, 'Data Retention: Commission takes Germany to Court Requesting that fines be imposed' IP/12/530, 31.05.2012.

from the fact that Article 1 of the Directive provides that the relevant data retained is destined for the competent national authorities in specific cases and in accordance with national law, without, however, listing any such authorities. This provision allows ample room for national discretion where Member States may choose to widen data access beyond law enforcement authorities and in any case they regard it appropriate. Such sloppy drafting of the Directive implies that apart from law enforcement authorities, both natural and legal persons may often obtain access to confidential data retained under Directive 2006/24/EC. This practice of 'function creep' was approved by the CJEU in a judgment delivered on 19 April 2012 from a preliminary reference made by the Supreme Court of Sweden on the interpretation of Articles 3 to 5 and 11 of Directive 2006/24/EC on the enforcement of intellectual property rights.[41]

In this case Bonnier Audio, a copyright holder of audio books, requested access to retained telecommunications data (name, address, and IP address) from an Internet service provider in order to identify a subscriber whose Internet Protocol address had been used for intellectual property infringing purposes. In the absence of a provision in Directive 2006/24 which prevents a party to a civil dispute from being ordered to disclose subscriber data to someone other than a public authority, the CJEU held that Member States are not precluded from using the Directive to enforce intellectual property rights. The CJEU held that the right to respect private and family life inherent in Article 7 of the EU Charter of Fundamental Rights has to be balanced against the protection of intellectual property enshrined in Article 17 of the Charter. The CJEU further established for future cases that in the event a private party requests access to personal data, such access would have to be ordered by a national judge taking into account the principle of proportionality. The language of proportionality employed here by the CJEU is reminiscent of that in *Rottmann*.[42] The proportionality assessment suggested by the CJEU in both cases lacks detail and guidance and, as such, leaves Member States considerable leeway to undermine the fundamental rights of their citizens in favour of large-scale data retention.

5. CONCLUSION

The purpose of this chapter was to unveil the main complex issues surrounding the so-called Data Retention Directive as well as the CJEU's contribution in assessing the internalities of the blanket harmonisation of the length of time that telecom operators and Internet providers must retain data under EU legislation. The chapter has provided insight into the blurry scope and objectives of the Data

[41] Case C-461/10, *Bonnier Audio AB and Others v Perfect Communication Sweden AB*, Judgment of the Court, 19.04.2012.

[42] Case C-135/08, *Janko Rottman v Freistaat Bayern* [2010] ECR I-01449. See also T Konstadinides, 'La Fraternité Européenne? The Extent of National Competence to Condition the Acquisition and Loss of Nationality from the perspective of EU Citizenship' (2010) 35(3) *European Law Review* 401.

Retention Directive and, by extension, the future of telecommunications data retention in Europe which will have to be proportionality-friendly and subject to judicial oversight. It has been argued that the regime forged by Directive 2006/24 lacks adequate legal safeguards in order to limit the risk of abuses of a host of rights guaranteed by both EU primary and secondary law as well as the European Convention of Human Rights (ECHR).[43] This is all the more crucial since certain studies on the application of the Directive in the Member States have demonstrated that blanket harmonisation of the length of time that telecom operators and Internet providers must retain data has proven to be superfluous for the investigation and prosecution of serious crime.[44] The empirical evidence to support the necessity of data retention is overall poor. This is confirmed by the very revealing consultation paper published in late 2011 by the European Commission services on reforming the Directive.[45] Among other things it is noted that the alleged value of historic communications data in terrorism or other cases involving serious crime has only been confirmed by eleven out of the twenty-seven Member States. It is also reported that the lack of clarification by EU institutions with regard to the type of data retained for combating crime or business purposes has resulted in confusion. For instance, some Member States have encouraged the storage of data (such as instant messaging and chat) which falls outside the scope of Directive 2006/24. As such, clarity with reference to the purpose and scope of the Directive as well as the establishment of safeguards for access and use of the retained data constitute high priority areas.

In light of these developments, the present author welcomes alternative legal instruments to Directive 2006/24 – in particular, the proposal on data preservation put through by Peter Schaar, the German Federal Commissioner for Data Protection and Freedom of Information. The proposal, also mentioned by the Council's Working Party on Data Protection and Information Exchange, suggests the substitution of the Directive on data retention with a 'quick freeze' system, which would make data storage dependent on a court order.[46]

[43] The right to protection of personal data exists in Article 16 TFEU, which includes provisions for a general application in areas such as judicial cooperation in criminal matters and Article 39 TEU where data protection is relevant in the sphere of Common Foreign and Security Policy. See also Directives 95/46/EC and 2002/58/EC; Regulation (EC) 45/2001 and Articles 7 and 8 of the EU Charter of Fundamental Rights.

[44] See Working Party on Data Protection and Information Exchange (DAPIX – Data Protection) Evaluation report on the Data Retention Directive (Directive 2006/24/EC of 15 March 2006 on the retention of data generated or processed in connection with the provision of publicly available electronic communications services or of public communications networks and amending Directive 2002/58/EC), 4 May 2011, DG H 2B, 10806/11; European Digital Rights, Shadow evaluation report on the Data Retention Directive (2006/24/EC), 17 April 2011, p.4. Available at www.edri.org/files/shadow_drd_report_110417.pdf.

[45] Council of the EU, Commission Services, 'Consultation on Reform of Data Retention Directive: Emerging themes and next steps', 18620/11,15 Dec 2011.

[46] The Federal Commissioner for Data Protection and Freedom of Information, Press Release: 'Peter Schaar: "Quick Freeze" instead of data retention', 14.06.2010. Available at: www.bfdi.bund.de/EN/PublicRelations/PressReleases/2010/22_%22QuickFreeze%22.html?nn=410156. See also note 40 above with regard to the relevant report by the Working Party on Data Protection and Information Exchange.

Such a *Kadi*-equivalent system would allegedly constitute a more efficient arrangement from the rule of law point of view, for the prosecution of serious cross-border crime than the current framework on blanket data retention. Such a system would discourage intense and all-encompassing telecommunications surveillance. It would also be fit for resolving civil disputes, which are unrelated to the fight against terrorism and organised crime. But still, in order to do so, the EU legislature has to come to a decision as to what constitutes 'serious crime' – a term which lies undefined in the Directive and, as seen in *Bonnier Audio AB*, gives complete discretion to Member States to hijack the Directive by using retained data for infringements which lie outside the scope of criminal investigation. This study indicates that the lack of an exact determination of the area of data necessary for the identification of natural or legal persons ('related data') does not merely constitute a transposition problem that can simply be remedied through national legislation in one Member State. Data controllers established in several Member States will still have to make themselves familiar with diverse national legislation within the EU. The result is a fragmented legal environment that not only results in legal uncertainty but is also incredibly expensive for businesses.[47]

Despite the overall dark picture painted in this chapter with regard to the alleged necessity of large-scale retention of traffic data, the new proposal for a Directive on the protection of individuals vis-à-vis the processing of personal data by law enforcement authorities for crime prevention is a positive development.[48] If adopted, such a Directive will give meaning to Article 16 TFEU both as a source of the right to protection of personal data and as a specific legal basis for the adoption of rules on the protection of personal data within the context of judicial co-operation in criminal matters and police co-operation. The character of the proposal is generally innovative in that it goes further than Directive 95/46/EC.[49] For instance, it provides for the 'right to be forgotten' that allows individuals to demand that data collectors delete their retained data when there are no legitimate grounds to retain data. What is more, Article 54 provides for compensation by the Member States, controllers or processors for the damage suffered in cases of an unlawful data processing operation. The proposed Directive may not, however, be met with enthusiasm by all national governments

[47] See Commission Staff Working Paper, Executive Summary of the Impact Assessment on the proposal for a Directive on the protection of individuals with regard to the processing of personal data by competent authorities for the purpose of prevention, investigation, detection or prosecution of criminal offences or the execution of criminal penalties, and the free movement of such data, Brussels, 25 Jan 2012 SEC (2012) 73 final.

[48] See the Commission's Proposal for a Directive on the protection of individuals with regard to the processing of personal data by competent authorities for the purpose of prevention, investigation, detection or prosecution of criminal offences or the execution of criminal penalties, and the free movement of such data, Brussels, 25 Jan 2012, COM (2012) 10 final.

[49] Directive 95/46/EC of the European Parliament and of the Council of 24 October 1995 on the protection of individuals with regard to the processing of personal data and on the free movement of such data [1995] OJ L 281/31.

which may be reticent towards witnessing the conduct of their public authorities being restrained by EU law. This is because the proposed Directive would extend the scope of data protection rules to 'domestic' processing.

To reflect on the title of this edited volume, it seems that the once cooperative model of 'European Police and Criminal Law' has shifted towards a coercive one. Such a model is based on rapid and intrusive action against potentially serious security threats. The EU is, therefore, promoting a system whereby mere suspicion suffices to resort to actions, such as intense and all-encompassing telecommunications surveillance. Judging from the infringement proceedings against a host of Member States, it appears that not all national governments are ready to adapt to the coercive EU criminal law model (although Commission infringement proceedings against them gradually force them to do so). As seen in this chapter, the effective transposition of the Directive goes further than merely establishing a legislative framework for the free flow of personal data in the internal market. The proposed Directive on data protection with regard to the processing of personal data by competent authorities may provide some relief to certain Member States with reference to the protection of individual privacy. It then depends on whether, in every day practice, national governments will choose the pervasive Orwellian surveillance state model over one based on a high threshold of individual data protection rights.

6

Ne bis in idem *in Criminal Proceedings*

ALEXANDROS-IOANNIS KARGOPOULOS*

1. INTRODUCTION – *NE BIS IN IDEM* AS A FUNDAMENTAL PRINCIPLE OF CRIMINAL PROCESS

'*Ne bis in idem*' or the right against '*double jeopardy*' as it is also known[1], is a fundamental principle of criminal process[2] found in almost every legal

* Judge of First-Instance (Civil/Criminal Division) Greece, PhD candidate (Democritus Un), LLM (Democritus Un), LLM (Un College London), LLB (Un of Kent), Dipl of Human Rights (Acad of Eur Law-EUI), email: kargopoulos@gmail.com.

[1] The principle is widely known under the first heading in civil law systems and under the second in common law systems. See S Trechsel, *Human Rights in Criminal Proceedings*, The Collected Courses of the Academy of European Law, Vol. XII/3 (Oxford, Oxford University Press, 2005) 382, J Sprack, *A Practical Approach to Criminal Procedure*, 12th edn (Oxford, Oxford University Press, 2008) 280–1, L Daqun, 'Double jeopardy' in A Cassese (ed), *Oxford Companion to International Criminal Justice*, (Oxford, Oxford University Press, 2009) 305, J-L De La Cuesta, 'Concurrent National and International Criminal Jurisdiction and the Principle "ne bis in idem", General Report', (2002) 73 *RIDP* 707, 709. In civil law systems, the principle is associated with the *res judicata* of criminal judgments that is attained when all available means of appeal have been exhausted, which, in principle, are available to both the defence and the prosecutor alike. In contrast, in common law systems the prosecutor is not in principle able to challenge a judgment issued by a court – a fact which is explained by the functioning of the jury system and the legitimacy that those judgments bear – and therefore, the protection against double jeopardy is seen as an impenetrable and absolute rule, although it has been qualified in some jurisdictions, M Chiavario, in M Delmas-Marty and JR Spencer (eds), *European Criminal Procedures,* (Cambridge, Cambridge University Press, 2002) 573. As such, in common law systems the principle of *ne bis in idem* is also intrinsically associated with what is known in civil law systems as the *non reformatio in pejus* principle, which is seen as a side-effect of appeals and protects the defendant from being put in an worse position by the higher court (ie by imposing a higher sentence or convicting him of a more serious crime). However, the greatest differences exist between the different conceptions of the principle found in systems belonging to the same legal family, Tallgreen and A Reisinger Coracini, 'Article 20 Ne bis in idem', in O Triffterer (ed), *Commentary on the Rome Statute of the International Criminal Court*, 2nd edn, (CH Beck/Hart/Nomos, 2008), 673, as, for example, between the Greek and the German system. However, in the author's view the alleged differences between common and civil law systems are over-exaggerated as the principle may identified with *the prohibition of a second evaluation of a criminal act of a certain perpetrator once this has been assessed by the competent judicial bodies and no other regular procedural avenues for the reversal of their judgement exist*. Similarly, raising the point about misconceptions over the alleged discrepancies between common law and civil law systems, see C Van Den Wyngaert & G Stessens, 'The International non bis in idem principle: resolving some of the unanswered questions' (1999) 48 *ICLQ* 779, 790.

[2] Its roots can be traced back to ancient Attic law, as evident by the speech of Demosthenes, Peri Ateleias pros Leptinin [On imperfection to Leptinis], XX:147 'Now the laws forbid the same man

system.[3] It literally means 'not twice for the same' and protects the individual from being tried a second time (the 'bis' element) for the same criminal act (the 'idem' element). In essence, the principle amounts to a self-imposed limitation on the *ius puniendi* of states, which is exhausted when criminal proceedings are finally discontinued or when the defendant is finally acquitted or convicted on the criminal charge that was brought against him. The principle is founded on a two-fold basis; on the need to ensure legal certainty and the systemic integrity of national criminal systems by shielding the finality of judgements (*res judicata pro veritate accipitur*) and on the protection of the liberty of the individual from consequent criminal proceedings for the same charge.[4]

An important distinction should be drawn however, between the principle when applied domestically and the principle when applied between states with concurring criminal jurisdictions (usually termed as '*horizontal*' *ne bis in idem*). EU law guarantees the latter, while most international instruments guarantee the former. *Ne bis in idem* may be an impenetrable guarantee with very few and strict exceptions, when applied within a single jurisdiction, but when it comes to the effect of foreign criminal judgements, *ne bis in idem* is the exception rather than the rule. For, due to the principle of national sovereignty and sovereign equality[5], states are not bound to comply with foreign judgements[6] and, in reality, they

to be tried twice on the same issue, be it a civil action, a scrutiny, a contested claim, or anything else of the sort', and Against Timocrates, XXIV:55, 'The legislator does not permit any question once decided by judgement of the court to be put a second time'. It is also found in the Justinian's Digest where it is provided that 'Isdem criminibus, quibus quis liberatus est, non debet praeses pati eundem accusari', D.48.2.7.2 ('on the same charges that a man was set free, no other charge can be brought against him').

[3] Some states, such as Germany, Cyprus and Portugal have afforded constitutional status to the principle, while most countries, like France, Belgium and Greece have inserted it in provisions of their criminal codes or codes of criminal procedures. See for details the extensive national reports on the issue, XVIIth International Congress of Penal Law, 'Concurrent National and International Criminal Jurisdiction and the Principle "Ne bis in idem"' (2002) 73 *RIDP*.

[4] The Latin legal maxim is found in the Justinian's Digest, D.50.17.207 ('Where a matter has been decided, it is considered as true.'), for the twofold basis of the principle see, *inter alia*, Opinion of Adv Gen R-J Colomer, in Cases C-436/04, *Léopold Henri van Esbroeck*, [2006] ECR I-02333, para 19, Opinion of Adv Gen R-J Colomer, in Joined Cases C-187/01, *Hüseyin Gözütok* and C-385/01, *Klaus Brügge*, [2003] ECR I-01345, para 49, I Anagnostopoulos, 'Ne bis in idem' (2002) 73 *RIDP* 965, 966, L Daqun, (2009), above n 1, I Tallgreen and A Reisinger-Coracini (2008), above n 1, 673–4, J Vervaele, 'Case Comment in Cases C-187/01 and C-385/01' (2004) 41 *CML Rev* 796, 801, M Wasmeier, 'The Principle of ne bis in idem' (2006) 77 *RIDP* 121, 121, D Spinellis, 'The ne bis in idem principle in "global" instruments' (2002) 73 *RIDP* 1149, 1150, note 4. The independence of the judiciary is also safeguarded through *ne bis in idem*, while it is further being advocated that the prohibition of proceedings for the second time is justified as a 'sanction' against state bodies for their failure to ensure the effective scrutiny of the case at hand in the proceedings, since failure of the state should never be used to the detriment of the individual, S Trechsel, (2005), above n 1, 383.

[5] This principle is manifested in Article 2(7) of the UN Charter, 24 October 1945, UNTS 1.XVI, also see ICJ, *Military and Paramilitary Activities in and Against Nicaragua, (Nicaragua v The United States of America)*, Merits, [1986] ICJ Reports 108, para 205.

[6] A Cassese, *International Criminal Law*, 2nd edn (Oxford, Oxford University Press, 2008) 338–9, S Trechsel (2005), above n 1, 386, A Colangelo, 'Double Jeopardy and Multiple Sovereigns: A Jurisdictional Theory' (2009) 86 *Wash U L Rev* 769, 797–8, U Neumann, 'The principle of Universal Jurisdiction' in I Manoledakis and C Prittwitz (eds), *Internationalisation of Criminal Law* (Ant Sakkoulas publ, 2003)

rarely do so.[7] In such instances, the *ratio* behind *ne bis in idem* vanishes. The need to ensure the integrity of the legal system is lacking as different legal orders are involved,[8] while the protection of the individual yields to the legitimate interest of states to punish the perpetrator. To mitigate these shortcomings in cross-border cases when *ne bis in idem* is inapplicable, the principle of 'deduction' usually comes into play and the sentence imposed is reduced by the term served abroad. Concluding, it is noted that horizontal *ne bis in idem* is not merely a fundamental principle of criminal process, but a complex jurisdictional rule regulating the exercise of the *ius puniendi* of states.[9]

2. *NE BIS IN IDEM* IN THE CONTEXT OF CRIMINAL PROCEEDINGS UNDER EU LAW

2.1 Legal Background to the Principle

Ne bis in idem has been originally enshrined in Article 14(7) of the ICCPR[10] and Article 4 of Protocol 7 of the ECHR.[11,12] Nevertheless, both instruments

4, C Milonopoulos, *International Criminal Law. Territorial Limits of Criminal Laws* (Ant Sakkoulas publ, 1993) 56, D Spinellis, 'Supra-national Application of the Ne Bis in Idem Principle' (2004) *Poinika Chronika* 673, 673. On the contrary, states are, in principle, bound to recognise the *res judicata* of judgements issued by international criminal tribunals due to the 'primary' jurisdiction of the latter and thus, are obliged to afford the *ne bis in idem* protective effect to their judgements (the so-called '*vertical ne bis in idem*'). On the International Criminal Court, see Articles 17 in conjunction with 15, 18, 19 of the Rome Statute of the International Criminal Court, UN Doc A/CONF.183/9 (17 July 1998) and UN, Report of the Ad Hoc Committee on the Establishment of an International Criminal Court, GAOR (Fiftieth Session) Suppl No 22, UN Doc A/50/22, p 9, para 43, I Tallgreen & A Reisinger Coracini (2008), above n 1, p 686. See also, Int'l Criminal Tribunal for the former Yugoslavia, UN SC Res 827 (1993), 25 May 1993, Annex, Articles 9 and 10, Int'l Criminal Tribunal for Rwanda, UN SC Res 955 (1994), 8 Nov 1994, Annex, Articles 8 and 9.

[7] U Neumann (2003), ibid, 4, A Colangelo (2009), ibid, 779, D Spinellis (2004), ibid, 673, A Obore-Odora, 'Competence of the International Criminal Tribunal for Rwanda' (1999) 6 *Murdoch Electronic Law Journal* 3, para 81, I Tallgreen and A Reisinger Coracini (2008), above n 1, 673–4, and 677, L Daqun (2009), above n 1, 305, J-L De La Cuesta (2002) above n 1, 707, 717, 732, S Trechsel, above n 1, 386, ICTY, Case No IT-94-1, *Prosecutor v Duško Tadić*, Decision on the Defence motion on the principle on non-bis-in-idem , 14 Nov 1995, para 9.

[8] C Van Den Wyngaert and G Stessens (1999), above n 1, 792.

[9] A sovereign state can exercise its criminal jurisdiction in all instances of permissible jurisdictional bases, subject to any exceptions to the contrary, such as immunity of officials. These bases would be the territoriality principle, active and passive personality principles, as well as the principles of protection and universal jurisdiction. For details, A Cassese (ed), *Oxford Companion to International Criminal Justice* (Oxford, Oxford University Press, 2009), under the relative key words, M Shaw, *International Law*, 6th edn (Cambridge, Cambridge University Press, 2008) 652 et seq, M Akehurst, 'Jurisdiction in International Law' (1972–1973) 46 *BYIL* 145, CM Bassiouni, 'Theories of Jurisdiction and their Application in Extradition Law and Practice' (1974/1) 5 *Cal W Int'l LJ* 3, Harvard Research in International Law, 'Jurisdiction with Respect to Crime', (Supp. 1935) 29 *AJIL* 435, 495.

[10] International Covenant on Civil and Political Rights, GA Res 2200A (XXI), 16 Dec 1966, 999 *UNTS* 171.

[11] Protocol No 7 to the Convention for the Protection of Human Rights and Fundamental Freedoms, Strasbourg, 22.XI.1984, ETS No 117.

[12] The 'bis' element has been understood to mean that there must have been a final decision by a competent court or tribunal. Final is 'A decision is considered final, when no further ordinary

followed[13] the established rule under international law dictating that states could not be bound by the finality of foreign criminal judgements and thus, embodied the traditional conception of the principle which is applied within a single state only.[14]

The first attempts to introduce a true 'horizontal' *ne bis in idem* accruing from foreign criminal judgements came within the framework of the Council of Europe. The first of those instruments was the European Convention on the International Validity of Criminal Judgements of 1970,[15] followed later by the European Convention on the Transfer of Proceedings in Criminal Matters of 1972.[16] Unfortunately, these were ratified only by a small number of states.[17] Noteworthy is also the European Convention on Extradition of 1957, which lays down *ne bis in idem* as a valid ground for the refusal of an application for extradition once a final judgement has been passed in the requested state.[18] Similarly, *ne bis in idem* was introduced as a ground for refusal of an application for judicial assistance in the Convention on Laundering, Search, Seizure and Confiscation of the Proceeds from Crime 1990.[19]

remedies are available or when the parties have exhausted such remedies or have permitted the time-limit to expire without availing themselves of them'. Explanatory Report to Protocol No 7 of the Convention for the Protection of Human Rights and Fundamental Freedoms, Strasbourg, 22.XI.1984, ETS No 117, paras 22 and 29. In this regard, see ECtHR, *Sergey Zolotukhin v Russia* [GC], Judgment of 10 Feb 2009 (appl no 14939/03), paras 107–8, *Tsonyo Tsonev v Bulgaria* (no 2), Judgment of 14 Jan 2010 (appl no 2376/03), para 53. The 'idem' element has been interpreted by the ECtHR along the lines of the '*idem factum*' to cover all the material facts assessed by the first Court, irrespective of their legal characterisation, ECtHR, *Sergey Zolotukhin v Russia* [GC], Judgment of 10 Feb 2009 (appl no 14939/03), paras 78–84.

[13] J Vervaele (2004), above n 4, 801 and 804, I Tallgreen and A Reisinger Coracini (2008), above n 1, 678. S Trechsel (2005), above n 1, 386.

[14] This is mainly due to normative force of the phrase 'with the law and penal procedures of each country/of that State'. On the ECHR Article 4 of Protocol 7, see Explanatory Report on Protocol No 7, ETS No 117, para 27, ECmsHR, *Gestra v Italy*, Decision of 16 Jan 1995 (appl no 21072/92), Concurring Opinion of Judge Sicilianos, in *Tomasović v Croatia*, Judgment of 18 Jan 2012 (appl no 53785/09), 3rd sent, On the ICCPR Article 14(7), see Communication no 204/1986, *A.P. v Italy*, UN Doc CCPR/C/OP/2 at 67 (1990) paras 7.3 and 8, Communication no 692/1996 (6 Feb 1996), *A.R.J. v Australia*, UN Doc. CCPR/C/60/D/692/1996, para 6.4, ICTY, Case No IT-94-1, *Prosecutor v Duško Tadić*, Decision on the defence motion on the principle on non-bis-in-idem, 14 Nov 1995, para 9, see also its *travaux préparatoires,* GA (fourteenth session) A/C.3/SR.963, p 3 in M Bossuyt and J Humphrey, *Guide to the Travaux Préparatoires of the International Covenant on Civil and Political Rights* (Martinus Nijhoff Publishers, 1987) 316.

[15] European Convention on the International Validity of Criminal Judgements, The Hague, 28.V.1970, ETS No 70, Article 53.

[16] European Convention on the Transfer of Proceedings in Criminal Matters, Strasbourg, 15.V.1972, ETS No 73, Article 35.

[17] The former has been ratified by 22 member states of the Council of Europe and the latter by 25, although few of them are actually Member States of the EU. For the contracting state parties and the ratification status of those Conventions see the website of the Council of Europe, at conventions.coe.int/.

[18] European Convention on Extradition, Paris, 13.XII.1957, ETS No 24, Article 9.

[19] Convention on Laundering, Search, Seizure and Confiscation of the Proceeds from Crime, Strasbourg, 8.XI.1990, ETS No 141.

2.2 Establishment of the Principle under EU Law

In the context of the European Communities, it soon became evident to certain Member States that a closer union required the abolition of internal borders and that such a development would also inevitably entail the recognition of foreign *res judicata* as otherwise the free movement of persons would be hindered.[20] This resulted in the drafting and signing by a small group of Member States of the Schengen Agreement in 1985[21] supplemented by the Convention Implementing the Schengen Agreement in 1990[22] (*herein after 'CISA'*) that introduced the revolutionary and horizontal *ne bis in idem* in its Articles 54–58. However, the Schengen Conventions were enacted outside the Community framework, lacking therefore all the characteristics of EU law. Their normative status within Member States varied significantly according to national law precepts, while their interpretation inevitably rested solely on the variable approaches followed by national courts.[23] Hence, with the conclusion of the Schengen Agreements, no real transfer of sovereign powers on the regulation of criminal jurisdictions to the EC took place. On the contrary, what was achieved was a common agreement with mutual compromises and a cooperative framework within which national criminal justice authorities could pursue their own agendas.[24] During the 1990s, the double jeopardy principle also figured in two Conventions concluded within the framework of the newly created Third Pillar, although its scope of application was limited to the crimes proscribed by those instruments.[25]

Subsequently, national competence on the regulation of conflicts of criminal jurisdictions was effectively transferred to the EU with the conclusion of the Amsterdam Treaty. This was achieved with Article 31, laying down the European

[20] See also in this regard the first attempts made by the European Parliament, Resolution on obstacles at the frontiers and freedom of movement for traffic in the community, [1984] OJ C 104/150 and Resolution on the Declaration of Fundamental Rights and Freedoms, [1989] OJ C 120.

[21] Agreement between the Governments of the States of the Benelux Economic Union, the Federal Republic of Germany and the French Republic on the gradual abolition of checks at their common borders, signed at Schengen on 14 June 1985, [2000] OJ L 239/13.

[22] Convention implementing the Schengen Agreement of 14 June 1985 between the Governments of the States of the Benelux Economic Union, the Federal Republic of Germany and the French Republic on the gradual abolition of checks at their common borders, [2000] OJ L 239/19. It was preceded by the Convention between the Member States of the European Communities on Double Jeopardy, Brussels, 25.5.198, which was nevertheless quite unsuccessful as it was ratified by only five Member States and thus, never came to force as such.

[23] Similarly F Leidnmuhler, 'The incorporation of the Schengen *acquis* into the framework of the EU by example of the "ne bis in idem" principle' (2002) 2 *European Legal Forum* 253, 256.

[24] On this last point see, E Wagner, 'The Integration of Schengen into the Framework of the European Union' (1998) 25 *Issues of European Integration* 1, 2.

[25] Convention..., on the protection of the European Communities' financial interests, [1995] OJ C 316/49, Article 7, Protocol of 27 September 1996, ..., to the Convention on the protection of the European Communities' financial interests, [1996] OJ C 313/2, Article 7 (2) and Second Protocol of 19 June 1997,..., to the Convention on the protection of the European Communities' financial interests, [1997] OJ C 221/12, Article 12(2), Convention of 26 May 1997,..., on the fight against corruption involving officials of the European Communities or officials of Member States of the European Union, [1997] OJ C 195/2, Article 10.

Union's competence to *prevent* those conflicts, coupled with the elaboration of the Schengen *acquis* to directly applicable EU law. Horizontal *ne bis in idem* became exclusively an issue of EU law and the CJEU was afforded jurisdiction to rule on its interpretation. The Schengen Agreements were incorporated into the *acquis communautaire* by virtue of the Second Protocol to the Treaty of Amsterdam[26] followed by the respective implementing acts, which defined the sum of what constituted the Schengen *acquis* and determined their appropriate legal basis.[27] Accordingly, Articles 54–58 of CISA were to have as their legal basis Articles 31 and 34 of the Treaty of Amsterdam.[28] The transfer of competence was finally completed with the signing of the Lisbon Treaty, which introduced the principle of mutual recognition of criminal judgements in Article 67(3) TFEU and amended Article 82(1) TFEU extending the European Union's competence from the mere *prevention* to the *resolution* of conflicts of criminal jurisdictions between Member States.

Notwithstanding all the above, the European Union legislator also introduced double jeopardy in Article 50 of the Charter of Fundamental Rights of the European Union (*herein after* 'CFR'),[29] which, by virtue of Article 6(1) TEU, has acquired the same legal force as the Treaties, thus transforming, the traditional principle of criminal procedure to a fundamental right with higher normative status. This distinction is not only of significant symbolic value emphasising the principle's importance within the EU's legal order, but of determinative practical effect, since, according to the distinction of Article 52(5) CFR, rights can be directly invoked by individuals, while principles can only be implemented through legislative or executive acts and become significant only when such acts are interpreted or reviewed.[30] In the meantime, *ne bis in idem* was also incorporated in the European Arrest Warrant framework-decision as mandatory and optional grounds for the non-execution of EAWs,[31] as well as in many other pieces of secondary EU legislation[32] in a similar fashion as a ground for

[26] Treaty of Amsterdam, amending the Treaty on European Union, the Treaties Establishing the European Communities and Related Acts, Protocol (no 2) integrating the Schengen acquis into the framework of the European Union, [1997] OJ C 340.

[27] Council Decision 1999/435/EC, concerning the definition of the Schengen acquis…, [1999] OJ L 176/1, Council Decision 1999/436/EC, determining, …, the legal basis for each of the provisions or decisions which constitute the Schengen *acquis*, [1999] OJ L 176/17, as well as the act The Schengen Acquis, as referred to in Article 1(2) of Council Decision 1999/435/EC of 20 May 1999, [2000] OJ L 239/1.

[28] In this regard see Opinion of Adv Gen DR-J Colomer, in Joined Cases C-187/01, *Hüseyin Gözütok* and C-385/01, *Klaus Brügge*, [2003] ECR I-01345, para 8.

[29] Charter of Fundamental Rights of the European Union, [2010] OJ C 83/389.

[30] Explanations on the Charter of Fundamental Rights, [2007] OJ C 303/2, Explanation on Article 52, p 35. In any case, the CJEU had already recognised that Articles 54–58 CISA were directly applicable and did not require further implementing measures, CJEU, Joined Cases C-187/01, *Hüseyin Gözütok* and C-385/01, *Klaus Brügge*, [2003] ECR I-01345, paras 36–37.

[31] Council Framework Decision 2002/584/JHA of 13 June 2002 on the European arrest warrant and the surrender procedures between Member States, [2002] OJ L 190/1, Article 3 (2), Article 4 (3) (5).

[32] These are Framework Decision 2003/577/JHA, on the execution in the European Union of orders freezing property or evidence, [2003] OJ L 196/45 (Article 7(1)(c)), Framework Decision

refusal of various forms of legal assistance in criminal matters. Without adding anything to the substantial content of the principle, these instruments merely expanded its application in specific criminal sub-procedures established by EU law, which would otherwise be unaffected by final criminal judgements issued in other Member States.

2.3 *Ratio Legis* of Double Jeopardy in EU Law

Double jeopardy in EU law has a residual legal nature. First, it is considered to be a general principle of law emanating from the criminal legal systems of the Member States[33] sharing therefore, the same *ratio* with the domestic principle. Hence, it rests on the need to ensure legal certainty and the protection of the individual,[34] not only within a single state but within the whole territory of the European area of freedom, security and justice.[35]

Within the framework of EU law, the principle is also identified with further principles and objectives tailoring its conceptual content and practical application accordingly. The principle primarily '... is aimed at enhancing European integration and, in particular, at enabling the Union to become more rapidly the area of freedom, security and justice which it is its objective to maintain and develop'.[36] This distinct operation of *ne bis in idem* within the EU has led the CJEU

2005/214/JHA, on the application of the principle of mutual recognition to financial penalties, [2005] OJ L 076/16 (Article 7 (2)(a)), Framework Decision 2006/783/JHA on the application of the principle of mutual recognition to confiscation orders, [2006] OJ L 328/59 (Article 8(1)(a)), Framework Decision 2008/909/JHA on the application of the principle of mutual recognition to judgements in criminal matters imposing custodial sentences or measures involving deprivation of liberty for the purpose of their enforcement in the European Union, [2008] OJ L 327/27 (Article 9 (1)(c)), Framework Decision 2008/947/JHA, on the application of the principle of mutual recognition to judgements and probation decisions with a view to the supervision of probation measures and alternative sanctions, [2008] OJ L 337/102 (Article 11(1)(c)), Framework Decision 2008/978/JHA, on the European evidence warrant for the purpose of obtaining objects, documents and data for use in proceedings in criminal matters, [2008] OJ L 350/72 (Article 13 (1)(a)), and Framework Decision 2009/829/JHA on the application, between Member States of the European Union, of the principle of mutual recognition to decisions on supervision measures as an alternative to provisional detention, [2009] OJ L 294/20 (Article 15(1)(b)), as well as Framework Decision 2009/948/JHA, on prevention and settlement of conflicts of exercise of jurisdiction in criminal proceedings, [2009] OJ L 328/42, which sets out the modalities that can facilitate the application of *ne bis in idem*. The most recent is Directive 2011/99/EU of the European Parliament and of the Council of 13, December 2011 on the European protection order, [2011] OJ L/2, Article 10(1)(g) issued under the Lisbon Treaty, which abolished framework decisions as a form of secondary EU legislation.

[33] Opinion of Adv Gen DR-J Colomer, in Cases C-436/04, *Léopold Henri van Esbroeck*, [2006] ECR I-02333, para 21.

[34] CJEU, Case C-150/05, *Jean Leon Van Straaten against Staat der Nederlanden and Republiek Italië*, [2006] ECR I-09327, para 59, Opinion of Adv Gen DR-J Colomer, in Joined Cases C-187/01, *Hüseyin Gözütok* and C-385/01, *Klaus Brügge*, [2003] ECR I-01345, paras 49–50

[35] Opinion of Adv Gen DR-J Colomer, in Case C-150/05, *Jean Leon Van Straaten against Staat der Nederlanden and Republiek Italië*, [2006] ECR I-09327, para 61

[36] CJEU, Joined Cases C-187/01, *Hüseyin Gözütok* and C-385/01, *Klaus Brügge*, [2003] ECR I-01345, para 36-37, Case C-467/04, *Giuseppe Francesco Gasparini*, Judgment of 28 Sep 2006, [2006]

to adopt a teleological interpretive approach on the issue, which, '... is the only interpretation to give precedence to the object and purpose of the provision rather than to procedural or purely formal matters,..., and to ensure that the principle has proper effect'.[37] In other words, as Advocate-General Colomer has put it, '... the wording of the provisions has no axiomatic force'.[38] In particular, *ne bis in idem* is inextricably associated with the free movement of persons with the latter being ensured by the application of the former.[39] Moreover, it is also identified with the principle of mutual trust between Member States and mutual recognition forcing the acceptance of criminal judgements issued in other Member States, even when the outcome would be different under the law of the recognising state.[40] Naturally, these principles never underpinned the traditional state-centred version of the principle in cross-border cases under which foreign criminal judgements were recognised only if their outcome was similar to that of a domestic judgement.

3. INTERPRETATION AND APPLICATION OF THE *NE BIS IN IDEM* PRINCIPLE

3.1 Key Provisions and Normative Remarks

The main provisions of EU law establishing *ne bis in idem*, as noted already, are Article 50 of the Charter and Articles 54–58 CISA. Article 50 CFR reads that 'No one shall be liable to be tried or punished again in criminal proceedings for

ECR I-09199, paras 27–28, Opinion of Adv Gen DR-J Colomer, of 19 Sep 2002, in Joined Cases C-187/01, *Hüseyin Gözütok* and C-385/01, *Klaus Brügge*, [2003] ECR I-01345, para 44, Opinion of Adv Gen DR-J Colomer, of 20 Oct 2005, C-436/04, *Léopold Henri van Esbroeck*, [2006] ECR I-02333, paras 23–25, Opinion of Adv Gen DR-J Colomer, of 8 June 2006, in C-150/05, *Jean Leon Van Straaten against Staat der Nederlanden and Republiek Italië*,[2006] ECR I-09327, para 59.

[37] CJEU, Joined Cases C-187/01, *Hüseyin Gözütok* and C-385/01, *Klaus Brügge*, [2003] ECR I-01345, para 35, Case C-469/03, *Filomeno Mario Miraglia*, Judgment of 10 Mar 2005, [2005] ECR *I*-0200, para 31.

[38] Opinion of Adv Gen DR-J Colomer of 8 Apr 2008, in C-297/2007, *Staatsanwaltschaft Regensburg v Klaus Bourquain*, [2008] ECR I-09425, para 3.

[39] CJEU, Joined Cases C-187/01, *Hüseyin Gözütok* and C-385/01, *Klaus Brügge*, [2003] ECR I-01345, paras 36–38, Case C-469/03, *Filomeno Mario Miraglia*, Judgment of 10 Mar 2005 [2005] ECR I-0200, para 32, Case C-436/04, *Léopold Henri van Esbroeck*, [2006] ECR I-02333, paras 33–34, Opinion of Adv Gen DR-J Colomer, of 8 Jun 2006, in C-150/05, *Jean Leon Van Straaten*,[2006] ECR I-09327, para 62, Opinion of Adv Gen DR-J Colomer, of 20 Oct 2005, C-436/04, *Léopold Henri van Esbroeck*, [2006] ECR I-02333, paras 26, 45 and 52.

[40] CJEU, Joined Cases C-187/01, *Hüseyin Gözütok* and C-385/01, *Klaus Brügge*, [2003] ECR I-01345, paras 33–35, Case C-436/04, *Léopold Henri van Esbroeck*, [2006] ECR I-02333, para 30, Case C-467/04, *Giuseppe Francesco Gasparini*, Judgment of 28 Sep 2006, [2006] ECR I-09199, para 30, C-150/05, *Jean Leon Van Straaten*, [2006] ECR I-09327, para 43. Also, Opinion of Adv Gen DR-J Colomer, of 19 Sep 2002, in Joined Cases C-187/01, *Hüseyin Gözütok* and C-385/01, *Klaus Brügge*, [2003] ECR I-01345, paras 124–125, and Opinion of Adv Gen DR-J Colomer, of 8 Jun 2006, in C-150/05, *Jean Leon Van Straaten*,[2006] ECR I-09327, para 62, where he stated that 'In a project as ambitious as the European Union, the States must trust in the adequacy of their partners' rules and also trust that they apply them correctly, accepting their consequences, even though they may produce different outcomes; that concept implies taking those outcomes into consideration, one corollary of which is the ne bis in idem principle' and paras 63 and 73.

an offence for which he or she has already been finally acquitted or convicted within the Union in accordance with the law.' It effectively transforms the procedural principle to a fundamental right within EU law with the status of primary EU legislation, which, according to Articles 47 and 51(2) CFR, can be directly invoked by individuals, even to the annulment of secondary EU legislation. Article 50 CFR corresponds to the *acquis* in EU law and namely, to the provisions of Articles 54–58 of CISA.[41] In particular, the main provision of CISA, Article 54, lays down that

> A person whose trial has been finally disposed of in one Contracting Party may not be prosecuted in another Contracting Party for the same acts provided that, if a penalty has been imposed, it has been enforced, is actually in the process of being enforced or can no longer be enforced under the laws of the sentencing Contracting Party.

Article 55(1) frames the margin that Contracting States enjoy in introducing permissible derogations from the rule contained in Article 54.[42] Article 56 includes the principle of 'deduction' (or 'set-off' as it is also known) by laying down that the sentence served in the first state must be deducted from the sentence imposed in the second state. Article 57 imposes the obligation for international cooperation between Contracting States in exchanging relative information, while Article 58 allows them to provide for greater protection on their discretion than that offered by Article 54.

Due to their intrinsic correspondence, Article 50 CFR should be interpreted and implemented conjunctively with Articles 54–58 CISA and the limitations prescribed by the latter, since CISA has not lost its status as directly applicable EU law. Hence, any limitations included in Articles 54–58 CISA must be objectively justified under the conditions laid down by Article 52(1) CFR. These limitations should 'respect the essence of those rights and freedoms' and will be upheld 'only if (a) they are necessary and (b) genuinely meet objectives of general interest recognised by the Union or (c) the need to protect the rights and freedoms of others'. Given all that, it has been correctly held that derogations from the rule of Article 54 CISA, enacted under Article 55(1) CISA, reflect purely national interests and thus, have been impliedly abolished by the Charter as these are neither necessary, nor do they meet objectives of general interest recognised by the European Union.[43]

[41] Explanations on the Charter of Fundamental Rights, [2007] OJ C 303/2, Explanation on Article 50, p 31.

[42] CISA, art 55(1) (a) 'where the acts to which the foreign judgement relates took place in whole or in part in its own territory; in the latter case, however, this exception shall not apply if the acts took place in part in the territory of the Contracting Party where the judgement was delivered; (b) where the acts to which the foreign judgement relates constitute an offence against national security or other equally essential interests of that Contracting Party; (c) where the acts to which the foreign judgement relates were committed by officials of that Contracting Party in violation of the duties of their office'. Also of importance is (2) which reads that 'The exceptions which were the subject of a declaration under paragraph 1 shall not apply where the Contracting Party concerned has, in connection with the same acts, requested the other Contracting Party to bring the prosecution or has granted extradition of the person concerned.'

[43] Areios Pagos (*in pleno*) 1/2011, (2011) 59 *Nomiko Vima* 1620 with comments by D Kioupis, (2011) *Poinika Chronika* 500 with comments by I Anagnostopoulos.

All the above, should apply *mutatis mutandis* to the provisions of the fraud and corruption Conventions. Notwithstanding the different territorial and temporal scope of those instruments that should always be taken into account, their provisions should, in view of Articles 53 CFR and 58 CISA, apply only to the extent they offer greater protection than that offered by Articles 54–58 CISA and Article 50 CFR, since the latter provisions prevail over the former, due to their higher normative status.[44]

3.2 Scope of Application

Ne bis in idem is strictly a subjective right and applies only to persons that were defendants in the first proceedings and not to any accomplices who were never prosecuted in the Member State where the first decision was issued.[45] It is doubtful though, whether the principle should also benefit legal persons.[46] In any case, when a natural person has been found guilty this should not in any way preclude the imposition of sanctions on the legal person that benefited from his acts. Moreover, it has been held that *ne bis in idem* is applicable at the time when the act in question is being evaluated by the authorities of the second Member State. Consequently, double jeopardy applies *retroactively* to acts carried out and to judgements issued even before when coming into force of CISA,[47] provided CISA (or CFR) is in force at the time when proceedings are brought in the second Member State. What is more, the place where the act in question was committed and the location of the court that issued the first judgement are unimportant for the application of the principle. *Ne bis in idem* applies as long as the first

[44] On the contrary, see S Peers, *EU Justice and Home Affairs Law*, 3rd edn (Oxford, Oxford University Press, 2011) 837. The author does not take any position on this and leaves open the issue of whether the provisions of these Conventions are *lex specialis* to Articles 54–58 CISA or the latter prevail over them. In my view, it is clear that Articles 50 CFR (by virtue of Article 6 (1) TEU) and 54 CISA (as directly applicable EU law) clearly supersede the respective provisions of the Conventions, which are merely international conventions lacking the characteristics of EU law. In any case, there is no need to resort to a *lex specialis* approach since the Conventions do not provide for any *special* regulation over the issue of *ne bis in idem* and thus, through a parallel application of Articles 50 CFR, 54 CISA and the respective provisions of the Conventions, Articles 53 CFR and 58 CISA come into play, as explained above.

[45] CJEU, Cases C-467/04, *Giuseppe Francesco Gasparini*, Judgment of 28 Sep 2006, [2006] ECR I-09199, paras 35 and 37 and operative part, Opinion of Adv Gen DR-J Colomer, of 20 Oct 2005, C-436/04, *Léopold Henri van Esbroeck*, [2006] ECR I-02333, para 31, para 123, Opinion of Adv Gen DR-J Colomer, 8 Jun 2006, C-150/05, *Jean Leon Van Straaten against Staat der Nederlanden and Republiek Italië*, [2006] ECR I-09327, paras 83–85.

[46] For more argumentation on the issue see S Peers (2011), above n 44, 842. In any case it should be taken into consideration that some Member States have not enacted provisions establishing criminal liability of legal persons (eg Greece).

[47] CJEU, Case C-436/04, *Léopold Henri van Esbroeck*, Judgment of 9 Mar 2006, [2006] ECR I-02333, paras 22–24 and operative part, Case C-150/05, *Jean Leon Van Straaten v Staat der Nederlanden and Republiek Italië*, [2006] ECR I-09327, Case C-491/2007, *Vladimir Turansky*, Judgment of 22 Dec 2008, [2008] ECR I-11039, para 27, Case C-297/07 *Staatsanwaltschaft Regensburg v Klaus Bourquain*, Judgment of 11 Dec 2008, [2008] ECR p I-09425, para 28.

judgement was issued by a court of a Member State that had jurisdiction over the case, regardless of the physical location of its seat.[48]

The most striking aspect of *ne bis in idem* in EU law, mentioned previously, is its horizontal application obliging Member States to recognise and abide by the *res judicata* of criminal judgements issued within the EU. This aspect is apparent in the wording of both provisions of Articles 54 CISA and 50 CFR. It may be true that Article 51(1) CFR limits the application of the Charter to EU bodies or Member States in the implementation of EU law. Nevertheless, Article 50 CFR also applies to purely national proceedings having no connection at all with the implementation of EU law.[49] In any case, cross-border criminal cases inevitably impinge on the free movement of persons in many respects and have, therefore, an abstract, but sufficient nexus with the implementation of EU law that brings them 'within the scope' of EU law as required for by Article 51(1) CFR.[50]

Quite significantly, drawing on the wording of the respective provisions (*'criminal proceedings' 'punished' 'acquitted/convicted', 'sentence'*) and the relevant part of the TFEU, which speaks of cooperation in 'criminal' matters (*'Title V, Chap. 4'*), the principle is currently considered to apply strictly to criminal proceedings.[51] It exclusively emanates from the *res judicata* of decisions issued in the context of criminal proceedings and bars only subsequent criminal proceedings with reference to their domestic qualification.[52] Nevertheless, it is strongly debated whether punitive administrative proceedings should be caught in the protective web of Articles 54 CISA and 50 CFR.

[48] CJEU, Case C-297/07 *Staatsanwaltschaft Regensburg v Klaus Bourquain*, [2008] ECR p I-09425, paras 29–31 and operative part, in which case the initial trial for a murder committed in Algeria took place in a military court in that country belonging, however, to the French state. On the irrelevance of the place of commission, S Peers (2011), above n 44, 841.

[49] Explanations, [2007] OJ C 303/2 , Explanation of Article 50, p 31 '[i]n accordance with Article 50, the "non bis in idem" rule applies not only within the jurisdiction of one State but also between the jurisdictions of several Member States.'

[50] CJEU, Case C-617/10, *Åklagaren v Hans Åkerberg Fransson*, Judgment of 26 Feb 2013, unpubl., available at curia.europa.eu, paras 19–20, Explanations, [2007] OJ C 303/2 , Explanation of Article 51, p 35.

[51] Commission of the European Communities, Commission staff working document – Annex to the Green Paper on conflicts of jurisdiction and the principle of ne bis in idem in criminal proceedings COM(2005) 696 final, Brussels, 23.12.2005, SEC(2005) 1767 , p 46, 52 and 61, J Vervaele (2004), above n 4, p 811, B VanBockel, Case Comment on Cases C-436/04, C-150/05 and C-467/04, (2008) 45 *CMLRev* 223, 241, P Nikoloudis, 'Extradition Request and ne bis in idem', (2004) *Poinika Chronika* 1098, 1099, S Peers (2011), above n 44, 842.

[52] CJEU, Cases C-187/01, *Hüseyin Gözütok* and C-385/01, *Klaus Brügge,* [2003] ECR I-01345, paras 27–28, as the Court accepted that ne bis in idem flows from '... a procedure by which the prosecuting authority, on which national law confers power for that purpose, decides to discontinue criminal proceedings' and that 'the prosecution is discontinued by the decision of an authority required to play a part in the administration of Criminal Justice', Case C-491/07, *Vladimir Turanský*, Judgment of 22 Dec 2008, [2008] ECJ I-11039, para 34, as well as para 32, where the Court clarified that 'a decision must, in order to be considered as a final disposal for the purposes of Article 54 of the CISA, bring the criminal proceedings to an end and definitively bar further prosecution.', Opinion of Adv Gen R-J Colomer in C-187/01, *Hüseyin Gözütok* and C-385/01, *Klaus Brügge,* [2003] ECR I-0134, paras 80 and 84, where he referred to a '...procedure which... is a way of administering criminal justice' and that 'the fact that, in a settlement, no court exercises its power to give judgement, does not have a "dejudicialising" effect'.

3.3 The 'Bis' Element (Final Judgement)

The 'bis' element has been broadly interpreted by the CJEU. The Court by taking a substantive approach has focused on the actual exhaustion of the *ius puniendi* of the Member State whose authorities examined the case first, rather on the formal exhaustion of all means of appeal. It has relatively held that 'a decision must, in order to be considered as a final disposal for the purposes of Article 54 of the CISA, bring the criminal proceedings to an end and definitively bar further prosecution'.[53] This is taken to include even decisions discontinuing the proceedings that '...are adopted without the involvement of a court and do not take the form of a judicial decision'[54] and thus, decisions issued by prosecutors or investigative judges that ultimately discontinue the proceedings and bar further prosecution, are also regarded to fall within the scope of Article 54 CISA.[55] The final character of a decision must therefore be assessed in the light of the legislation of the Member State whose authorities have issued the decision at hand.[56] This 'substantive' approach on the 'bis' element is the outcome of the operation of the principle of mutual recognition on which *ne bis in idem* lies, that compels the recognition of judgements issued in other Member States, even when the outcome under the applicable national law would be different.[57] Its adoption also appears necessary in order to rule out the paradoxes that a strict literal interpretation would produce.[58]

[53] CJEU, Case C-491/07, *Vladimir Turanský*, Judgment of 22 Dec 2008, [2008] ECJ I-11039, para 34, as well as para 32, Joined Cases C-187/01, *Hüseyin Gözütok* and C-385/01, *Klaus Brügge*, Judgment of 11 Feb 2003, [2003] ECR I-01345, para 38.

[54] CJEU, Case C-187/01, *Hüseyin Gözütok* and C-385/01, *Klaus Brügge*, [2003] ECR I-01345, paras 38, 31, 34, 42 and operative part.

[55] In the words of the Advocate-General, 'When that provision speaks of a person whose case has been 'finally disposed of' ([a person who has been] rechtskräftig abgeurteilt, onherroepelijk vonnis, définitivement jugée, juzgada en sentencia firme, giudicata con sentenza definitiva ordefinitivamente julgado), in spite of the literal meaning of the Spanish version, it does not refer to a decision taken by a court in the form of a judgement delivered after proceedings providing all the safeguards laid down in Article 6 of the European Convention on the Protection of Human Rights, but, more generically, to any pronouncement made in the legal sphere, by which the State's final word on the acts being prosecuted and the guilt of the perpetrator is expressed, whether by a court in its role as judge, or by an examining magistrate as the result of his investigations or by a Prosecutor bringing the prosecution against the criminal acts', Opinion of Adv Gen DR-J Colomer, of 19 Sep 2002, in C-187/01, *Hüseyin Gözütok* and C-385/01, *Klaus Brügge*, [2003] ECR I-01345, para 103. Noteworthy is that under EU law both tribunals and prosecutors were already considered as 'judicial authorities' see CISA, Article 53, and the EU Convention on Mutual Assistance in Criminal Matters of 29/5/2000, [2000] OJ C 197/1, Article 6. Furthermore, see the Explanatory Reports to the European Convention on Extradition of 13/12/1957, ETS no 24, and the European Convention on Mutual Assistance in Criminal Matters of 20/4/1959, ETS no 30, to which those EU Conventions refer.

[56] CJEU, Cases C-491/07, *Vladimir Turanský*, Judgment of 22 Dec 2008, [2008] ECJ I-11039, para 34, as well as para 35, C-297/07 *Staatsanwaltschaft Regensburg v Klaus Bourquain*, Judgment of 11 Dec 2008, [2008] ECR p I-09425, paras 40–42.

[57] CJEU, Cases, C-436/04, *Léopold Henri van Esbroeck*, [2006] ECR I-02333, para 29, C-467/04, *Giuseppe Francesco Gasparini*, Judgment of 28 Sep 2006, [2006] ECR I-09199, para 30

[58] CJEU, Joined Cases C-187/01, *Hüseyin Gözütok* and C-385/01, *Klaus Brügge*, [2003] ECR I-01345, para 40, Opinion of Adv Gen R-J Colomer, of 19 Sep 2002, in C-187/01, *Hüseyin Gözütok* and C-385/01, *Klaus Brügge*, [2003] ECR I-01345, paras 110–112.

Ne bis in idem, although not evident in the wording of Article 54 CISA, has been held to cover both acquittals and convictions.[59] Article 50 CFR is clear on this matter (*'finally acquitted or convicted'*). The elements defining a conviction are twofold: the substantial ruling on the guilt of the defendant for a criminal act and the imposition of a criminal sanction. A sanction is to be regarded as 'criminal' provided that it is of 'punitive' character and is imposed within the context of criminal proceedings.[60] Sanctions as such include the deprivation of liberty, monetary fines, and the confiscation of property, as well as alternative sanctions, like community service.[61]

An acquittal, on the other hand, has a broader meaning and covers a wide spectrum of decisions discontinuing criminal proceedings. The rest international instruments have taken the approach whereby an acquittal is qualified as 'finally disposing the trial', only when the relative judgement has been passed 'on the merits of the case'.[62] This approach has also been suggested as being the most appropriate for the interpretation of Articles 54–58 CISA.[63] Such a view, however, disregards the fact that in reality criminal proceedings are discontinued not only where the commission of the act has not been established, but for a variety of other reasons precluding the defendant's criminal liability altogether.[64] The weight should therefore rest on the overall non-establishment of criminal liability.[65]

This also seems to be the approach of the CJEU, which focuses solely on the exhaustion of the *ius puniendi* as being the sole appropriate criterion in assessing the finality of an acquittal, given that the wording of the respective provisions

[59] CJEU, Case C-467/04, *Giuseppe Francesco Gasparini*, Judgment of 28 Sep 2006, [2006] ECR I-09199, sent. 1 and para 24. Opinion of Adv Gen R-J Colomer, of 8 Jun 2006, in C-150/05, *Jean Leon Van Straaten κατά Staat der Nederlanden*, [2006] ECR I-09327, para 53. Also, Commission of the European Communities (2005), above n 51, p 46.

[60] This is clearly implied by CJEU, in Joined Cases C-187/01, *Hüseyin Gözütok* and C-385/01, *Klaus Brügge*, Judgment of 11 Feb 2003, [2003] ECR I-01345, paras 28–29, 39. See also Opinion of Adv Gen R-J Colomer, of 19 Sep 2002, in C-187/01, *Hüseyin Gözütok* and C-385/01, *Klaus Brügge*, [2003] ECR I-01345, paras 50 and 87 focusing in particular on the deterrent effect of the sanction.

[61] All these have naturally already been characterised as criminal sanctions in EU legislation, Framework Decision 2005/214/JHA, on the application of the principle of mutual recognition to financial penalties, [2005] OJ L/16, Framework Decision 2006/783/JHA, on the application of the principle of mutual recognition to confiscation orders, [2006] OJ L 328/59, Framework Decision 2008/909/JHA, on the application of the principle of mutual recognition to judgements in criminal matters imposing custodial sentences or measures involving deprivation of liberty for the purpose of their enforcement in the European Union, [2008] OJ L 327/27.

[62] ECtHR, *Yelena Pavlova Smirnova and Irina Pavlova Smirnova v Russia*, Decision (Appl no 46133/99 and 48183/99), para 3 where the discontinuance of the proceedings by the prosecutor was held not to fall within the scope of Article 4 of Protocol 7.

[63] C Van Den Wyngaert and G Stessens, (1999), above n 1, 798, since for a judgement to result to an acquittal, an assessment of the merits must have taken place.

[64] R Lööf, '54 CISA and the Principles of ne bis in idem' (2007) *Eur J Crime Cr L Cr J* 309, 324. On the clarification on what a decision on the merits stands for, see Opinion of Adv Gen R-J Colomer, of 8 Jun 2006, in C-150/05, *Jean Leon Van Straaten against Staat der Nederlanden and Republiek Italië*, [2006] ECR I-09327, paras 65–67.

[65] S Trechsel (2005), above n 1, 388–9, R Lööf (2007), ibid, 324, Commission of the European Communities, Brussels, 26 July 2000, COM(2000) 495 final, 4–5, para 3.1.

makes no reference to the content of the judgement that has become final.[66] This is further implied by the principle of mutual recognition that requires the acceptance of foreign judgements regardless of their outcome.[67] By following this approach, the Court has already held that decisions, which permanently discontinue proceedings due to a time bar of the criminal acts in question fall within the notion of a 'final judgement'.[68] The same applies to decisions where the defendant is discharged of his charges due to the lack of evidence[69] and decisions where the criminal proceedings are discontinued following a criminal settlement.[70]

In *Miraglia*, the Court held that the discontinuance of proceedings without an examination of the merits of the case because prosecution for the same facts had already been brought against the defendant in another Member State, could not have been regarded as 'finally disposing the trial'.[71] The *Miraglia* case in reality was a necessary exception to the rule and should not be seen as blurring the general approach of the Court by requiring the first court to have issued a judgement on the merits. There could be many other instances where a national court might decline from its jurisdiction to hear a case and/or discontinue proceedings on purely procedural and jurisdictional grounds, such as in cases of foreign officials who enjoy immunity, lack of international jurisdiction, discontinuance of proceedings due to inadmissibility of a criminal suit because of procedural irregularities or due to the cooperation offered by the defendant in providing information to the authorities, etc. In such marginal cases, despite the existence of a final criminal judgement, the application of *ne bis in idem* should be precluded[72] for the reason that the *ius puniendi* of the state that first brought proceedings was non-existent altogether or could not, in reality, have been exercised.[73]

[66] CJEU, Case C-467/04, *Giuseppe Francesco Gasparini*, Judgment of 28 Sep 2006, [2006] ECR I-09199, para 24, Case C-150/05, *Jean Leon Van Straaten v Staat der Nederlanden and Republiek Italië*, [2006] ECR I-09327, para 56, Opinion of Adv Gen R-J Colomer, of 8 Jun 2006, C-150/05, *Jean Leon Van Straaten against Staat der Nederlanden and Republiek Italië*, [2006] ECR I-09327, paras 51–55.

[67] CJEU, Case C-467/04, *Giuseppe Francesco Gasparini*, Judgment of 28 Sep 2006, [2006] ECR I-09199, paras 29–30.

[68] CJEU, Case C-467/04, *Giuseppe Francesco Gasparini*, Judgment of 28 Sep 2006, [2006] ECR I-09199, paras 28, 33 and operative part. *Contra*, Opinion of the Adv Gen E Sharpston of 15 June 2006, in C-467/04, *Giuseppe Francesco Gasparini*, paras 90 *et seq*.

[69] CJEU, Case C-150/05, *Jean Leon Van Straaten v Staat der Nederlanden*, ECR 2006 I-09327, operative part.

[70] CJEU, Case C-187/01, *Hüseyin Gözütok* and C-385/01, *Klaus Brügge*, Judgment of 11 Feb 2003, [2003] ECR I-01345, operative part.

[71] CJEU, Case C-469/03, *Filomeno Mario Miraglia*, Judgment of 10 Mar 2005, [2005] ECR I-0200, paras 30 and 35 and operative part.

[72] This is similar to the established position on the recognition of foreign criminal judgements in the UK according to common law, Bar Council of England and Wales, Response to the Commission's December 2005 Green Paper COM (2005) 696 final on: Conflicts of Jurisdiction and the Principle of ne bis in idem in Criminal Proceedings, 29/03/2006, p 9.

[73] This approach is in many ways similar to that proposed by S Peers (2011), above n 44, 845–6 according to whom the current approach of the CJEU is uncertain and the criterion should focus on whether the Court terminated the proceedings had an *opportunity* to decide the case on the merits. The author S Peers, however, does not determine whether this opportunity should be examined in

3.4 The 'Idem' Element (Identity of Facts)

The CJEU has interpreted the 'idem' element in line with the 'idem factum' criterion by following an approach based 'strictly on the facts',[74] while it substantially added to its content by drawing a quite detailed and elaborated definition.

The Court by reference to the wording of Article 54 CISA,[75] has held accordingly that the only decisive element for the interpretation of the 'idem' element, are the material acts in dispute and not their legal classification or the underlying protected legal interest.[76] Additionally, it has stated that any other interpretation would run contrary to the goal pursued by the respective provision rendering it ineffective in practice.[77] In reaching this conclusion, the CJEU has made particular use of the principle of mutual recognition, which obliges Member States to recognise foreign judgements, even if the outcome would be different under their national legislation, in light also of the lack of harmonisation in the respective field which necessitates such an approach.[78] Hence, according to the established case law,

> [t]he only relevant criterion for applying the concept of 'the same acts' within the meaning of Article 54 of the CISA is identity of the material acts, understood as the existence of a set of concrete circumstances which are inextricably linked together in time, in space and by their subject-matter.[79]

the abstract or in the concrete facts of the case. Under the latter alternative, even cases of time-barred proceedings should be ruled out, since the first national court would be precluded *ab initio* to examine the case. In any case, according to the present author, there is no uncertainty with regard to the current approach taken by the Court, since the exhaustion of the *ius puniendi* and the non-establishment altogether of the criminal liability of the defendant by the first court is clear enough for the second national court to assess and rests on an *ad hoc* and *ex post* examination of that decision, which is line with the operation of mutual recognition. On the other hand, the opportunity-based approach advocated by S Peers, even by an *in abstracto* examination, would lead to an examination of hypothetical procedural scenarios that might have evolved in the first Member State, which would only trouble the second court and lead to uncertain results.

[74] B VanBockel (2008), above n 51, 238.

[75] CJEU, Case C-436/04, *Léopold Henri van Esbroeck*, [2006] ECR I-02333, paras 27–28 and operative part, Opinion of Adv Gen R-J Colomer, of 20 Oct 2005, in C-436/04, *Léopold Henri van Esbroeck*, [2006] ECR I-02333, para 44 referring to the wording of all respective European languages, C-150/05, *Jean Leon Van Straaten*, [2006] ECR I-09327, paras 41–42.

[76] CJEU, Cases C-436/04, *Léopold Henri van Esbroeck*, [2006] ECR I-02333, paras 27–36, C-150/05, *Jean Leon Van Straaten*, [2006] ECR I-09327, paras 41–47, C-288/2005, *Jurgen Kretzinger*, [2007] ECR I-06441, paras 29, 31–34, Opinion of Adv Gen R-J Colomer, of 20 Oct 2005, C-436/04, *Léopold Henri van Esbroeck*, [2006] ECR I-02333, paras 44–58, Opinion of Adv Gen R-J Colomer, 8 Jun 2006, C-150/05, *Jean Leon Van Straaten*, [2006] ECR I-09327, para 73.

[77] CJEU, Case-436/04, *Léopold Henri van Esbroeck*, [2006] ECR I-02333, paras 34–36 and operative part, Case C-150/05, *Jean Leon Van Straaten*, [2006] ECR I-09327, paras 45–46, Case C-288/2005, *Jurgen Kretzinger*, [2007] ECR I-06441, para 33, Opinion of Adv Gen R-J Colomer, of 20 Oct 2005, in C-436/04, *Léopold Henri van Esbroeck*, [2006] ECR I-02333, para 45.

[78] CJEU, Case C-436/04, *Léopold Henri van Esbroeck*, [2006] ECR I-02333, paras 31–32, 35–36 and operative part, Case C-150/05, *Jean Leon Van Straaten*, [2006] ECR I-09327, paras 44 and 47.

[79] CJEU, Cases, C-436/04, *Léopold Henri van Esbroeck*, [2006] ECR I-02333, paras 36, 38, 42 and operative part, C-467/04, *Giuseppe Francesco Gasparini*, Judgment of 28 Sep 2006, [2006]

If there is unity in all these dimensions, the substantive facts should not be divided artificially into separate episodes.[80] The existence of the three respective elements is examined disjunctively and the identity of the material act does not change, even if these three elements change in the course of the action.[81] The term 'space' is considered to encompass the whole territory of the European Union including all the territories of its Member States.[82] Consequently, the export and import, and the trafficking of illegal goods or narcotic drugs, etc, conducted within the territories of multiple EU Member States, are considered to be the same act.[83] Also, both the import and subsequent sale and distribution of narcotic drugs and/or illegal goods from the same bulk are acts that may fall under the notion of 'the same acts'.[84] Moreover, it has been held that 'in the case of offences relating to narcotic drugs, the quantities of the drug that are at issue in the two Contracting States concerned or the persons alleged to have been party to the acts in the two States are not required to be identical',[85] provided that these are part of the same initial quantity. Naturally, this reasoning should apply *mutatis mutandis* to illegal goods, illegal firearms, etc.

Finally, Article 50 CFR should also be interpreted in line with the 'idem factum' criterion followed by the CJEU, notwithstanding its differentiated wording that points at a different reading,[86] given that the Charter was not meant to establish new rights but to manifest, albeit in a written text of higher normative status, those already recognised in the jurisprudence of the CJEU.[87]

ECR I-09199, para 54 and operative part, C-150/05, *Jean Leon Van Straaten against Staat der Nederlanden and Republiek Italië*, [2006] ECR I-09327, paras 48, 53 and operative part, C-288/2005, *Jurgen Kretzinger*, [2007] ECR I-06441, paras 35–37.

[80] Opinion of Adv Gen R-J Colomer, 8 Jun 2006, C-150/05, *Jean Leon Van Straaten*, [2006] ECR I-09327, para 79.

[81] Ibid, para 80.

[82] Opinion of Adv Gen R-J Colomer, 8 Jun 2006, in C-150/05, *Jean Leon Van Straaten against Staat der Nederlanden and Republiek Italië*, [2006] ECR I-09327, para 52 'it is ludicrous to refer to import and export in a territory governed by a legal system which, in essence, is designed to remove borders for both persons and goods.', Opinion of Adv Gen E Sharpston, 5 Dec 2006, in C-288/05, *Jürgen Kretzinger*, [2007] ECR I-06441, para 38. See also the 'silent' acceptance by the CJEU of this position, in Case C-436/04, *Léopold Henri van Esbroeck*, Judgment of 9 Mar 2006, [2006] ECR I-02333, para 41.

[83] CJEU, Case, C-436/04, *Léopold Henri van Esbroeck*, [2006] ECR I-02333, paras 37, 42 and operative (narcotic drugs), Case C-150/05, *Jean Leon Van Straaten*, [2006] ECR I-09327, paras 51, 53 and operative (narcotic drugs), Case C-288/05, *Jürgen Kretzinger*, [2007] ECR I-06441, para 37 and operative part (illegal goods).

[84] CJEU, Case C-467/04, *Giuseppe Francesco Gasparini*, Judgment of 28 Sep 2006, [2006] ECR I-09199, para 57 and operative part.

[85] CJEU, Case C-150/05, *Jean Leon Van Straaten*, [2006] ECR I-09327, paras 49, 53 and operative part.

[86] B VanBockel (2008), above n 51, 243, R Lööf (2007), above n 64, 328. This difference in the wording may be explained by the fact that the drafters of the Charter had the equivalent wording of the ECHR in mind, R Lööf (2007), above n 64, 331, Commission of the European Communities, (2005), above n 51, 57.

[87] CFR Preamble, fifth sent of Adv Gen E Sharpston, of 18 Oct 2012, in Case C396/11, *Ciprian Vasile Radu,* unpubl, available at curia.europa.eu, paras 51–52, In this regard, House of Lords, European Union Committee, The Treaty of Lisbon: an impact assessment, Vol I: Report, HL Paper

This particularly holds true for Article 50 that was meant to correspond to the Schengen *acquis*.[88]

3.5 The Enforcement of the Sentence Condition

The final condition on which the application of *ne bis in idem* rests, is the enforcement of the first judgement be it a conviction. According to Article 54 CISA, subsequent proceedings are barred 'provided that, if a penalty has been imposed, it has been enforced, is actually in the process of being enforced or can no longer be enforced under the laws of the sentencing Contracting Party.' In general, it was common for national legislators to render dependent the recognition of foreign and final criminal judgements on such a condition. Within the CISA framework though, this condition has been interpreted and applied in a significantly more liberal manner. Nevertheless, in view of Article 50 CFR which does not include it as such, its validity is being challenged.

It is clear that where the sentence has been fully served and in particular when the convicted person has fully served his prison term, paid his monetary fine or completed his community service, the condition is fulfilled. It is also quite clear that the penalty imposed is 'in the process of being enforced', when the defendant is serving his prison term, doing his community service or paying the instalments of the monetary fine, when such a possibility is provided for by national law. Moreover, it is also quite clear that when a defendant has only partially served his sentence, the condition is not fulfilled and thus, subsequent proceedings can be brought against him in another Member State in which case the principle of 'deduction' comes into play.[89] Besides, it has been held that

> in so far as a suspended custodial sentence penalises the unlawful conduct of a convicted person, it constitutes a penalty within the meaning of Article 54 of the CISA. That penalty must be regarded as 'actually in the process of being enforced' as soon as the sentence has become enforceable and during the probation period. Subsequently, once the probation period has come to an end, the penalty must be regarded as 'having been enforced' within the meaning of that provision.[90]

62-I, 2008, pp 92–93, num 5.37–5.43, pp 98–101, num 5.69–5.80. Also, this derives from Article 53 CFR which provides that the Charter sets up a 'minimum' level of protection thus, precluding a restrictive interpretative approach on the rights contained therein.

[88] Explanations on the Charter of Fundamental Rights, [2007] OJ C 303/2, Explanation on Article 50, p 31. Moreover, in support of the above, it should be borne in mind that the ECtHR has also interpreted under the prism of 'idem factum' criterion, the respective provision of Article 4 of Protocol 7 which shares a similar wording to Article 50 CFR, ECtHR (GC), *Sergey Zolotukhin v Russia*, Judgment of 10 Feb 2009, Appl no 14939/03, paras 80–81.

[89] Opinion of Adv Gen E Sharpston, of 5 Dec 2006, in Case C-288/05, *Jürgen Kretzinger*, [2007] ECR I-06441, paras 68–69.

[90] CJEU, Case C-288/05, *Jürgen Kretzinger*, [2007] ECR I-06441, para 42 and operative part. Opinion of Adv Gen E Sharpston, of 5 Dec 2006, in Case C-288/05, *Jürgen Kretzinger*, [2007] ECR I-06441, paras 49–50. Notable is that all the Governments which intervened in the case and the Commission adhered to this view, Case C-288/05, *Jürgen Kretzinger*, [2007] ECR I-06441, para 41.

This rationale should also be applied to any provisional suspension or release following conviction, since the initial judgement is actually being enforced according to its terms.[91] Nevertheless, the initial judgement becomes enforceable anew, once the terms of the suspended sentence or the provisional release are breached and a decision revoking either the suspension or the release is issued. This results in the enforcement condition not being observed anymore. All other Member States regain thus, in this instance, their power to bring criminal proceedings and to impose any new sentence, subject again to the application of the 'deduction' principle.

A time-barred sentence should always be regarded as a sentence that can no longer be enforced. This is notwithstanding that in reality the particular sentence was never enforceable because a retrial was required according to the applicable national law, such as when the initial judgement was issued in default.[92] According to the Court, 'the words "no …longer" refer to the time when the new proceedings begin' before the second Member State and thus, the enforcement condition is complied with, when, at the time the second proceedings are brought, the sentence imposed can no longer be enforced according to the applicable national legislation.[93] On the contrary, a sentence that is not enforced due to pardon or amnesty should be regarded as falling short of the enforcement condition, due to the intrinsic political character of those measures.[94] However, in view of Article 58 CISA, the application of favourable national law to the contrary is not ruled out in these cases.

The Court has also held that a sentence imposed by a court of a Member State should not be considered as being or having been enforced in a case where the defendant has been held in police custody and/or held on remand pending trial, given that police or pre-trial detention precede the final judgement and the imposition of any sentence, the latter being the necessary pre-condition for the recognition of criminal judgements.[95] Nevertheless, it has been advocated that pre-trial detention must be regarded as fulfilling the enforcement condition in two instances; the first is where the time spent in detention in one Member State is equal to or greater than the time of the sentence imposed in another Member State and the second is where the detention is followed by the actual serving of the sentence imposed.[96] This view, however, is quite superfluous. In

[91] OLG München, [2001] NStZ 614 = [2001] StV 495 and note by B Hecker, StV (2002) 71.

[92] CJEU, Case C-297/07 *Staatsanwaltschaft Regensburg against Klaus Bourquain*, Judgment of 11 Dec 2008, [2008] ECR I-09425, operative part.

[93] CJEU, Case C-297/07 *Staatsanwaltschaft Regensburg against Klaus Bourquain*, Judgment of 11 Dec 2008, [2008] ECR I-09425, paras 47–48 and operative part.

[94] Opinion of Adv Gen D R-J Colomer of 8 Apr 2008, in C-297/07 *Staatsanwaltschaft Regensburg against Klaus Bourquain*, Judgment of 11 Dec 2008, [2008] ECR I-09425, paras 77–82 and, in particular, para 83. It accordingly follows that proceedings that have been discontinued due to pardons or amnesties, should not bar subsequent proceedings in other Member States as these should not be considered to follow within the notion of 'final' judgement.

[95] CJEU, Case C-288/05, *Jürgen Kretzinger*, [2007] ECR I-06441, para 52 and operative part.

[96] Opinion of Adv Gen E Sharpston, of 5 Dec 2006, in Case C-288/05, *Jürgen Kretzinger*, [2007] ECR I-06441, paras 65–67.

the latter scenario, a sentence has been actually imposed in the first Member State, so the argument raised is devoid of any practical significance. The second court will examine whether the sentence imposed is being or has been enforced and will not assess the pre-trial detention as a separate issue. In the first scenario, the duration of the detention does not absolve it from its character as pre-trial detention. Therefore, it cannot be regarded as a 'penalty' for the purposes of Article 54 CISA and, as such, it cannot operate to the fulfilment of the enforcement condition, regardless of its duration. Member States though are not precluded from deducting the time spent in pre-trial detention in the first Member State from the sentence imposed by applying more favourable national provisions to this effect.

4. PARTICULAR ISSUES OF INTEREST

4.1 Is the Enforcement Condition Still in Force?

An issue of great importance that has been raised, especially in view of the now legally binding Charter, is whether and to what extent the enforcement condition of Article 54 CISA is still in force. Both views have already been expressed, in the literature and in national jurisprudence, arguing either in favour of the silent abolition of the enforcement condition or in support of its enduring validity. The CJEU has not yet dealt with the issue in the light of the Charter, but has ruled in the past in favour of the validity of the enforcement condition.

The first view advocating the abolition of the enforcement condition is based on the three following main points. First, on the wording of Article 50 CFR, since, contrary to that of Article 54 CISA, it does not include the enforcement condition. Hence, given the higher normative status of the former, it has been suggested that the enforcement condition has been abolished altogether. This reasoning has already been expressed in a judgement issued by the Athens Court of Appeal.[97] Secondly, it is argued that the enforcement condition cannot be justified under the terms of Article 52(1) CFR. This point has been underlined by the Commission, which has clearly opted in favour of the abolition of this condition in view of the Charter by considering that it does not meet with the requirements of necessity and proportionality required by Article 52(1) CFR.[98] Thirdly, it is suggested that the *ratio* behind the enforcement condition has become redundant under the overall legal framework of EU law in criminal

[97] Court of Appeal (Crim Fellonies Div) 674/2011, (2011) 6 *Poiniki Dikaiosini* 702 with comments by P Tsiridis.

[98] Commission of the European Communities, Green Paper on conflicts of jurisdiction and the principle of *ne bis in idem* in criminal proceedings COM(2005) 696 final, Brussels, 23.12.2005, pp 9–10, Commission of the European Communities, (2005), above n 51, pp 47–48 and p 58. It should also be noted that the Commission is advancing this view more on a *de lege ferenda* basis and this must be taken into account in assessing its weight.

matters. The enforcement condition echoes national concerns for the effective enforcement of criminal decisions and is justified in the context of traditional international cooperation in criminal matters.[99] Yet, the many legal instruments available under current EU law and namely, the EAW, effectively guarantee the enforcement of any criminal measure or sanction within EU thus rendering the enforcement condition unnecessary.[100] Thus, it is further suggested that the enforcement condition constitutes a disproportionate limitation on the application of *ne bis in idem*. In particular, this last point has been behind the Commission's and other commentators' rationale on the abolition of the enforcement condition.

Nevertheless, the above view faces quite strong criticism clearly pointing in a different direction. The opposite view claims that the enforcement condition of Article 54 CISA is still in force. In particular, the above arguments are rendered invalid by the following. First, indeed the wording of Article 50 CFR, which is of higher normative status than Article 54 CISA, does not literally include the enforcement condition, but this does rule not out its implicit inclusion. The 'Explanations' on the Charter are quite clear in suggesting exactly that last point; Article 50 CFR was meant to correspond to the Schengen *acquis* and namely to the provisions of Articles 54–58 CISA, while the very limited exceptions in those Conventions permitting '[M]ember States to derogate from the 'non bis in idem' rule [such as the enforcement of the sentence condition] are covered by the horizontal clause in Article 52(1) of the Charter concerning limitations'[101]. Thus, the enforcement condition should not be regarded to have been tacitly abolished by Article 50 CFR. Secondly, the enforcement condition is still justified under Article 52 (1) CFR because it pursues a *general interest* recognised by the European Union, namely the suppression of criminality, which coincides with the attainment of security within the area of freedom, justice and security proclaimed in the Treaties and, in particular, in Article 3(2) TEU and Articles 67(3), 83, 84, 85(1), 86(5), 87(2) and 88(1) TFEU. Thirdly, the *ratio* behind the enforcement condition still remains strong. For it may well be so that under the current legal regime there are many instrumentalities facilitating the enforcement of criminal judgements across the EU, however, this does not necessarily mean that judgements are indeed enforced.

It should be noted in this regard that the CJEU in *Kretzinger*[102] by adopting the concurring view of Advocate-General E. Sharpston[103] and through an extensive argumentation ruled that the execution of judgements through the EAW mechanism is not enough to render redundant the enforcement condition,

[99] For this *ratio* see C Van Den Wyngaert/G Stessens (1999), above n 1, p 799.

[100] R Lööf (2007), above n 64, 327, I Anagnostopoulos, 'The enforcement of sentence in Article 54 CISA', (2008) *Poinika Chronika* 111, 116.

[101] Explanations on the Charter of Fundamental Rights, [2007] OJ C 303/2, Explanation on Article 50, p 31.

[102] CJEU, Case C-288/05, *Jürgen Kretzinger*, [2007] ECR I-06441, paras 59–62.

[103] Opinion of Adv Gen E Sharpston, 5 Dec 2006, in C-288/05, *Jürgen Kretzinger*, [2007] ECR I-06441, paras 87–88.

which can be said to be of general interest to the EU for the suppression of crime. The Court of Justice thus paved the way for the maintenance and justification of the enforcement condition under the general limitation clause of Article 52(1) CFR. In particular, the CJEU noted that the enforcement condition of Article 54 CISA has not been repealed by the EU legislator, but, on the contrary, it has also been included in the *ne bis in idem* version of the EAW thus revealing its enduring validity.[104] In short, it would be absurd to suggest that the EAW mechanism abolished the enforcement condition as regards the application of *ne bis in idem*, since it has actually preserved it *verbatim*. Also, the following points should be added in this line of argumentation. Firstly, the view advocating the abolition of the enforcement condition does not take into account the fact that most of the respective (Third Pillar) measures rest on the discretion of Member States to implement them in practice. For example, the EAW is not issued automatically once criminal charges have been brought, but authorities are free to neglect it and, in practice, do so quite often. Secondly, not all (Third Pillar) legislation on criminal cooperation has actually been 'ratified' by Member States. Thirdly, the purported view rests on a fundamental antithesis, which causes legal uncertainty and was aptly noted by the CJEU.[105] Usually, all mutual recognition instruments like the EAW can be activated only in cases of serious criminality determined either by the seriousness of the crimes involved or by the severity of the penalties imposed. Hence, enforcement of judgements is usually guaranteed in those instances, but not in cases of minor criminality. According to that view therefore, in cases of mirror criminality the application of *ne bis in idem* would either still depend on the enforcement condition, since no effective means to enforce those judgements currently exist at EU level, or the enforcement condition would not apply at all thus creating a major gap in criminal law enforcement, since the defendant would benefit from *ne bis in idem*, but the relative measures and sanctions would be left unexecuted. Naturally, the second alternative should be rejected. On the other hand, what a paradox it would be for *ne bis in idem* to apply in cases of serious criminality without requiring the *in concreto* enforcement of the sentence, due to an *in abstracto* but uncertain possibility of enforcement, while in cases of minor criminality, the defendant would be placed in a more disadvantageous position, since for *ne bis in idem* to apply, the enforcement condition would have to be complied with. This paradoxical outcome, however, must also be ruled out.

In conclusion, it becomes evident that the position arguing in favour of the enforcement condition and its enduring validity, even under the current legal regime, is far more persuasive than the alternative supporting its implied abolition. The 'Explanations' make clear that Article 50 CFR impliedly includes the enforcement condition. The rationale of the relative judgement of the CJEU, although issued before the Charter came into force, reveals the importance of the enforcement condition and its compatibility with Article 52(1) CFR. The

[104] CJEU, Case C-288/05, *Jürgen Kretzinger*, [2007] ECR I-06441, paras 60–61.
[105] Ibid, para 62.

opposite view fails to take into account important factors clearly pointing in the opposite direction. The enforcement of national criminal judgements is of general interest for the EU as a whole, since this is the *raison d'être* of the area of freedom, security and justice. Their enforcement must be guaranteed under the present regime in every single instance. Hence, the enforcement of sentence remains valid as a necessary precondition for the application of *ne bis in idem* in cross-border cases.

4.2 Should Punitive Administrative Proceedings be Included in the Scope of Article 50 CFR?

4.2.1 The Debate and the Arguments over the Issue

Another quite important question raised is whether punitive administrative proceedings should be considered to fall within the scope of Articles 50 CFR and 54 CISA barring therefore subsequent criminal proceedings brought for the same acts within the same or different Member States or vice-versa. Again, both views can be advocated, the first suggesting an affirmative answer to the above, the second, a negative.

The first view supporting the inclusion of punitive administrative proceedings under the notion of criminal proceedings is based on a proposed interpretive alignment of Articles 50 CFR and 54 CISA to the jurisprudence of the ECtHR on Articles 6 and 4 of Protocol 7. Under the so-called conformity clause of Article 52(3) CFR, the CJEU is obliged both on an *a priori* and *ex post* basis to take fully into account and follow the rulings of the Strasbourg Court in the interpretation of any corresponding Charter rights.[106] In its established case

[105] In particular the preamble, filth sentence provides that 'This Charter reaffirms..., the rights as they result, in particular, from..., the case-law...of the European Court of Human Rights.' making thus explicitly clear the indispensable association between the Charter rights and the respective jurisprudence of the ECtHR as the normative content of the former, while it has been laid down that 'The purpose of Article 52 is to set the scope of the rights and principles of the Charter, and to lay down rules for their interpretation...The meaning and the scope of the guaranteed rights are determined not only by the text of those instruments, but also by the case-law of the European Court of Human Rights and by the Court of Justice of the European Union.', Explanations relating to the Charter of Fundamental Rights, [2007] OJ C 303/2 , p 17, Explanation to Article 52. Also, the last sentence of the provision of Article 52(3) *a contrario* implies that Union law is prevented from providing more restrictive protection than that as guaranteed by the Convention and in effect, by the jurisprudence of the Strasbourg Court. On the issue, see CJEU, Case C-400/10 PPU, *V.Mcb. v L.E.*, Judgment of 5 Oct 2010, unpubl., available at curia.europa.eu, para 53, where the Court ruled that '...it follows from Article 52(3) of the Charter that, in so far as the Charter contains rights which correspond to rights guaranteed by the ECHR, their meaning and scope are to be the same as those laid down by the ECHR...Article 7 of the Charter must therefore be given the same meaning and the same scope as Article 8(1) of the ECHR, as interpreted by the case-law of the European Court of Human Rights'. Also, CJEU, Joined Cases C-92/09 and C-93/09, *Volker und Markus Schecke GbR and Hartmut Eifer v Land Hessen*, unpubl, available at curia.europa.eu, paras 51, 52 and 72, 87. See also, The European Convention, Chairman of WG II, 22 Oct 2002, Final Report of Working Group II, Brussels, 22 Oct 2002, CONV 354/02, p 7, Secretariat, Summary of the meeting held on 17.9.2002, CONV 295/02, Brussels, 26 Sep 2002, 2, R van der Linden, 'The

law, the ECtHR consistently holds that *ne bis in idem* applies to different types of proceedings, albeit within a single state, barring subsequent administrative or criminal proceedings, provided that the charge in question is qualified as criminal in nature according to the autonomous meaning of the notion criminal based on the *Engel* criteria,[107] which are transposed from Articles 6 and 7 ECHR to Article 4 P7 ECHR.[108] Hence, by virtue of Article 52(3) CFR, it has been suggested that the notion criminal found in Articles 50 CFR and 54 CISA should be interpreted autonomously in line with the ECtHR's jurisprudence, catching therefore in its protective web national administrative proceedings, provided these fulfil the relevant *Engel* criteria.[109] This argumentation is further

relationship between the Charter and the ECHR', Working Group II Working Document 12, Brussels, 25 Jul 2002, Speech given by Former President G-C Rodríguez Iglesias, Strasbourg, 31 January 2002, 31, in European Court of Human Rights, Annual Report 2001, Registry of the European Court of Human Rights Strasbourg, 2002, by whom the term conformity clause was used, Judge V Skouris, 'Union protection and the Charter of Fundamental Rights of the European Union', Thessaloniki, 23/2/2012, 2, paper presented at the conference of the Hellenic National School of Judges, *Contemporary issues relating to the protection of Fundamental Rights at the European Level*, Thessaloniki, 23–4/2/2012, Speeches by Mr Schoo and JCPiris in Auditions of MM Schoo, Piris and Petite, Working Group II Working Document 13, Brussels 5 Sep 2002, part I and III, EU Network of Independent Experts on Fundamental Rights – Coordinator O De Schutter, *Commentary of the Charter of Fundamental Rights of the European Union*, (June 2006), 17–8, the Examination of witness Dr Cl Ladenburger, Q383, E82, and Memorandum by Fair Trials International, E148, para 33, both in House of Lords, European Union Committee, *The Treaty of Lisbon: an impact assessment*, Vol. II: Evidence, HL Paper 62-II, 2008, E64-E83, E146 *et seq*. Moreover, A Balfour, 'Eliminating Conflicting interpretations of the European Convention on Human Rights by the European Court of Justice and the European Court of Human Rights: The PDIQ System as a Preventative Solution', (2007) 2 *Intercultural Hum Rts L Rev* 183, 194, Hon. Mr Justice JL Murray, 'The Influence of the European Convention on Fundamental Rights on Community Law', (2011) 33 *Ford. Int'l Law J* 1388, 1401, L Rincón – Eizaga, 'Human rights in the EU. Conflict between the Luxembourg and Strasbourg Courts regarding interpretation of Article 8 of the ECHR', (2008) 11 *Int Law Rev Colomb Derecho Int* 119, 148, W Weiß, 'Human Rights in the EU: Rethinking the Role of the European Convention on Human Rights After Lisbon', (2011) 7 *Eu Const* 64, 81.

[107] Eg ECtHR, *Engel and Others v the Netherlands*, 8 June 1976, Series A no 22, *Tomasović v Croatia*, Judgment of 18 Jan 2012 (appl no 53785/09), para 20. These are the legal classification of the offence under national law, the very nature of the offence and the degree of severity of the penalty that the person concerned risks incurring, which are examined disjunctively, although a cumulative approach of all three criteria, where each separate criterion does not suffice, is possible, ECtHR, *Jussila v Finland* [GC], appl no 73053/01, ECHR 2006-XIV, paras 30–31.

[108] See, *inter alia*, ECtHR, *Haarvig v Norway* (dec), 11 Dec 2007 (appl no 11187/05), *Rosenquist v Sweden* (dec.), 14 Sep 2004 (appl no 60619/00), *Manasson v Sweden* (dec), 8 April 2003 (appl no 41265/98), *Göktan v France,* appl no 33402/96, ECHR 2002-V, para 48, *Malige v France,* 23 Sep 1998, ECHR 1998-VII, para 35, and *Nilsson v Sweden* (dec), 13 Dec 2005 (app no 73661/01), ECHR 2005-XIII, *Tomasović v Croatia,* Judgment of 18 Jan 2012 (appl no 53785/09), para 19. See also, ECtHR, *Mamidakis v Greece*, Judgment of 11/1/2007 (appl no 35533/04), 10 *Poiniki Dikaiosini* (2007) 855 with by S Trekli, *Giannetaki & S. Metaphoriki Ltd and Giannetaki v Greece*, Judgment of 6 Dec 2007 (appl no 29829/05), *Chatzinikolaou v Greece*, Judgment of 21 Feb 2008 (appl no 33997/06), 56 Nomiko Vima (2008) 1361, *Västberga Taxi Aktiebolag and Vulic v Sweden*, Judgment of 23 Jul 2002 (appl no 36985/97), *Janosevic v Sweden*, Judgment of 23 July 2002 (appl no 34619/97), *Sergey Zolotukhin v Russia* [GC], Judgment of 10 Feb 2009 (appl no 14939/03) *Ruotsalainen v Finland,* Judgment of 16 June 2009 (appl no 13079/03).

[109] S Peers (2011), above n 44, 843, I Ziemele in EU Network of Independent Experts on Fundamental Rights, *Commentary* (2006), above n 106, 385, A Biehler, R Kniebóhler, J Lelieur-

reinforced with the application by the CJEU of Article 6 ECHR guarantees to administrative proceedings on the basis of the autonomous notion of 'criminal' fashioned by the ECtHR's jurisprudence[110] and through the explicit expansion by the EU legislator of the scope of application of the right to a fair trial, established in Articles 47 and 48 CFR, to all sorts of proceedings.[111]

Nevertheless, the above view is quite simplistic as it fails to take into account the distinct and special nature of the horizontal *ne bis in idem* in EU law and the overall framework of criminal cooperation within the European Union. Moreover, such a view would entail severe repercussions on the administration of national justice systems with unpredictable results. The ECtHR's jurisprudence should indeed be applauded, since a restrictive interpretation of the right to a fair trial and *ne bis in idem* based solely on the domestic characterization of the procedures would contravene the very meaning and purpose of the Convention, rendering ineffective its safeguards in practice. Nevertheless, it would be inappropriate to transpose the approach taken by the ECtHR regarding this particular aspect of *ne bis in idem* to the interpretation and implementation of its horizontal EU law counterpart.

The *ne bis in idem* principle of Article 4 of Protocol 7 ECHR and that of Articles 50 CFR and 54 CISA are in reality by their nature quite distinct and have a different scope of application, not suitable for alignment. The first is an expression of the traditional state applied principle of criminal process, which affords protection to the individual and ensures legal certainty, while the latter is a unique supranational principle with horizontal application that regulates the criminal jurisdictions of states and the recognition of foreign judgments, aimed further at enhancing European integration. Consequently, although both versions of double jeopardy share a common core, it would be paradoxical to transpose the idiomatic characteristics of the first, which applies only within a single legal order, to the second. The legal basis for this argument can be established on Article 52(3) itself and Article 53 of the Charter; the Charter may, in principle, offer greater protection than that of the ECHR system, such as Article 50 CFR offers by affording horizontal effect to the *ne bis in idem* principle. Such an additional protection though, should be strictly governed by EU law precepts and should be kept confined within the limits prescribed by EU law, since it is in excess of the protection offered by the Convention. In plain words, the *ne bis in idem* principle guaranteed by Articles 50 CFR and 54 CISA *does not correspond* to its ECHR equivalent of Article 4 of Protocol 7, in so far as the latter is applied strictly 'within the same Member State' and not horizontally.

Fischer, and S Stein (eds), *Freiburg Proposal on Concurrent Jurisdictions and the Prohibition of Multiple Prosecutions in the European Union*, (Max-Planck-Institut, 2003), 20 *et seq* (albeit on *de lege ferenda* basis).

[110] CJEU, C-235/92 P, *Montecatini SpA v the Commission* [1999] ECR I-4539 paras 175–176.

[111] D O'Connell, in EU Network of Independent Experts on Fundamental Rights, *Commentary* (2006), above n 106, 374.

Unequivocal support for this argument is clearly provided by the 'Explanations' on the Charter, which explicitly distinguish between the horizontal application of the principle and its application within a single state, by laying down that *ne bis in idem* has the same meaning and the same scope as the corresponding right in the ECHR, only when it is applied within the same Member State and not between different Member States.[112] That being so, the relative jurisprudence of the ECtHR should not be used for the interpretation of Articles 50 CFR and 54 CISA in an unqualified manner. The scope of application of the respective provisions in particular, should be assessed and construed independently of each other. Accordingly, the term criminal proceedings found in Articles 50 CFR and 54 CISA should be interpreted without taking into account the respective jurisprudence of the ECtHR on the issue.

Another conclusive argument against an unqualified interpretive alignment between the Charter and the ECHR versions of the *ne bis in idem* principle can be inferred from the identification of *ne bis in idem* with mutual recognition of judgements and from the overall legal framework within which the principle operates. In the field of cooperation in criminal matters and, in particular, in the regulation of conflicts of jurisdiction between the Member States, harmonisation is subordinate to mutual recognition. Harmonisation should be used only as a means for the facilitation of mutual recognition of judgements and only through the enactment of secondary legislation.[113] In this regard, it has to be underlined that Article 67(1) TFEU and Article 82(2) TFEU specifically lay down that the establishment of the area of freedom, security and justice and of any relative rules shall respect '... the differences between the legal traditions and systems of the Member States'. If however the CJEU adopted an autonomous meaning of criminal proceedings with respect to the application of *ne bis in idem*, this would in reality amount to a *de facto* horizontal harmonising effect of the various national legislations of Member States dealing with the administration of justice, disregarding 'the differences between the legal traditions and systems of the Member States' involved. This would also result in a twofold creeping competence; first, the CJEU would substitute the EU legislature in its task of enacting legal instruments of mutual recognition and harmonisation in the field of criminal matters, while, secondly, the limitation set up by the Treaties

[112] Explanations, [2007] OJ C 303/2 , Explanation on Article 50, p 31, where it is provided that 'As regards the situations referred to by Article 4 of Protocol No 7, namely the application of the principle within the same Member State, the guaranteed right has the same meaning and the same scope as the corresponding right in the ECHR'.

[113] TFEU, Article 82(1) 'Judicial cooperation in criminal matters in the Union shall be based on the principle of mutual recognition of judgments and judicial decisions and shall include the approximation of the laws and regulations of the Member States... to prevent and settle conflicts of jurisdiction between Member States' Article 82(2) 'To the extent necessary to facilitate mutual recognition of judgments and judicial decisions and police and judicial cooperation in criminal matters having a cross-border dimension, the European Parliament and the Council may, by means of directives adopted in accordance with the ordinary legislative procedure, establish minimum rules. Such rules shall take into account the differences between the legal traditions and systems of the Member States'.

that gives priority to the use of mutual recognition in criminal matters over the use of harmonisation, would be exceeded. Such an outcome however, must be precluded.

In this regard, Article 52(2) CFR should also be noted. According to that provision, 'rights recognised by this Charter for which provision is made in the Treaties shall be exercised under the conditions and within the limits defined by those Treaties'. It may well be true that double jeopardy is not guaranteed as such by the Treaties themselves; however, its legal basis is found therein and, in particular, in Articles 67(3) and 82(1) TFEU. What is more, the Schengen *acquis* and Articles 54–58 CISA to which Article 50 CFR was meant to correspond have the previous Treaty Articles as their basis. Consequently, the norm of Article 52(2) CFR should also apply in this instance and thus, the limits drawn by Articles 67(3) and 82(1) TFEU according to which only a restrictive interpretation of the notion criminal proceedings is permissible, should inevitably delineate the scope of application of the right against double jeopardy as guaranteed by the Charter.

What is more, the application of fair trial guarantees outside the strict criminal context by the CJEU cannot lead to the conclusion that the notion criminal found in Articles 50 CFR and 54CISA should be similarly expanded. Indeed, the guarantees of the right to a fair trial should apply to procedures outside the strict criminal context. This acknowledgement however, does not mean *ipso jure* that these guarantees inescapably lead to a *res judicata* effect, which bars subsequent proceedings, since to be exact, double jeopardy is quite distinct from the right to a fair trial.[114] On the contrary, the unequivocal expansion of the right to a fair trial by the EU legislature to cover administrative proceedings, in contrast to *ne bis in idem* that was not extended in a similar fashion, leads to the inevitable conclusion that under EU law these proceedings neither were meant, nor should be covered by Articles 54 CISA and 50 CFR, since the EU legislature would have amended or drafted these provisions accordingly

A rationale similar to that argued so far was articulated by Advocate-General Yves Bot in the *Melloni* case. Notwithstanding the clauses of Article 52(3)(4) pointing in a parallel and conforming interpretation of the Charter to the ECHR, Advocate-General Yves Bot adopted an elaborated line of reasoning justifying a differentiated interpretation of Charter rights. In particular, according to the Advocate-General Bot:[115]

> Although it is true that the interpretation of the rights protected by the Charter must tend towards a high level of protection, as may be inferred from Article 52(3) of the Charter and from the explanatory remarks concerning Article 52(4) of the Charter, it is nevertheless important to state that this must be a level of protection which accords with European Union law, ... That is a reminder of a principle that has long guided

[114] S Trechsel (2005), above n 1, 385, where in pointing at the distinct nature of the two states that *ne bis in idem* '... is not a guarantee which requires a specific quality of the trial, but leads to a consequence that there should be no trial at all'.

[115] Opinion of Adv Gen Y Bot in C-399/11, *Stefano Melloni,* unpublished, available at curia.europa.eu, paras 106–112.

> the interpretation of fundamental rights within the Union, namely that the protection of fundamental rights within the Union must be ensured within the framework of the structure and objectives of the Union. In that regard, it is not irrelevant that the preamble to the Charter refers to the main objectives of the Union, including the creation of an area of freedom, security and justice. It is therefore not possible to reason only in terms of a higher or lower level of protection of human rights without taking into account the requirements linked to the action of the Union and the specific nature of European Union law... The fundamental rights to be protected and the level of protection to be afforded to them reflect the choices of a society...and cannot therefore be transposed automatically to other contexts... the level of protection for fundamental rights to be achieved cannot be separated from the context in which it is carried out... As regards the assessment of the level of protection for fundamental rights which must be guaranteed within the legal order of the European Union, the specific interests which motivate the action of the Union must be taken into account... Those specific interests cause the level of protection for fundamental rights to be adjusted depending on the different interests at stake.

Although this reasoning was used to reject the transposition of the interpretation given to national Constitutional rights to their equivalent Charter rights, it can also be used to reject a complete interpretive alignment between Charter and ECHR rights and to adopt a differentiated interpretation between the two instruments. For the Advocate-General made an explicit mention not only of Article 52(4) CFR relating to national Constitutions, but also of Article 52(3) CFR on the basis of which the interpretation of Charter rights must be aligned to that of their corresponding rights in the ECHR. Thus, he clearly stated that a differentiated interpretation between Charter and ECHR is necessitated by holding that 'the assessment of the level of protection for fundamental rights to be achieved [should be] carried out within the framework of the implementation of EU law'.[116]

That said, the conclusion should be drawn that the approach arguing for an interpretive alignment of *ne bis in idem* to the case-law of the ECtHR in order to cover punitive administrative proceedings should be rejected.

4.2.2 *The Case-law on the Issue*

The above approach rejecting the application of Articles 50 CFR and 54 CISA on administrative proceedings is evident, albeit with important differences, in the recent Opinion of Advocate-General Cruz Villalón in the case of *Åklagaren v Hans Åkerberg Fransson*.[117] The Opinion clearly states that Article 50 CFR does not prevent a person from being sanctioned in criminal proceedings for facts

[116] Opinion of Adv Gen Y Bot in C-399/11, *Stefano Melloni*, unpublished, available at curia.europa.eu, para 135.

[117] Opinion of Adv Gen C Villalón, of 12 June 2012, in Case C-617/10 *Åklagaren v Hans Åkerberg Fransson*, unpublished, available at curia.europa.eu.

in respect of which a final penalty has already been imposed in administrative proceedings. In this case, the Swedish authorities imposed on Mr Fransson an administrative fine for tax offences, which after becoming final was followed by criminal prosecution for the same acts. The national court referred a preliminary question asking, in effect, whether national law was in breach of Articles 50 CFR and Article 4 Protocol No 7 ECHR bearing in mind the facts of the case. Initially, the Advocate-General argued that the Court lacked jurisdiction to rule over the preliminary question referred to it, since he regarded that the case fell short of the necessary connection with EU law required by Article 51(1) CFR. In his view, 'the connection in the case between Union law, which is in principle being implemented, and the exercise of the public authority of the State, was extremely weak and is not, in any event, a sufficient basis for a clearly identifiable interest on the part of the Union in assuming responsibility for guaranteeing that specific fundamental right vis-à-vis the Union'[118] since the punishment of the conduct in the present case was merely occasionally related to EU law and not casually.[119] Although, there was a connection between the effectiveness of tax collection under the relevant Directive and the penalties involved, the imposition of the latter rested solely upon the discretion of Member States and therefore was not an issue pertaining to the implementation of EU law. This was so as

> the mere finding that the exercise of the power of the State to impose penalties in a particular case is ultimately based on a provision of Union law is not, of itself, sufficient for the purposes of transferring the review of any constitutional guarantees applicable to the exercise of that power from the sphere of responsibility of the Member States to that of the Union.[120]

Next, the Advocate-General tried to answer the question in its substance. In this regard, he first noted that not all Member States have ratified Protocol 7 ECHR and that many have specifically limited its application only to criminal offences. He thus achieved to demonstrate the considerable lack of agreement between the Member States regarding the problems resulting from the imposition of both administrative and criminal penalties in respect of the same offence by further underlying its agreed exclusion from the accession process of the EU to the ECHR.[121] For all those reasons, he suggested that the requirement imposed by Article 52(3) CFR for an interpretive alignment with the ECtHR's jurisprudence should be qualified when it comes to *ne bis in idem*.[122] The Advocate-General opted for a 'partially autonomous interpretation' of Article 50, taking into consideration the case law of the ECtHR, but tailoring its protective threshold according to an independent interpretation which should be based exclusively on the wording and scope of Article 50 of the Charter.[123] Next, he concluded

[118] Ibid, para 57.
[119] Ibid, paras 61–65.
[120] Ibid, para 54.
[121] Ibid, paras 71–74.
[122] Ibid, para 85.
[123] Ibid, para 87.

that Article 50 CFR does not preclude the institution of criminal proceedings following the imposition of an administrative penalty for the same material facts, provided that the criminal court is in a position to take into account the prior existence of an administrative penalty for the purposes of mitigating the punishment to be imposed by it. However, the extent to which the second condition is complied with shall be left to the national court to assess.[124] He based his conclusions on the wording of Article 50 CFR and on the reasoning suggesting that the imposition of criminal penalties, after taking into account the administrative penalties already imposed do not infringe the principles of proportionality and the prohibition of arbitrariness.[125]

It is made clear from the above Opinion that the Advocate-General suggests that a comparison of double jeopardy in the Charter and the ECHR reveals a different scope of application. This inevitably leads to an independent and distinct interpretation of Article 50 CFR and Article 4 Protocol 7 ECHR, precluding the barring of administrative proceedings under the former.

However, according to the Opinion, there could be instances involving the implementation of EU law and the cumulative imposition of administrative and criminal penalties that could fall within the ambit of the *ne bis in idem* principle. Moreover, the Advocate-General concluded that the application of Article 50 CFR on administrative proceedings depended on whether these were to be taken account by the criminal court. As such, although the general approach of the Opinion which distinguishes *ne bis in idem* under the two texts is to be applauded, particular aspects of its rationale and the suggested outcome must be rejected. By moving the focus from the barring of subsequent proceedings to the carrying out of a set-off between the two, many questions remain unanswered. First and foremost, what if the criminal proceedings are brought before the imposition of administrative sanctions? What if national legislation does not provide for a set-off between the two? Moreover, what if, in the absence of specific provisions to this effect, the national court silently takes into account prior administrative penalties? What should be the case with Member States that have ratified Protocol 7 ECHR? All these puzzling questions reveal the overall weakness of the Advocate-General's argumentation, which lies on a mistaken assumption. The set-off presupposes the opening of further proceedings, while *ne bis in idem* precludes them altogether. It would be thus a *contradictio terminis* to assess the violation of *ne bis in idem* on whether a set-off has actually taken place or not. The latter is actually a distinct principle to the former, it is guaranteed by a different legal provision (Article 56 CISA) and comes into play only when *ne bis in idem* is inapplicable

The Advocate-General disregarded the fact EU law solely establishes the horizontal *ne bis in idem,* leaving the internal aspect to Member States. Although the Charter's wording may be misleading in this respect ('*within the Union*'), Article 54 CISA, which the Charter meant to manifest, is quite clear on

[124] Ibid, paras 93 and 96, and part VII, conclusion.
[125] Ibid, paras 94–95.

that. This is more so evident by the drafting history and the *ratio* behind double jeopardy in Articles 50 CFR and 54 CISA, which were meant to contribute to the establishment of the area of freedom, security and justice where persons would freely exercise their right to free movement. Also, he completely disregarded the overall legal framework regarding cooperation of Member States in criminal matters as stipulated by the Treaty and all the relevant arguments drawn by it, as analysed previously. In essence, it seems that the Opinion echoed national voices on the issue against the stance taken by the ECtHR and provided for an alternative rationale to that jurisprudence, while it left the pre-condition of the set-off to be decided by national courts. In other words, in practice national courts could rule out any violation of *ne bis in idem* due to the cumulative imposition of sanctions. If the Advocate-General had adopted the view focusing on the different nature and scope of application of Article 50 CFR than its ECHR equivalent, it would have been much easier to draw the same conclusion, without leaving any gaps that may cause further confusion. In the present case, it should have been suggested that the Court lacked jurisdiction, given that the sanctions were imposed within a single state only and the imposition of the criminal sanctions was not dictated by EU law. Moreover, the exclusion of administrative proceedings from the ambit of Articles 50 CFR and 54 CISA could have been based on the wording of those provisions and on the previous arguments deriving from the overall legal framework. This would not have left any gaps that could trigger uncertain developments in the case-law.

The Court in its respective judgement[126] in trying to give a conclusive solution to the issue, departed from the Opinion of the Advocate-General and ruled that the case had the necessary connection with EU law as required from by Article 51(1) CFR, but avoided making a qualification of the administrative proceedings in question by holding that this was 'a matter which is for the national court to determine'. It also tacitly rejected the reasoning suggested by the Advocate-General according to which the infringement of *ne bis in idem* would be precluded when a 'set-off' is carried out by the criminal court by taking into account the prior existence of the administrative penalty imposed.

In particular, the CJEU in *Fransson* adopted an expansive approach on the interpretation of Article 51(1) CFR by holding that the definition of the field of application of the Charter is to be interpreted according to the 'Explanations' on the Charter, which lay down that 'the requirement to respect fundamental rights defined in the context of the Union is only binding on the Member States when they act in the scope of Union Law'.[127] The Court thus, by referring to Articles 6(1) TEU and 52(7) CFR has affirmed the normative interpretive value of the 'Explanations' on the Charter, since in this instance the wording of Article 51(1) CFR ('…implementing Union law') appears to imply a narrower

[126] CJEU, Case C-617/10, *Åklagaren v Hans Åkerberg Fransson*, Judgment of 26 Feb 2013, unpubl, available at curia.europa.eu.

[127] Ibid, paras 19–20.

construal of the scope of application of the Charter than the 'Explanations'. This expansive approach taken by the Court led it to hold that the disputed measures fell 'within the scope' of EU law because these were regarded to have been taken within the context of administrative and legislative measures to ensure the collection of VAT revenue in compliance with EU law and to counter fraud affecting the financial interests of the EU.[128] As such, the Court held that there was a direct link of those measures with EU law fulfilling the requirements of Article 51(1) CFR, notwithstanding the fact that the national legislation upon which the tax penalties and criminal proceedings in question were founded had not been adopted to transpose the respective Directive.[129] It should thus be inferred that a case will fall within the scope of the Charter, provided that the measures at issue can simply be considered to fall within a field that is regulated by EU law, without being necessary for those measures to implement specific regulations of EU law.

Next, in answering the question whether a tax penalty imposed can have a barring effect on subsequent criminal proceedings for the same acts in view of Article 50 CFR, the Court totally disregarded the reasoning followed by the Advocate-General and reached to important conclusions of its own. First, the Court affirmed that a tax penalty, which is criminal in nature and has become final, precludes, according to Article 50 CFR, subsequent criminal proceedings for the same acts.[130] Nevertheless, it pointed out that, as a rule:

> Article 50 of the Charter does not preclude a Member State from imposing, for the same acts ..., a combination of tax penalties and criminal penalties since in order to ensure that all VAT revenue is collected and, in so doing, that the financial interests of the European Union are protected, the Member States have freedom to choose the applicable penalties...[which]...may therefore take the form of administrative, criminal penalties of a combination of the two.[131]

Next, the Court went on further to weaken its first preposition on the inclusion of administrative proceedings within the scope of Article 50 CFR; although it reaffirmed that the notion criminal is to be assessed in line with the three *Engel* criteria, it undermined the significance of that conclusion by holding that their examination rests solely on the national court and it should be carried out in relation to possible higher national standards of protection of fundamental rights.[132] In essence thus, the Court held that, in a case like *Fransson*, where the impugned measures bear a direct link with EU law, but were imposed as a matter of national law and not in the implementation of EU law, the assessment of the criminal character of these measures is to be made only with reference to national higher standards, given that EU law permits the cumulative imposition

[128] Ibid, paras 24–26.
[129] Ibid, paras 26–28.
[130] Ibid, paras 33–34.
[131] Ibid, paras 33–34.
[132] Ibid, paras 34–36 and operative part.

of administrative and criminal measures. Such an assessment moreover, falls solely within the competence of the national court. As a result, the determination of the criminal nature of punitive administrative measures is deferred to the national courts, while the reference to the *Engel* criteria appears to have been merely *obiter* bearing no actual legal consequences, given that their examination is up to the national court which could easily reach to stricter formulations of these criteria or can even disregard them completely. Nevertheless, the Court did not stop there, but further ruled that even if a national court held by applying the above reasoning, that the measures at hand constitute a bar to further proceedings, the validity of such a conclusion would be upheld 'provided that… the primacy, unity and effectiveness of European Union law are not thereby compromised…as long as the remaining penalties are effective, proportionate and dissuasive'.[133] It follows therefore, that even measures qualified as criminal in nature will still not be capable of barring subsequent proceedings, if such a bar to proceedings undermines the effectiveness of EU law. Thus, the Court managed to insert a further condition which can be used to render ineffective the general proposition that measures, criminal in nature, should be caught within the protective net of Article 50 CFR. This last condition would probably serve the Court to preclude parallel proceedings from being barred, in future cases where administrative and criminal measures are imposed directly in the implementation of EU law.

On the issue at hand, the similar case of *Łukasz Marcin Bonda*[134] regarding the imposition of both administrative and criminal sanctions, should also be noted. In that case, the Court, although it ruled that the relative penalties imposed as of Article 138(1) of Regulation No 1973/2004 where not of criminal nature, it did not examine them under Articles 50 CFR and 54 CISA, but merely in relation to the national provisions of the code of criminal procedure.[135] The Court after having established that the relative measures imposed by virtue of the respective Regulation constituted a 'specific administrative instrument...intended to ensure the sound financial management of EU public funds' that 'may be applied independently of any criminal penalties',[136] it then ruled out their inclusion under the concept of criminal proceedings of Article 4(1) of Protocol 7 ECHR. In particular, by applying the *Engel* criteria, the CJEU noted that the respective measures could not be termed as criminal, given that these were not regarded as criminal in nature by EU law, their purpose was not punitive, but was essentially to protect the management of EU funds, and since their sole effect was to deprive the farmer in question of the prospect of obtaining aid.[137]

Even so, the actual application by the CJEU of the *Engel* criteria in *Bonda* reveals confusion on the part of the Court to properly delineate and apply these

[133] Ibid, paras 29 and 36.

[134] CJEU, Case C-489/10, *Łukasz Marcin Bonda*, Judgment of 5 Jun 2012, unpublished, in curia.europa.eu.

[135] Ibid, paras 26–27 and operative part.

[136] Ibid, paras 27–35 and operative part.

[137] Ibid, paras 43–47 and operative part.

criteria. First and foremost, the CJEU has not made clear whether these criteria should only apply disjunctively or whether a cumulative approach is possible, where separate analysis of each criterion does not make it possible to reach a clear conclusion as to the existence of a criminal charge, as the ECtHR has already ruled in similar cases.[138] In addition, contrary to what the CJEU has held, the fact that a measure seeks to protect a certain objective, such as the management of EU funds, should not automatically rule out its qualification as of punitive character, since any criminal offence actually serves to protect an underlying legitimate objective. Under the facts of the case in particular, it was clear that the respective criminal offence aimed at protecting the same objective with the administrative measures imposed and namely, the proper management of subsidies.[139] Moreover, according to the ECtHR the examination of the criminal character of a given measure rests not only on its punitive character, but also on its deterrent effect and on whether the measure is directed towards all citizens rather than towards a group possessing a special status.[140] Accordingly, the ECtHR has held that when a fee imposed can be seen as a punishment to deter re-offending, then it is to be regarded as criminal.[141] Unfortunately, the CJEU has not made any reference whatsoever to the element of deterrence in the assessment of the character of the measures in question. It should be pointed out though that the conclusion that the CJEU has reached in *Bonda* was correct, notwithstanding the particular weaknesses of its rationale, since the administrative measures at hand merely deprived the interested party temporarily from a benefit that he would be otherwise able to claim.

By juxtaposing the two judgements, the following conclusions should be made. First, it is noteworthy that the CJEU has not examined the issue in the *Bonda* case by reference to Articles 50 CFR/CISA and this could be taken to imply that these provisions should never be brought in cases evolving within one single state with the only applicable rules being the national provisions in force. However, as ruled in *Fransson*, when the case at hand bears the necessary connection with EU law, such as when it relates to issues regulated by EU law, then Article 50 CFR becomes applicable. Accordingly, subsequent proceedings should be barred, when the relevant offence is qualified as criminal in nature. Two distinctions should be drawn at this point; between measures imposed directly by EU law on the one hand, such as those analysed in *Bonda*, and measures imposed on the discretion of EU Member States that fall 'within the scope of EU law' as

[138] Eg ECtHR, *Jussila v Finland* [GC], appl no 73053/01, ECHR 2006-XIV, paras 30–31, *Ezeh and Connors v the United Kingdom* [GC], nos 39665/98 and 40086/98, ECHR 2003-X, paras 82–86, *Tomasović v Croatia*, Judgment of 18 Jan 2012 (appl no 53785/09), para 20.

[139] CJEU, Case C-489/10, *Łukasz Marcin Bonda*, Judgment of 5 Jun 2012, unpubl, in curia.europa.eu, para 20.

[140] Eg ECtHR, *Ezeh and Connors v the United Kingdom* [GC], nos 39665/98 and 40086/98, ECHR 2003-X paras 102 and 105, ECtHR, *Tomasović v Croatia*, Judgment of 18 Jan 2012 (appl no 53785/09), para 22, *Västberga Taxi Aktiebolag and Vulic v Sweden*, Judgment of 23 Jul 2002 (appl no 36985/97), para 79.

[141] ECtHR, *Ruotsalainen v Finland*, Judgment of 16 Jul 2009 (appl no 13079/03), para 46.

contemplated in *Fransson*. The Court will assess itself whether the penalties involved are considered as criminal in nature by taking into account the *Engel* criteria, only to the extent the relative sanctions are imposed directly by provisions of EU law. In such an occasion, the Court will not examine their character with reference to Articles 50 CFR and 54 CISA, but independently on the basis of the provisions these penalties are prescribed. If on the contrary, the relative provisions are within the scope of EU law as contemplated in *Fransson*, but have been imposed by the Member States themselves acting on their discretion and not in the implementation of EU law, then the qualification of those measures will rest solely on national courts. In such an instance moreover, as mentioned already, the examination of the criminal nature of the measures in question would be made only with regard to national higher standards, given that EU law permits, as a rule, the cumulative imposition of administrative and criminal measures for the same acts. Thus, national standards would determine in such an instance the criminal nature of the measures in question and not an autonomous notion of criminal based on Article 50 CFR. This outcome must be applauded for it has been established that an autonomous notion of criminal proceedings would have the effect of a two-fold creeping competence disregarding the differences of the national legal systems of Member States and would go way beyond what has been envisaged by the respective Treaty framework on the establishment of the area of freedom, security and justice. Nevertheless, the adoption by the Court of the *Engel* criteria, despite the fact it has actually rendered them ineffective in *Fransson*, together with their uncertain application in *Bonda*, does not clarify, but rather complicates the interpretation and application of Article 50 CFR and 54 CISA to proceedings that lie outside the *stricto sensu* criminal context. The reasoning adopted in both these judgements could be easily misapplied by national courts and could lead to further confusion, given that at this time many other substantive questions regarding the interpretation and application of the horizontal *ne bis in idem* principle remain unanswered. It would have been straightforward and unambiguous, as strongly advocated, to hold that Articles 50 CFR and 54 CISA are quite distinct than Article 4 of Protocol 7 ECHR, having a different scope of application not suitable for alignment and thus, to rule that only proceedings being classified as criminal according to their domestic classification should fall within the ambit of Articles 50 CFR and 54 CISA. Both the reasoning expressed by Advocate-General Yves Bot and the arguments delivered so far, have established that such a formulation is not at odds with the *ratio* of Articles 51(1), 52(3) and 53 CFR, but, on the contrary, coincides with the overall Treaty framework established by Articles 67 and 82 TFEU.

4.3 *Lis pedens*

Ne bis in idem and *lis pedens* are intrinsically associated, since in reality the latter is an incomplete version of the former. *Lis pedens* in particular bars further proceedings due to prior and ongoing proceedings for the same acts, provided that all the requirements of *ne bis in idem* are fulfilled, with the exception of the existence of a final judgement, since ongoing proceedings suffice. So, there must be factual identity, personal identity and identical ongoing procedures. It should also logically follow that an EU-wide *lis pedens* would not require the enforcement of the sentence condition to be complied with, since the latter presupposes the existence of a final judgement.

Under current EU law though, in contrast to civil, commercial and matrimonial cases[142] and despite various efforts to this direction,[143] no general binding rule of *lis pedens* exists as regards ongoing criminal proceedings in numerous Member States based on the same acts. The general rule is that Member States are not barred by virtue of Articles 54–58 CISA or 50 CFR to institute parallel criminal proceedings or preliminary investigations against the same person in respect of the same acts.[144] Besides certain pieces of legislation dealing with particular criminal acts, which address the conflict of concurrent jurisdictions by requiring the cooperation of the Member States involved with a view to allocate jurisdiction to one of them,[145] no general norm exists. Hence,

[142] Council Regulation 44/2001, of 22 December 2000, on international jurisdiction, recognition and enforcement of judgements in civil and commercial cases, [2001] OJ L 12/1, Articles 27–30, Council Regulation (EC) No 2201/2003 of 27 November 2003 concerning jurisdiction and the recognition and enforcement of judgments in matrimonial matters and the matters of parental responsibility, repealing Regulation (EC) No 1347/2000, [2003] OJ L 338/1, Article 19, Council Regulation (EC) No 4/2009 of 18 December 2008 on jurisdiction, applicable law, recognition and enforcement of decisions and cooperation in matters relating to maintenance obligations, [2009] OJ L 007/1, Articles 12–13, Council Regulation (EU) No 650/2012 of the European Parliament and of the Council of 4 July 2012 on jurisdiction, applicable law, recognition and enforcement of decisions and acceptance and enforcement of authentic instruments in matters of succession and on the creation of a European Certificate of Succession, [2012] OJ L 201/0107, Preamble lit 35, Articles 17–18.

[143] Commission of the European Communities (2005), above n 98, 9–10, Commission of the European Communities, (2005), above n 51.

[144] CJEU, Case C-491/07, *Vladimir Turanský*, Judgment of 22 Dec 2008, [2008] ECJ I-11039, paras 34 and 44, W Schomburg, 'Are we on the Road to a European Law-Enforcement Area? International Cooperation in Criminal Matters. What Place for Justice?' (2000/1) 8 *Eur J Crime Cr L Cr J* 51, 56, M Fichera and C Janssens, 'Mutual Recognition of judicial decisions in criminal matters and the role of the national judge' (2007) 8 *ERA Forum* 177, 191, European Parliament, Directorate-General Internal Policies, Policy Unit C, Citizens' rights and constitutional affairs: Briefing Paper – The application of the ne bis in idem principle in the area of implementation of third pillar instruments, IP/C/LIBE/FWC/2005-26 of 14-02-2006, PE 378278, 7.

[145] Council Framework Decision 2000/383/JHA of 29 May 2000 on Increasing Protection by Criminal Penalties and other Sanctions against Counterfeiting in Connection with the Introduction of the Euro, [2000] OJ L 140/1, Article 7 (3), Council Framework Decision 2002/475/JHA of 13 June 2002 on Combating Terrorism, [2002] OJ L 164/3, Article 9(2), Council Framework Decision 2005/222/JHA of 24 February 2005 on attacks against information systems, [2005] OJ L 69/67, Article 4(11), Council Framework Decision 2005/667/JHA of 12 July 2005, to strengthen the criminal-law framework for the enforcement of the law against ship source pollution, [2005] OJ L 255/164, Article 7(4)(5), Convention on the protection of the European Communities' financial interests, [1995] OJ C 316/49, Article 6, Convention on the Fight against Corruption Involving Officials of the European Communities or Officials of Member States of the European Union, [1997] OJ C 195/2, Article 9. For a detailed reference of those provisions see the Annex in Commission of the European Communities (2005), above n 51.

the rule seems to be that of 'first come, first served', since a Member State, which succeeds to issue a final judgement first, precludes all other Member States from taking further proceedings.[146]

So far, under EU law, only general guidelines and procedures are provided for determining the appropriate Member State to conduct the prosecution, which are mainly established by a Framework Decision of 2009.[147] This process involves the communication of the authorities of the Member States in order to reach to a common decision by consensus as to which state should prosecute or where ongoing proceedings should be concentrated. Its main aspects are the obligation to contact, the obligation to reply, the obligation to enter into direct consultations and the obligatory exchange of a specific minimum set of information. Eurojust may play an important role in this procedure, provided that the authorities of the Member States request its assistance. The relevant criteria, which should be considered in choosing the appropriate forum, are the place of the commission of the crime, the place where the damage occurred, the habitual residence of the defendant, the availability of evidence and witnesses, the interests of the victims and the length of the proceedings.[148] The severity of the legislation and of the sentences to be imposed should not play any role in determining the appropriate forum where criminal proceedings should take place.[149] What is also of great interest is the attempt by the Framework Decision to bypass the obstacle of mandatory prosecution adopted by Member States that obliges national prosecuting authorities to institute criminal proceedings once reasonable grounds exist, by proclaiming in its Preamble that this is deemed to be fulfilled when any Member State ensures the criminal prosecution of a particular criminal offender through the use of the procedures established under its provisions.

The existing framework has been negatively criticised.[150] Its shortcomings are many. Mainly, these relate to the disproportionate burden that the defendant may bear due to the parallel ongoing proceedings and the overall lack of efficiency and predictability of the current mechanism. In particular, the 2009 Framework Decision has also been heavily criticised, since, in practice, it does ensure that multiple prosecutions are avoided, but risks further proceedings

[146] Commission of the European Communities (2005), above n 51, 3, M Fichera and C Janssens (2007) above n 144, 191, R Lööf (2007), above n 64, 332.

[147] Council Framework Decision 2009/948/JHA, of 30 November 2009, on prevention and settlement of conflicts of exercise of jurisdiction in criminal proceedings, [2009] OJ L 328/42.

[148] Council Framework Decision 2009/948/JHA, [2009] OJ L 328/42, Preamble, Commission of the European Communities, (2005), above n 98, 7–8, Commission of the European Communities (2005), above n 51, 35 and following, Eurojust, Annual Report 2003, 63 available atwww.eurojust.eu.int.

[149] Eurojust, ibid, 63.

[150] European Criminal Bar Association, Response to the Green Paper on Conflicts of Jurisdiction and the Principle of ne bis in idem in Criminal Proceedings COM (2005) 696, Bundesrechtsanwaltskammer, European Affairs Committee and Criminal Law committee, Position on the GREEN PAPER on Conflicts of Jurisdiction and the Principle of ne bis in idem in Criminal Proceedings COM (2005) 696, March 2006, BRAK Position no 07/2006, Bar Council of England and Wales (2006) above n 72, 4–6.

to take place, since authorities may more easily become aware of cases over which they may establish jurisdiction.[151] No general obligation to concentrate proceedings is imposed on the Member States, which are neither legally bound to waive or accept jurisdiction, nor to suspend their own proceedings in favour of another Member State, even despite the conclusion of consultations. Also, the requirement of mandatory prosecution has not been surpassed, since the respective proclamation in the Preamble of the 2009 Framework Decision lacks any solid legal content providing no more than an uncertain interpretive guideline to national authorities. Moreover, as mentioned previously, the individual instruments, which include relevant rules, share exactly the same drawbacks; they merely set out a general obligation to cooperate with a view of concentrating proceedings and nothing more.

Nevertheless, besides the inexistence of an EU-wide *lis pedens* rule, Member States can certainly fill this void by applying their own law instead. It is noteworthy that in the *Miraglia* case, the competent national authorities discontinued criminal proceedings due to ongoing criminal proceedings in another Member State.[152] This decision to discontinue proceedings was not deemed by the CJEU as being contrary to EU law. Quite the contrary, the Court succeeded with its judgement to rule out any possible shortcomings that such discontinuances of proceedings may have in the future.[153] So, when *lis pedens* is provided for by national law, national courts should be expected to apply it in cross-border cases within the EU, despite the absence of any relevant EU legislation. Member States are allowed to bar further proceedings due to ongoing proceedings in another Member State, since, in this instance they would be offering greater protection to the defendant than that offered from Articles 50 CFR and 54 CISA, in line with Articles 53 CFR and 58 CISA. It should also be borne in mind that in the field of international cooperation in criminal matters, it is usual for gaps to exist in the respective instruments that are filled by the analogous application of national provisions. In other words, when ongoing proceedings are taking place in two or more Member States, there is indeed no actual reason to reject the plea of *lis pedens* raised by the defendant, save in exceptional cases of important gravity where parallel proceedings may prove useful to gather evidence or prevent the commission of further crimes.

Contrary to what the CJEU has supported so far, it may also be advocated that the application of *lis pedens* is dictated by the principle's own very nature and its inextricable association with *ne bis in idem* with which it should be considered to be part and parcel. In particular, it is common ground that unnecessary parallel criminal proceedings could result in an infringement of the principle of *ne bis in idem*. *Lis pedens* though, aims at securing the finality of judgements and at ensuring the application *ne bis in idem* by pre-emptively barring parallel

[151] S Peers (2011), above n 44, 842.

[152] CJEU, Case C-469/03, *Filomeno Mario Miraglia*, Judgment of 10 Mar 2005, [2005] ECR I-0200, para 18.

[153] Ibid, paras 30 and 35 and operative part.

proceedings from the initial stage. This has even led jurisdictions, which do not guarantee *lis pedens* explicitly in their legislation, to establish the principle in their case law, by viewing it as a necessary corollary of *res judicata* and *ne bis in idem*. It could be further supported that *lis pedens* should be applied within the EU as a general principle of law according to Article 6(3) TEU. It is certainly undisputed that *lis pedens* is a general principle of law common to the legal systems of the EU Member States. Also, it has to be underlined that EU law has regulated the mutual recognition of pre-trial measures in criminal cases and the mutual recognition of orders for the gathering of evidence in the context of ongoing cross-border criminal proceedings,[154] a fact which obviously implies that not only final judgements, but ongoing criminal proceedings as well are an issue of EU law. This is evident by the wording of Article 82(1) TFEU, which affords competence to the EU to prevent and settle conflicts of jurisdictions. From all these, it may well be inferred that *lis pedens* can be applied both as a general principle of EU law emanating from the national legal systems of the Member States and as an integral component of *ne bis in idem* itself. Such an approach would be in conformity with the objective of Articles 67(3) and 82(1) TFEU to effectively ensure mutual recognition of criminal judgements and judicial orders.

Nevertheless, emphasis should be given on the fact that by applying a *lis pedens* rule in the absence of specific rules allocating jurisdiction within the EU, the '*first come, first served*' rule is kept intact. In reality, the only change would be to move the focus of that rule from the first court issuing the final judgement to the first court initiating criminal proceedings. Moreover, one could easily raise the argument that the *ratio* of *lis pedens* within a single legal order rests mainly on the allocation of territorial jurisdiction in favour of one the courts involved. This may quash any argument in favour of establishing such a rule within the EU legal order in the absence of relevant legislation, given that territorial concerns bear no impact on parallel proceedings taking place in different Member States, which have established legitimate jurisdictional bases to bring prosecutions. Even so, further shortcomings due to parallel proceedings are avoided and this would be to the overall benefit of the defendant. What is more, the application of *ne bis in idem* is safely reassured *a priori*. In any case, by bearing in mind the above considerations, the concentration of ongoing criminal proceedings in a particular Member State should be considered as a legal commitment that Member States should adhere to and a primary objective that the EU should further legislate on.

[154] Framework Decision 2008/978/JHA, on the European evidence warrant for the purpose of obtaining objects, documents and data for use in proceedings in criminal matters, [2008] OJ L 350/72, Framework Decision 2003/577/JHA, on the execution in the European Union of orders freezing property or evidence, [2003] OJ L 196/45, Framework Decision 2009/829/JHA on the application, between Member States of the European Union, of the principle of mutual recognition to decisions on supervision measures as an alternative to provisional detention, [2009] OJ L 294/20.

4.4 Concurrence of Crimes and *ne bis in idem*

Concurrence of crimes occurs when in a concrete set of factual circumstances, multiple crimes can be established. In such an instance, the defendant may be prosecuted cumulative for those crimes. Concurrence of crimes plays an important role in the calculation of the sentence(s) to be imposed. In such instances, the individual sentences for any concurrent crimes may be added in full to form the final sentence ('consecutive sentencing'). Also, multiple sentences for multiple crimes may be served simultaneously ('concurrent sentencing') and thus, the convicted person may actually serve only the biggest of the sentences imposed. An intermediate solution to the above alternatives is to calculate the appropriate sentence by adding to the base sentence (usually that of the most serious crime) the individual sentences for any concurrent crimes, but by limiting their duration ('cumulative sentencing'). Different legal orders apply different rules on the calculation of the appropriate final sentence in such instances by using all possible combinations of the above techniques. Usually, some states impose as a rule a total (cumulative) sentence that is the result of various calculus, which vary according to the 'type' of concurrence.

Concurrence of crimes is usually distinguished between ideal concurrence (*'concours idéal des infractions'*), when multiple crimes are committed by the perpetrator with only a single act, and real concurrence (*'concours réel des infractions'*), when multiple crimes are committed with more than one act. Concurrence of crimes is also determined by the number of affected victims and by the underlying protected legal interest (legal fundament). Where, either the number of victims (eg. terrorist bombing with many victims) or the protected legal interest violated (eg. violation of red traffic light and manslaughter of innocent bystander) are multiple in number and distinct, then the defendant is accordingly thought to have committed more than one crime. In the latter instance, be it either a case of ideal or real concurrence, the defendant should be charged with each individual crime on the same proceedings and sentenced cumulatively or even consecutively. Finally, there is this sort of concurrence, where, at first, multiple crimes may seem to have been committed, but ultimately, only one crime can actually be established, since one of the applicable criminal provisions and usually the most severe, precludes the application of the others. For such a concurrence to be established, the crime which is to be precluded must have all of its material elements in common with the other applicable crimes, while the underlying legal values protected by the applicable provisions must be identical.[155]

In cross-border cases within the EU, concurrence of crimes, as regards the application of *ne bis in idem*, is a quite problematic issue with uncertain solutions.[156] This particularly holds true when the defendant may be held

[155] Eg such as theft and aggravated forms of theft or robbery which usually consists by theft and unlawful violence or threat of violence and precluding the establishment of the latter by absorbing them.

[156] B VanBockel (2008), above n 51, 239.

criminally liable for the same acts in more than one Member State, but for different crimes protecting different legal values. In a similar situation, within a single legal order that adheres to the *idem factum* criterion, no further proceedings can be brought in relation to any concurrent crimes not tried. Nevertheless, even in such instances, certain jurisdictions permit subsequent prosecution to take place for any concurrent crimes not assessed, provided those crimes violated a distinct legal value. In similar cases within the EU, it is highly possible for such a situation to occur. A defendant could be tried in one Member State, when, at the same time, he could also be held accountable for other concurrent crimes in another Member State, based on the same facts for which he was tried initially. In such an instance, the second Member State will naturally insist on prosecuting the defendant. In such a case of ideal concurrence, by applying the strict *idem factum* criterion adopted by the CJEU and thus, by completely disregarding both the legal qualification of the acts in question and their protected legal values,[157] further prosecution in another Member State should be completely barred.[158] This is notwithstanding, the possibility of qualifying differently those crimes under the legislation of the second Member State. More importantly, in a situation as such, any Member State, would be barred from instituting any further criminal proceedings, regardless of whether, it could have done so at its domestic level and despite of its inability to have prosecuted the defendant in an initial stage.[159] Neither a missed opportunity to prosecute the defendant, nor a different national regulation of the situation, could justify the opening of new criminal proceedings in respect of concurrent crimes not tried. An exception however, should be drawn in cases involving numerous victims, where, regardless of the existence of a final judgement in a Member State, further criminal proceedings can be instituted against the defendant in another Member State, as regards the victims that were not subjects of the first trial finally disposed of. Also, when the defendant has already been finally tried in a Member State for certain acts, the authorities of another Member State should not be barred to further prosecute him when the consequences of his acts that

[157] CJEU, Cases C-436/04, *Léopold Henri van Esbroeck*, [2006] ECR I-02333, paras 27–36, C-150/05, *Jean Leon Van Straaten*, [2006] ECR I-09327, paras 41–47, C-288/2005, *Jurgen Kretzinger*, [2007] ECR I-06441, paras 29, 31–34, Opinion of Adv Gen R-J Colomer, of 20 Oct 2005, C-436/04, *Léopold Henri van Esbroeck*, [2006] ECR I-02333, paras 44–58, Opinion of Adv Gen R-J Colomer, 8 Jun 2006, C-150/05, *Jean Leon Van Straaten*, [2006] ECR I-09327, para 73.

[158] In this regard see in particular, Opinion of the Adv Gen E Sharpston of 15 June 2006, in C-467/04, Giuseppe Francesco Gasparini, para 23, and CJEU, Case C-467/04, *Giuseppe Francesco Gasparini*, Judgment of 28 Sep 2006, [2006] ECR I-09199, paras 55–57 and operative part. It should be noted that although the Adv Gen argued that import of illegal goods in a Member State and subsequent sale in another Member State should be considered as two distinct crimes, the Court took the opposite approach. Moreover, all cases that concern the import and export to and from different Member States can be seen as cases of concurrent crimes, which are nevertheless viewed by the CJEU as involving only one single act, CJEU, Case, C-436/04, *Léopold Henri van Esbroeck*, [2006] ECR I-02333, paras 37, 42 and operative (narcotic drugs), Case C-150/05, *Jean Leon Van Straaten*, [2006] ECR I-09327, paras 51, 53 and operative (narcotic drugs), Case C-288/05, *Jürgen Kretzinger*, [2007] ECR I-06441, para 37 and operative part (illegal goods).

[159] This could be, for example, due to lack of available evidence or necessary procedural requirements or, simply, because of its failure to take prompt action.

were not examined in the first trial give rise to criminal liability for a distinct crime.[160] In other words, when the consequences of an act by a defendant were not assessed in the proceedings taken in a Member State, further prosecution is not barred as long as these consequences alter the nature of his crime or are capable of giving rise to a different crime.[161]

A certain leeway for allowing further prosecution for any concurrent crime not tried, despite the existence of a final judgement dealing with the same facts, could be drawn by adopting the approach taken by international criminal tribunals,[162] whereby multiple convictions entered under different statutory provisions, but based on the same conduct, are permissible only when each statutory provision involved has a materially distinct element not included in the other. An element could be regarded as distinct from another, when it requires proof of a fact not required by the other. However, even by adhering to the proposed approach, the margin drawn is actually quite narrower than it may appear at first. For it is quite difficult in cases of ideal concurrence to assess and establish the existence of a distinct material element, given that the CJEU prohibits further proceedings for the same acts, which are '...understood as the existence of a set of concrete circumstances which are inextricably linked together in time, in space and by their subject-matter'. When it comes to concurrent crimes committed by the perpetrator through a single act, these two notions (same acts-distinct material element) seem to be contradictory bearing in mind the broad interpretation given by the CJEU to the notion of same acts. Even acts that are traditionally considered to be distinct have been held by the CJEU to fall under the above definition.[163] Nevertheless, the all-encompassing approach adopted by the CJEU should not be rejected, even in view of the severe circumvention it has impacted on the power of Member States to bring further criminal proceedings in cross-border cases involving concurrent crimes. Quite the contrary; it should be applauded, because it reinforces the protection of the liberty of the individual and effectively guarantees the right to free movement within the EU. An alternative approach, which could endow Member States with a greater level of discretion in bringing further prosecutions, could be abused by national authorities to the detriment of the individual. This would be antithetic to the establishment of the area of freedom, security and justice and therefore, should be unwelcomed.

[160] Commission of the European Communities (2005), above n 51, 58.

[161] Ibid.

[162] For example, ICTY (AC), IT-96-21-A, *Delalić and others*, Judgment of 20 Feb 2001, paras 412, 423 ICTR (TC), ICTR-96-4-T, *Akayesu*, Judgment of 2 Sep 1998, para 468, ICTR-96-13-A, *Musema*, Judgment of 16 Nov 2001, paras 363, 366–367. This test was initially established by United States Supreme Court, *Blockburger v United States*, 284 U.S. 299= 52 S. Ct. 180, followed by USS, *U.S. v Dixon*, [1993] 113 S Ct 2849, 2856.

[163] All cases that concern the import and export to and from different Member States can be seen as cases of concurrent crimes, which are nevertheless viewed by the CJEU as involving only one single act, CJEU, Case C-436/04, *Léopold Henri van Esbroeck*, [2006] ECR I-02333, paras 37, 42 and operative (narcotic drugs), Case C-150/05, *Jean Leon Van Straaten*, [2006] ECR I-09327, paras 51, 53 and operative (narcotic drugs), Case C-288/05, *Jürgen Kretzinger*, [2007] ECR I-06441, para 37 and operative part (illegal goods).

5. EPILOGUE

In epitomising all the above, many important points should be underlined. The first is the unequivocal transformation of *ne bis in idem* by the Charter from a traditional principle of criminal procedure to a fundamental right, emphasising its undisputed importance for EU law. For a true area of freedom, security and justice can only be attained through the unqualified expansion of the binding force of final criminal judgments throughout the European Union. The identification of *ne bis in idem* with the principle of mutual recognition has played a crucial role in this process. Quite important also, it has been the Court, which by delivering quite unprecedented judgments has further shaped the principle's substantial content in a positive manner reinforcing its practical implementation. The important role of the Court in the process of European integration is revealed by the relative rulings. In particular, this is evident in the shaping of both the notion 'final' judgement and the notion 'same acts'. The CJEU's *lex dicta* and rationale have been so strong that they even influenced the ECtHR to change its own jurisprudence on the interpretation of *ne bis in idem* in a manner contrary to the explicit wording of the Convention and to align itself with the case law of the former. The issues surrounding *ne bis in idem* within the EU have not, however, been solved. The provisions in question still continue to raise difficulties in practice. The lack of substantial harmonisation in the respective field generates many problems and will continue to do so. The particularities of and differences between Member States inevitably vex the situation. However, if one is to abide by the principle's extrinsic and unique nature under EU law, most of these may find comprehensive solutions with doctrinal consistency and respect to the overall framework of cooperation in criminal matters under the Treaty and to the particularities of the various legal systems involved.

7

Mutual Trust and Political Intentions: The European Arrest Warrant and the Nordic Arrest Warrant

PER OLE TRÄSKMAN*

1. MUTUAL RECOGNITION

The European Commission launched the European Legal Area Project in 1995, resulting in a proposal called Corpus Juris. The proposal aimed primarily at the adoption of a number of penal provisions in order to protect the financial interests of the European Union, as well as procedural provisions considered necessary for an effective enforcement of the new penal regulations. The procedural provisions also included a proposal to establish a jurisdiction encompassing the whole of the territory of the European Union and to institute a European prosecution authority (European Public Prosecutor's Office), EP, with competence extended to all the Member States.[1] The reasons for this given in the proposal were mainly based on the efficiency requirement.[2]

> These rules will allow long, complex procedures of bilateral cooperation to be avoided; procedures all the more inefficient in that crime of this kind is very frequently multinational. International letters rogatory would also become unnecessary between Member States of the European Union, and similarly extradition, also rendered obsolete by the institution of the EP.

The Corpus Juris proposal was never realized as such, but the proposal laid one of the foundation stones for subsequent European cooperation, the conception of the whole European Area as one single jurisdiction. This conception has subsequently mainly been realized through the provisions on the mutual recognition of judgments and judicial decisions.

* Senior Professor, LLD, Faculty of Law, Lund University.

[1] P O Träskman, '"Corpus Juris" – ett frestande eller ett främmande förslag till enhetlig europeisk rättssfär?' (1997) *Nordisk Tidskrift for Kriminalvidenskab* 262.

[2] Ibid, 271.

The conception 'mutual recognition of judicial decisions' came into focus at the meeting of the European Council in Cardiff in June 1998. The principle of mutual recognition was further accentuated as a basic principle for European cooperation in the Action Plan adopted by the European Council in Vienna in the same year, and the importance of the concept of mutual recognition was further emphasized as the cornerstone of judicial cooperation at the Tampere Summit in 1999. In the Tampere Summit Conclusions the following is stated as point 33:

> Enhanced mutual recognition of judicial decisions and judgments and the necessary approximation of legislation would facilitate co-operation between authorities and the judicial protection of individual rights. The European Council therefore endorses the principle of mutual recognition which, in its view, should become the cornerstone of judicial co-operation in both civil and criminal matters within the Union. The principle should apply both to judgments and to other decisions of judicial authorities.

The principle of mutual recognition was deemed to be a necessary condition for the aim to create the area of freedom, justice and security.[3]

The principle of mutual recognition has later been emphasized and confirmed. The dignity of the principle can be observed by the fact that it has been confirmed in Article 82 of the Treaty on the Functioning of The European Union. According to this Article, judicial cooperation in criminal matters in the EU shall be based on the principle of mutual recognition of judgments and judicial decisions and shall include an approximation of the laws and regulations of the Member States in certain specific areas.

The Council Framework Decision on the European arrest warrant and the surrender procedures between Member States were the first tangible expression of the order based on the principle of mutual recognition.[4] The Framework Decision was approved in a strained procedure in June 2002, as a conclusion of an intensified period of preparation, which culminated after the terrorist attack in New York in 2001.[5] The adoption of the Framework Decision implied that the traditional system of extradition was replaced by a system of surrender between judicial authorities. In the Framework Decision on the European arrest warrant it is defined as 'a judicial decision issued by a Member State with a view to the arrest and surrender by another Member State of a requested person, for the purposes of conducting a criminal prosecution or executing a custodial sentence or detention order'.[6]

[3] J Vestergaard, 'Udlevering til strafforfølgning mv. – den europæiske arrestordre som udtryk for gensidig anerkendelse' (2004) *Festskrift til Hans Gammeltoft-Hansen* 627.

[4] P O Träskman, 'Den europeiska arresteringsordern i Sverige – med några utblickar till Danmark och Finland' (2007) *Nordisk Tidskrift for Kriminalvidenskab* 18, especially 19.

[5] Council Framework Decision 2002/584/RIF of 13 June 2002 on the European arrest warrant and the surrender procedures between Member States.

[6] The Framework Decision, Article 1.1.

1.1 From Extradition to Surrender

Extradition implies that a person is handed over from one state to another in order to make it possible to press criminal charges against him/her or to execute a punishment that has already been set. An extradition case is initiated when an accused or sentenced person is not present on the territory of the requesting State, and this state is dependent on the cooperation with the requested State in order to force the person to enter its territory. Extradition has been the last resort in order to carry out a procedure against a suspected person or to execute a punishment against a sentenced person as long as the wanted person has refused to enter the requesting State voluntarily.[7]

In Sweden extradition is regulated through different sets of rules. Provisions on extradition between Sweden and the other Nordic countries are included in a specific law from 1959 (1959:254; 'The Nordic Extradition Law). Extradition in general – between Sweden and all non-Nordic countries – is regulated in a law from 1957 (1957:668). But extradition between Sweden and all the other Member States was replaced with surrender on the basis of a European Arrest Warrant (law 2003:1156; The Arrest Warrant Law) in 2004.[8] This law replaced the specific regulations in the general extradition law concerning extradition between Sweden and the other Member States and today it is the provisions in the Arrest Warrant Law which shall be applied between the Member States (with certain exceptions in relation to the Nordic states).[9]

The Framework Decision on the European arrest warrant and the surrender procedures between Member States was adopted the 13th of June 2002.[10] This implied that the traditional extradition system as regards the relationship between the Member States was relegated to the realms of history and that the future system was based on the idea of surrender between the judicial authorities.

The introduction of the new surrender system was mainly due to dissatisfaction with the tardiness of the extradition system.[11] The aim of the new system with an arrest warrant was to establish a procedure, which made it possible to transfer an accused or sentenced person from one Member State to another. The introduction to the Framework Decision stipulates that the formal extradition procedure must be abolished 'among the Member States in respect of persons who are fleeing from justice after having been finally sentenced and extradition procedures should be speeded up in respect of persons suspected of having committed an offence'.

[7] K Påle, *Villkor för utlämning* (Uppsala, Iustus Förlag, 2003) 21.

[8] In addition to this law there are two more statutes with provisions concerning the surrender procedure: Ordinance (2003:1178) on surrender to Sweden on the basis of an European Arrest Warrant and Ordinance (2003:1179) concerning surrender from Sweden on the basis of an European Arrest Warrant.

[9] Government bill 2003/04:7, 57.

[10] The Framework Decision on the European arrest warrant and the surrender procedures between Member States.

[11] P O Träskman (2007, see note 4), 19–20.

The introduction of the European Arrest Warrant certainly resolved a real problem. The formal, traditional extradition procedure was both complicated and time-consuming. The international remedies, above all agreements and conventions on extradition, have not offered a satisfying basis for a secure, effective and rapid procedure to transfer a suspected or sentenced person from one jurisdiction to another. A rapid and sufficiently secure system from a human rights perspective lies in the interests of the judicial authorities, the suspected or sentenced person and the victim of an offence. The fact that one state approves the judgment or the judicial decision of another state and through that executes a request based on an arrest warrant is a very obvious manifestation of the principle of mutual approbation of judicial decisions.[12]

In order to indicate that this was a new system, which had been simplified to such an extent that it could no longer be classified as an extradition procedure, new terminology was also introduced. Thus, the 'requested State' is now 'the executing Member State' and the 'requesting State' is now 'the issuing Member State'. The new system is no longer labelled as 'extradition', the expression used is 'surrender'.[13] The system is based on the idea that surrender shall be executed if it is not legally impossible. What is possible or impossible is regulated with specific legal rules and the margin for own appreciation is very limited. The question of surrender is therefore much more of a judicial matter than a political one.

The most recent step is that the extradition system between the Nordic states has also has been relegated to the realms of legal history. A Convention on a Nordic Arrest Warrant was approved in June 2005.[14] Equivalent changes with regard to the conditions for surrender and in the terminology have now been introduced also when it comes to the relationship between the Nordic states.

A Nordic Arrest Warrant is defined in the Convention as '... a judicial decision issued by a Nordic State with the aim that another Nordic State shall apprehend and surrender a wanted person for a criminal procedure or for the execution of a sentence of imprisonment or another sanction consisting of the deprivation of liberty.'[15]

This means that it is only extradition to 'a third State', a state outside both the Nordic region and the European Union, which is still regulated through traditional extradition legislation. Nordic and European cooperation is instead based on the new surrender system founded on the principle of mutual trust.

2. THE EUROPEAN ARREST WARRANT

Since 1st January 2004, the traditional legislation on extradition is no longer applied in relation to other Member States instead it has been replaced by the

[12] Government bill 2003/04:7, 57.

[13] K Påle, *Villkor för utlämning* 379.

[14] The Convention of the 15th December 2005 on surrender between the Nordic States in criminal cases.

[15] The Nordic Convention Art 1.1.

Act (2003:1156) on surrender from Sweden according to a European Arrest Warrant and the Ordinance (2003:1179) on the same matter. Surrender from Sweden is regulated in the Act and the Ordinance. The rules concerning the process of surrender by the public prosecutors and the courts are included in these statutes. A process of surrender can be initiated for two different purposes: to enable the execution of a punishment already set or for the criminal process of an accused person.

The system of surrender according to a European Arrest Warrant is characterized by a process, which is as speedy and simple as possible, and also if possible, without any legal obstacles. This means that there is no general requirement of double criminality or no obstacle to surrender a State's own citizens.

The decision to surrender a person from Sweden is taken by a district court. The decision of the district court to surrender a person against his/her will, can be appealed to the court of appeal and to the Supreme Court. The district court shall in principle make its decision within 30 days from the day when the wanted person was apprehended. The decision shall, if the person gives his/her consent to the surrender, be made within 10 days from the day when the consent was given. The wanted person has the right to a public defence lawyer, and the procedure in the district court shall in general be oral.

The conditions necessary for surrender are regulated in the Act. The surrender of an accused person can be granted if the offence in question may entail imprisonment for one year or more according to the law in the issuing State. Surrender in order to execute a sanction already sentenced requires that the sanction consists of the deprivation of liberty for a period of four months or more. The main rule is also still that the requirement of double criminality is fulfilled; this means that the surrender of a person from Sweden is allowed only when the act giving cause to the surrender is also an offence according to Swedish law. However, surrender can also be executed in cases where the requirement of double criminality is not fulfilled, for example, when the act in question is included in the Annex attached to the Framework Decision, what is known as 'the list'. An additional condition is that according to the law in the issuing State the act may lead to a sentence of imprisonment for three years or more.

The Act on the European Arrest Warrant also contains an enumeration of a number of cases when surrender is not permitted. To take a few examples, when the wanted person has been sentenced for the offence in question in Sweden or in another Member State, when the offence on which the arrest warrant is based is covered by amnesty in the executing Member State (Sweden), when a decision to abstain from prosecution has been taken in Sweden, when the act, which is not an offence according to Swedish law, has been committed in Sweden, and when the period for prosecution has expired in Sweden. In some cases, when surrender is requested for the execution of a sanction, the person in question may serve his (or her) sentence in Sweden instead, and in some cases a person, who is surrendered for procedure in the issuing State, shall be brought back to Sweden for the execution of a sanction that has been determined abroad.

In the future, a European Arrest Warrant shall not be issued when it is a matter of surrender between the Nordic states, instead a Nordic Arrest Warrant shall be issued.

The new order with surrender on the basis of a European Arrest Warrant is not uncontroversial and the order has also been criticized. Some of the criticism has been more a matter of principle, and has primarily concerned the abolishment of some of the traditional obstacles to extradition, especially the abolishment of the requirement of double criminality and the opening for surrender also of a state's own citizens. Some other points of criticism have concerned practical problems, as well as a grave concern regarding the possible lack of mutual confidence between states concerning each other's justice systems. Is the mutual confidence between Member States really already so strong that a system can be based on it, a system, which is based on the mutual recognition of foreign judgments and judicial decisions?

There is a quick reply to the question of the possibility to surrender also a state's own citizens namely that this hindrance has already been abolished within the EU as an obstacle to extradition. The amendment to the earlier regulations was carried out when the new extradition treaty between the Member States was approved in 1996. The treaty was implemented as a part of the Swedish Extradition Act in 2001 through new provisions in Article 3 and 3a (2001:1158).

The problems linked to the abolishment of the general requirement of double criminality are more complicated. The requirement of double criminality is solidly based on the necessity to protect the rights of an accused person and strong arguments against the abolishment can easily be formulated.[16] These arguments can be summarized in three points: The requirement of double criminality emanates from basic norms in substantive international law. The prohibition with regard to interfering in the domestic matters of a foreign state is one of the fundamental pillars of international law, and, in general, making decisions concerning the criminalization of certain acts is a domestic matter. However, it is evident that this prohibition has become less strict over time mainly with reference to international human rights.

The requirement of double criminality has also been upheld with reference to reasons based on sound criminal policy. Crime policy and criminal law policy have been accepted as the domestic concern of a national state for a long time now. Political decisions made in these fields of policy only concern the state in question – what other states decide is 'not our business'. The requirement of double criminality can basically be said to be a means of assistance established when international cooperation (in the form of accepting jurisdiction over crimes committed abroad, in the form of extradition or in some other form of international legal aid) is appropriate or acceptable. Every decision concerning

[16] P O Träskman, 'Håller kravet på dubbel straffbarhet att bli rättshistoria?' in T Elholm, V Greve, P Asp, R Bragadottir, D Frände og A Stradbakken (eds.), *Liber amicarum et amicorum Karin Cornils – Glimt af Nordisk straffrätt og straffeprocessrett* (2010) 469, especially 473.

the criminalization of an act is based on a balance between the interests of society to criminalize an act and the interests of the individual to have his or her freedom.

Moreover, last but not least the requirement of double criminality has an important function as a guarantee for fair justice. It means that a person cannot be accused of an act, which is not a crime where the act was committed. The requirement upholds and realizes the fundamental requirement of foresight in the criminal justice system of the consequences of how you behave and what you do.

The adoption of the European Arrest Warrant implied that the requirement of double criminality would be abolished in the relations between different Member States. This was because the reason for elaborating the system of surrender instead of extradition was basically founded on the principle of mutual trust. It can be concluded that the abolishment of the requirement of double criminality was very logical if you really want to realize the principle of mutual recognition of judgments and judicial decisions, but at the same time it is necessary to express some doubt about the timing: is the time really ripe enough for this step to be taken within the European Union. Is the common feeling of trust between the Member States as regards each other's criminal systems strong enough?

The question has very evidently been placed on the agenda with the case of Julian Assange. Julian Assange is suspected of rape in Sweden, but it has been impossible to complete the pre-trial investigation because Assange fled to England and has since refused to return to Sweden. A competent Swedish prosecutor decided on the basis of a European Arrest Warrant to request England to surrender him to Sweden. Assange was opposed to the decision to surrender him and he has used every legal possibility to reject the Swedish request. However, the competent supreme legal instances in England have also declared that surrender to Sweden is fully in accordance with the EAW provisions. The next turn in this case is that Assange has taken refuge at the Ecuadorian Embassy and Ecuador has also granted him political asylum in Ecuador.

2.1 What is so Interesting in this Peculiar Case?

Cooperation based on the EAW system is basically founded on the principle of mutual recognition of judgments and judicial decisions. This implies that the main rule inside the EU is that every judicial authority shall accept and execute judgments and judicial decisions made by competent authorities in the other Member States. This principle is as such based on the presumption that there is a common trust with respect to the justice systems in all the other Member States.

However, the Julian Assange case and the different legal proceedings in England concerning the validity of the decision of the Swedish prosecutor to request the surrender of Assange, demonstrates (as does the earlier debate in Sweden on the Calle Jonsson case, which basically concerned a deep Swedish mistrust of the criminal justice system in Greece) that this supposed mutual trust is not as strong as it was assumed when the relevant EU decisions were being made. It is appropriate to say that the 'superstructure' has been elaborated more rapidly than the base, and that the decision-makers have tried to promote mutual trust to a certain extent and also take it for granted to a degree, which is not in line with reality.

The Julian Assange case is important because it can be used as a test in a process consisting of diagnostic tests to find out how well the principle of mutual recognition of judicial decisions fulfils the function of a basic element in the cooperation between the Member States. What you have to ask yourself is whether the principle is based on reality or just on a chimera.[17]

The practical problems that have arisen in conjunction with an EAW have mainly concerned the fact that certain Member States have used the system in cases concerning relatively minor offences,[18] and that the procedural rights of an accused person have been too weakly protected.[19] These problems are mentioned in the 2011 report from the European Commission to both the European Parliament and the Council about the implementation from 2007 of the Council Framework Decision of 13 June 2002 on the European arrest warrant and the surrender procedures between Member States.[20]

The Council adopted a Resolution on a Roadmap for strengthening procedural rights of a suspected person in 2009.[21] The thinking behind this Resolution was that it was deemed necessary to correct the distortion between the possibilities to initiate criminal procedures inside the 'EU jurisdiction' and the legal possibilities for suspected and accused persons to defend themselves against accusations:

> Discussions on procedural rights within the context of the European Union over the last few years have not led to any concrete results. However, a lot of progress has been made in the area of judicial and police cooperation on measures that facilitate prosecution. It is now time to take action to improve the balance between these measures and the protection of procedural rights of the individual. Efforts should be deployed to strengthen procedural guarantees and the respect of the rule of law in criminal proceedings, no matter where citizens decide to travel.

The measures given priority in the Resolution are the following:[22]

A) Translation and Interpretation

The suspected or accused person must be able to understand what is happening and to make him/herself understood. A suspected or accused person who does

[17] See P Asp, *Dagens Juridik*, www.dagensjuridik.se/2012/05/assange-visar-att-tilliten-mellan-Staterna-kanske-inte-ar-sa-stark-som-eu-lagstiftaren-har-f.

[18] This criticism is especially focused on Poland.

[19] See K Liatsou, 'Överlämnande på grund av brott – den europeiska och den nordiska arresteringsordern', Master thesis at the University of Lund 2012. www.jur.lu.se.

[20] COM(2011) 175 final, 6.

[21] Resolution of the Council of 30 November 2009 on a Roadmap for strengthening procedural rights of suspected or accused persons in criminal proceedings (2009/C 295/01).

[22] Resolution of the Council of 30 November 2009 (2009/C 295/01), 3.

not speak or understand the language that is used in the proceedings will need an interpreter and translation of essential procedural documents. Particular attention should also be paid to the needs of suspected or accused persons with hearing impediments.

B) Information on Rights and Information about the Charges
A person that is suspected or accused of a crime should get information on his/her basic rights orally or, where appropriate, in writing, eg by way of a Letter of Rights. Furthermore, that person should also receive information promptly about the nature and cause of the accusation against him or her.

C) Legal Advice and Legal Aid
The right to legal advice (through a legal counsel) for the suspected or accused person in criminal proceedings at the earliest appropriate stage of such proceedings is fundamental in order to safeguard the fairness of the proceedings; the right to legal aid should ensure effective access to the aforementioned right to legal advice.

D) Communication with Relatives, Employers and Consular Authorities
A suspected or accused person who is deprived of his or her liberty shall be promptly informed of the right to have at least one person, such as a relative or employer, informed of the deprivation of liberty, it being understood that this should not prejudice the due course of the criminal proceedings.

E) Special Safeguards for Suspected or Accused Persons who are Vulnerable
In order to safeguard the fairness of the proceedings, it is important that special attention is shown to suspected or accused persons who cannot understand or follow the content or the meaning of the proceedings, owing, for example, to their age, mental or physical condition.

F) A Green Paper on Pre-Trial Detention
The time that a person can spend in detention before being tried in court and during the court proceedings varies considerably between the Member States. Excessively long periods of pre-trial detention are detrimental for the individual, can prejudice the judicial cooperation between the Member States and do not represent the values for which the European Union stands. Appropriate measures in this context should be examined in a Green Paper.

Some of these measures have already been implemented. The Directive (2010/64/EU) on the right to interpretation and translation in criminal proceedings was adopted in October 2010, and the Directive (2012/13/EU) on the right to information in criminal proceedings was adopted in May 2012. Two Annexes are attached to this Directive. The first one is an 'Indicative model Letter of Rights', whose purpose is to assist national authorities in drawing up their Letter of Rights at national level with written information which suspects or accused persons must be provided with. The second Annex is an 'Indicative model Letter of Rights for persons arrested on the basis of a European Arrest Warrant'. The first right, which must be granted, is the right to a lawyer:

> You have the right to speak confidentially to a lawyer. A lawyer is independent from the police. Ask the police if you need help to get in contact with a lawyer, the police shall help you. In certain cases the assistance may be free of charge. Ask the police for more information.

One step in the effort to improve the arrest situation for a suspected person is the adoption of the Framework Decision on mutual recognition of supervision measures as an alternative to provisional detention. The aim of this Framework Decision is to make it easier for a suspected person to continue to live in his or her normal surroundings, albeit with certain supervision measures while awaiting trial in another Member State.[23]

The Commission has also prepared a Green Paper on the application of EU criminal justice legislation in the field of detention. The aim of the Green Paper is to strengthen mutual trust in the European judicial area. The Commission wishes to explore the extent to which detention issues (following a criminal offence) have an impact on mutual trust, and consequently on mutual recognition and judicial cooperation in general within the European Union. It is stated that, [w]hilst detention conditions and prison management are the responsibility of the Member States, the Commission is interested in this issue because of the central importance of the principle of mutual recognition of judicial decisions for the area of freedom, security and justice. Is further action necessary and possible? If yes, what kind of action?[24] The document contains ten questions and the Commission wishes to receive an answer about how the rules in force are applied in the Member States concerning the deprivation of liberty both before and after trial and how the rules could be changed in order to improve the mutual trust between Member States.

The Commission stresses that to ensure an effective system of mutual recognition of judgments, the existence of real mutual trust between the authorities of the Member States is necessary.

> The principle of mutual recognition rests on the idea of mutual trust between Member States. Judicial decisions are to be recognised as equivalent and executed throughout the Union regardless of where the decision was taken. This is based on the presumption that criminal justice systems within the European Union, whilst not the same, are at least equivalent. Judicial decisions are usually executed by judges in the executing State. Those judges need to be satisfied that the initial decision was taken fairly (ie that the person's rights were not violated when the decision was taken) and that the person's rights will be respected fully when returned to another Member State.
>
> Without mutual confidence in the area of detention, European Union mutual recognition instruments that have a bearing on detention will not work properly, because a Member State might be reluctant to recognise and enforce the decision taken by another Member State's authorities. It could be difficult to develop closer judicial

[23] Report from the Commission to the European Parliament and the Council on the implementation since 2007 of the Council Framework Decision of 13 June 2002 on the European arrest warrant and the surrender procedures between Member (COM (2011) 175, 7.

[24] COM (2011) 327.

> cooperation between Member States unless further efforts are made to improve detention conditions and to promote alternatives to custody.

It is therefore of great importance that the Member States have knowledge of each other's criminal justice systems.[25] The questionnaire was directed to practitioners in the legal field, people involved in the legal systems, academics, NGOs and public authorities. Seventy-nine responses were submitted by Member State governments, prison administrations, and a wide range of NGOs and Civil Society groups interested in criminal justice. It was disappointing to note that only seventeen of the twenty-seven Member State governments responded to the Green Paper. The results of the questionnaire are being processed by the Commission.

Mutual trust must be ensured in order to continue with the system of the European Arrest Warrant. Therefore, the Commission is giving priority to the strengthening of the procedural rights of suspected and accused persons through a set of minimum guarantees for a fair trial. In an Annex to the manual of the European Arrest Warrant ('Staff Working Document') the Commission has included a part containing 'proportionality'.

> Confidence in the application of the EAW has been undermined by the systematic issue of EAWs for the surrender of persons sought in respect of often very minor offences. In this context, discussions in Council arising from the conclusions of the Member State evaluations show that there is general agreement among Member States that a proportionality check is necessary to prevent EAWs from being issued for offences which, although they fall within the scope of Article 2(1) of the Council Framework Decision on the EAW, are not serious enough to justify the measures and cooperation which the execution of an EAW requires. Several aspects should be considered before issuing the EAW including the seriousness of the offence, the length of the sentence, the existence of an alternative approach that would be less onerous for both the person sought and the executing authority and a cost/benefit analysis of the execution of the EAW. There is a disproportionate effect on the liberty and freedom of requested persons when EAWs are issued concerning cases for which (pre-trial) detention would otherwise be felt inappropriate. In addition, an overload of such requests may be costly for the executing Member States. It might also lead to a situation in which the executing judicial authorities (as opposed to the issuing authorities) feel inclined to apply a proportionality test, thus introducing a ground for refusal that is not in conformity with the Council Framework Decision or with the principle of mutual recognition on which the measure is based.[26]

Note that the remarks in the manual are only recommendations and therefore not binding. However, it is emphasized in the manual that the Member States must interpret the national regulation on the EAW in accordance with the Framework Decision.[27]

[25] COM (2011) 327, 2.

[26] 17195/1/10, COPEN 275, Revised version of the European handbook on how to issue a European Arrest Warrant, p 14, section 3.

[27] Rev Handbook, 3, footnote 1.

3. THE NORDIC COUNTRIES AND THE NORDIC ARREST WARRANT

Close international cooperation in criminal matters was already in the nineteen sixties and seventies elaborated between the Nordic states. At that time it was in many respects something rather unique. The crucial characteristics of this system of cooperation have been a respect for certain national differences combined with a demand for an effective system. The system has been based on the traditional forms of international cooperation in legal matters. It has been possible to transfer the proceedings from one Nordic state to another, it has been possible to extradite a person from one Nordic state to another, also when the requirement of double criminality is not fulfilled, and also when the extradition concerns a national in the requested State. It has also been possible to give legal aid and assistance in many other forms, and to transfer the execution of a punishment from one State to another. This possibility has been open both in respect of a penalty consisting of the deprivation of liberty as well as fines and community sanctions. The form of cooperation has in general been direct between the relevant authorities and without the use of diplomatic channels or central official authorities.

The experience of this cooperation has been positive – or even very positive. In the Nordic legal literature it is almost impossible be find a single example of problems in the legal cooperation between the Nordic states or any proposals of a completely different system than the existing one.[28]

Despite this – or maybe due to this – the Nordic states shortly after the adoption of the Framework Decision on the European Arrest Warrant took an initiative to start a project in order to launch a Nordic Arrest Warrant system. Already in June 2002 a decision was made at the meeting of the Nordic Ministers of Justice at Svalbard that the Nordic laws on extradition should be revised with the aim of obtaining at least the same degree of efficiency as the system of surrender with the use of the EAW system. Later at the meeting of the Nordic Ministers of Justice in Copenhagen, the Nordic states signed the Convention on the Nordic Arrest Warrant.[29]

This has resulted in a change from the traditional system of extradition to a system of surrender when the Nordic countries are concerned. Furthermore, there has also been a change in terminology in the Nordic system equivalent to the change after the adoption of the EAW.

In the Convention, a Nordic Arrest Warrant is defined as 'a judicial decision, issued by a Nordic State with the aim that another Nordic State shall arrest and surrender a wanted person for procedure or for execution of a sentence of imprisonment or another measure consisting of deprivation of liberty.'[30] The Convention has been implemented into Swedish national law through the Act on the Nordic Arrest Warrant ('nordiska arresteringsorderlagen').[31] The law will

[28] Träskman (1997, in note 1), 270.
[29] The Nordic Convention on a Nordic Arrest Warrant (June 2005).
[30] The Nordic Convention on NAW article 1.1.
[31] Law (2011:1165) on surrender from Swerden according to a Nordic Arrest Warrant.

come into force from the date decided by the government and at the same time the Nordic Extradition Law will be abolished.

What is new in the Nordic Arrest Warrant system? In short, the new Convention is slightly more developed than both the Framework Decision on the EAW and the earlier Nordic system. This is proof of the fact that there is far more advanced cooperation between the Nordic states than between the EU Member States in general. A comparison between the present Nordic system and the new system shows that a system based on optional cooperation in legal matters with few possibilities to reject cooperation is replaced by a compulsory system for surrender with some new possibilities to reject surrender. But the differences are not so remarkable. In the following passage only the most significant changes will be mentioned.

Similar to the procedure for surrender according to the EAW the Nordic Convention is based on the principle of mutual recognition. This implies a system shift in comparison with the earlier optional Nordic system. Now a request of surrender *shall* be approved by the executing State as long as there is no legal ground for refusal. [32] In the Swedish government bill on the new law on the Nordic Arrest Warrant, it was discussed whether it was appropriate to implement the Nordic Convention on a NAW by changing the present law on extradition between the Nordic states. However, the conclusion was that the Convention required such extensive changes with regard to a new basic structure for the system as well as the contents of the law that the best solution was to elaborate a completely new law.[33]

It was also discussed whether a possible solution was to change the national law on the EAW. The arguments in favour of this were that the Framework Decision on the EAW and the Nordic Convention on the NAW contain many similarities both with respect to the structure of the systems and the contents in general. But also here the conclusion was that there were after all certain basic differences too. The most important being that the criminal systems in the Nordic countries do not differ from each other as much as the systems of the EU do generally speaking. Furthermore, there is a long tradition of close cooperation in legal matters between the Nordic states and this kind of cooperation does not have the same reputation in the relations between Sweden and the other Member States of the EU as it does between Sweden and the Nordic ones. Therefore, there would be a great need for a specific regulation with respect to Nordic cases if the Nordic Convention were to be included in the national law on the European Arrest Warrant. This could result in an obvious risk for difficulties in applying the law in practice.[34]

The Nordic Convention involves reinforced cooperation both compared to the Framework Decision on the EAW and the earlier Nordic system. The most

[32] See above section 2.2.
[33] Government bill 2010/11:158, 60.
[34] Government bill 2010/11:158, 60.

important differences mentioned in the Swedish governmental bill concern the requirements for surrender, special provisions concerning own nationals, the number of grounds for refusal, the length of the time limits and the possibilities for an extended surrender.[35]

The conditions for surrender are more restricted in the Nordic system than in the European Arrest Warrant system. There is no requirement of double criminality in the Nordic system nor is there a requirement on a certain minimum when it comes to the crime or sentenced penalty which has given rise to the request of surrender. The only requirement is that the offence in question may result in a penalty consisting of deprivation of liberty, or when surrender is requested for the execution of a penalty that the sentence has resulted in a penalty of that kind.[36]

The three compulsory grounds for refusal are the same in both systems: amnesty, a prohibition of ne bis in idem and the condition that the person requested for surrender has reached a certain age and therefore is responsible for the offences he/she has committed.[37] But the Nordic Convention contains fewer optional grounds for refusal than the Framework Decision. There is no possibility to have a requirement of double criminality in the Convention, nor is there the possibility to refuse surrender referring to the requirement of double criminality or to deny surrender on the grounds of limitation due to lapse of time.[38]

Also the grounds for refusal based on the territoriality are different in the two systems. The Framework Decision (Article 4 (7)) contains two different optional grounds for refusal linked to the territoriality, namely (a) when the arrest warrant relates to offences which are regarded by the law of the executing Member State as having been committed in whole or in part in the territory of the executing Member State or in a place treated as such; or when the offences (b) have been committed outside the territory of the issuing Member State and the law of the executing Member State does not allow prosecution for the same offences when committed outside its territory.

In the Nordic Convention there is just one such ground. A request can be refused if the act in question has been committed inside the territory of the requested State and the act is not criminalized as an offence according to the law in that State.[39]

A Nordic Arrest Warrant shall be dealt with quickly. The time limit for a decision on surrender in a case where the wanted person consents to surrender is three days, compared with 10 days according to the European Arrest Warrant.[40] In other cases the time limit is 30 days, compared to 60 days according to

[35] Government bill 2010/11:158, 60–61.

[36] The Nordic Convention on NAW, Article 2.1.

[37] The EU Framework Decision Article 3(1)–(3) and The Nordic Convention on the NAW, Article 4(1)–(3).

[38] These grounds for refusal are included in the EU Framework Decision Article 4(1) and the Nordic Convention on the NAW, Article 4(4) respectively.

[39] The Nordic Convention on NAW Article 4.2.

[40] The Nordic Convention on NAW Article 14.2.

the EAW.[41] The time limit for the execution of the surrender is 5 and 10 days respectively.[42] The much shorter time limits can be explained with reference to the fact that the criminal systems in the Nordic states are quite similar and that there has existed very close cooperation between the Nordic authorities for a very long time. Despite this there are some situations where it is impossible to keep the time limits and for these situations there are some exemptions in the Convention, when the decision shall be made and the action shall be taken as soon as possible.[43] Equivalent exemptions are also included in the Framework Decision on the EAW, but here the time limit is fixed to 30 days.[44]

There are also some other differences between the Nordic Convention and the Framework Decision, inter alia concerning the extended surrender.

Traditionally, the fact that a case concerns a political crime has been an obstacle to extradition.[45] According to the general Swedish law on extradition, extradition cannot be granted, when the request concerns a political crime. Also according to the Swedish law on extradition between Sweden and another Nordic state there is a certain limit to grant extradition for a political crime. The extradition of a Swedish citizen for a political crime is only possible when the requirement of double criminality is fulfilled.[46] This obstacle has now been abolished in the new system of surrender. This is not considered to be a problem due to the fact, that the similarities between the criminal systems in the Nordic states are so great that such an obstacle lacks practical impact. The abolishment is interpreted as new proof of a closer cooperation between the Nordic States.[47] It is also obvious that it is difficult to argue for the need to have the obstacle to surrender a person for a political crime between the Nordic States when such an obstacle is abolished concerning surrender in the Framework Decision on the EAW. In Europe this obstacle was already abolished in the EU Convention on extradition in 1996.[48]

Both the Framework Decision on the EAW and the Nordic Convention contains provisions referring to the European Convention on Human Rights. If surrender is considered to be a breach of a provision in the Human Rights Convention, surrender cannot be granted.

4. WHAT SHALL WE DO WITH TWO DIFFERENT SYSTEMS OF ARREST WARRANTS?

It is well known that the model for the system of the European Arrest Warrant was taken from the Nordic system and the positive experiences of that system.

[41] Article 14.3 (EU Framework Decision) respectively article.17.3 (The Nordic Convention on NAW).

[42] Article 19.2 (The Nordic Convention on NAW) respectively Article 23.2 (EU Framework Decision).

[43] Article 14.4 (The Nordic Convention on NAW.

[44] Article 17.4, (The EU Framework Decision).

[45] Träskman (2007, see note 4), 25.

[46] The Nordic Extradition Law, Article 4.

[47] Government bill 2010/11:158, 65.

[48] Government bill 2000/01:83, 29.

This was also declared in the *travaux prépartoire* for the Framework Decision. So far, so good. However, there are still some good reasons to make certain reflections.

The first reflection is focused on the EU system. Nordic cooperation and the positive experience of this existed already when close cooperation in legal matters was formalized through Nordic legislation. Thus the legislation was firmly based on an existing and solid trust. There are good grounds to wonder whether that was also the case when the system with mutual recognition was adopted in the European Union. It is much more appropriate to claim that the introduction of the system with mutual recognition and the adoption of the European Arrest Warrant were political means used to shape and construct a common European sense of trust. All criticism against the European Arrest Warrant is proof of this.

The second reflection concerns Nordic cooperation. When the Framework Decision on the EAW was transposed into national legislation in the Nordic countries there was very little coordination with the aim of finding a 'Nordic solution'. The national Nordic laws on the European Arrest Warrant differ from each other on several points.[49] This may give rise to some astonishment and wonder. Why was there no political will to create a 'Nordic model' for the way in which the Framework Decision was implemented?

Against this background, it may also be astonishing that the Nordic decision was to establish a Nordic system with a Nordic Arrest Warrant based on a *convention*. The use of a convention has not been the traditional way of creating Nordic legal cooperation in the field of criminal law and criminal procedure. Earlier Nordic cooperation was not at all based on conventions but on common decisions aimed at the introduction of an homogeneous piece of regulation through national laws in every Nordic state. And finally it is necessary to ask: Why should you not be more radical and courageous in the Nordic countries if the purpose really was to accentuate that the Nordic states are a particular region inside the EU?

When he was the Prosecutor-General in Sweden, Fredrik Wersäll proposed the following in an article in 2006:[50]

> A vision of a boundless Nordic region contains a complete realization of the principle of mutual recognition and execution of decisions taken during the pretrial investigation and the criminal trial. A decision taken in one Nordic State during the pretrial investigation or during the criminal trial shall be recognized and approved for execution in all other Nordic States, without any reconsideration.
>
> Such a vision contains also that it shall be possible to bring a person with force across the State frontiers as easily as it is today to bring a person from one part of the country to another part during the pretrial investigation and the criminal trial.
>
> This implies that a decision to arrest a person taken by a court in a Nordic State can be executed, without any further national procedure, by the police in another Nordic

[49] See Träskman (2007, see note 4).

[50] F Wersäll, 'Straffrättsligt samarbete i ett gränslöst Norden' (2006) *Nordisk Tidskrift for Kriminalvidenskab* 122.

State if the person is found there. Such a system does not according to my opinion raise any apprehensions about risks concerning the legal safety. The legal safety guarantees granted for the wanted person can and shall satisfied by the authorities in the State where the procedure is carried out and not in the State where the person is found. An objection referring to *ne bis in idem* can for instance be as well, or even better, tried in the State of procedure. I do not believe that anyone contests if I claim that the legal safety is equally guaranteed in all the five Nordic States.

The crucial question is, why did the Nordic decision-makers not have enough courage to actually realize this vision?

5. CONCLUSION

In my opinion this is further evidence of the fact that the era you might call *the 'Golden Age of Nordic cooperation'*, and I am here referring to the period between 1960 and the year 2000, is over. It was during this period the Nordic model for cooperation in legal matters was shaped. There are many signs which indicate that this period has now elapsed.[51] The adoption of the Nordic Arrest Warrant and the contents of the Nordic Convention on it are a sign of this. The political will to make use of the possibilities for conducting Nordic pioneering work in the field of criminal law, criminal procedure and criminal policy is not put to good use. The decision-makers bow to and are content with insipid European solutions.

[51] P O Träskman, 'Finsk, svensk och nordisk straffrätt – och den europeiska – några reflektioner' in *Rikoksesta rangaistukseen. Juhlajulkaisu Pekka Viljanen 1952–26/8–2012* (Turun Yliopisto, Oikeustieteellinen tiedekunta 2012) 257–270.

Part III
EU Police Cooperation

8
EU Police Cooperation Post-Lisbon

ANNA JONSSON CORNELL*

Reinforcing law enforcement cooperation in the EU is one of the main goals of the policy area of Freedom, Security and Justice and it has been a priority since the adoption of the Tampere Programme by the European Council. One important aspect of law enforcement cooperation is the exchange of information between the law enforcement bodies of the Member States. The development of this field in the EU has been swift and substantial, starting with the Schengen Convention in 1990 on to the adoption of the Stockholm Programme in 2009. The development is continuing as a result of the entry into force of the Lisbon Treaty, although the preconditions are changing as will be discussed and described further in this chapter. The need to map out existing systems, evaluate their effectiveness and ensure coherence and consolidation concerning information exchange has been expressed on several occasions and it is an important strategic objective in the area of freedom, security and justice. As a means to achieve that goal the Commission issued a communication to the Commission and the Council on the European Information Exchange Model (EIXM) in December 2012.[1]

As a result of the entry into force of the Lisbon Treaty in December 2009, the pillar structure was removed. This has had a major impact on the policy area of freedom, security and justice. The area of freedom, security and justice is now a competence shared between the EU and its Member States, Article 4(2) j TFEU. Also, the legislative process has changed as well as the legal acts the EU is able to adopt in this particular policy area. Furthermore, the principles of direct effect and the supremacy of EU law together with the principles of subsidiarity and proportionality apply when the European Union exercises its powers. The main purpose of this chapter is to highlight these changes focusing on EU police cooperation from a constitutional law perspective, but also to discuss their implications for national law enforcements agencies and individuals who might be subjected to operational measures based on EU legislation.

* Senior Lecturer in Comparative Constitutional Law, Associate Professor in Constitutional Law and Research Director for Uppsala Forum for Democracy, Peace and Justice at Uppsala University.

[1] COM(2012) 735 final.

The chapter is divided into two parts. The first part deals with the EU's legislative procedures, strategy and operational planning, and competence issues relevant to police cooperation. One particular aspect of this is the difficulty of defining operational and non-operational police cooperation. The second part of the chapter focuses on the regulation of operational police cooperation in the EU with special attention being paid to the sharing of information and the challenges which still remain within this particular field. As will be shown and discussed further, police cooperation and operational police cooperation in particular raise important questions on the sharing of competence between the EU and its Member States, national sovereignty, democratic legitimacy, accountability, and the control and protection of fundamental rights. Serious concerns are raised by the following aspects: changes made to the EU's legislative procedures on police cooperation, the fragmented EU regulations, changes made relevant to the sharing of information and the very fact that operational police cooperation and the protection of fundamental rights must first and foremost be conducted according to and implemented by national law. Since EU police cooperation is an important policy area in its own right in the area of freedom, security and justice these issues deserve more attention than they have hitherto been granted, with special focus paid to policy planning and law-making.

Therefore let us start with a few remarks on policy, strategy, and national implementation in the area of freedom, security and justice in general in order to set the stage. The European Council has the overall responsibility for defining the strategic guidelines for legislative and operational planning, Article 68 TFEU. The Stockholm Programme, for example, was adopted under this provision. Moreover, Article 71 TFEU establishes a standing committee on internal security, COSI, whose main purpose is to ensure that operational cooperation on internal security is promoted and reinforced in the EU. The aim is that COSI with its operational focus shall facilitate the coordination of actions by national authorities in the area of freedom, security and justice. COSI has a coordinating responsibility for operational measures related to internal security which has raised certain questions as to the actual mandate of COSI as well as the implementation thereof. These aspects and their relevance for operational police cooperation will be elaborated further below.

With regard to the implementation of EU policies, the Commission may propose that the Council adopt measures enabling the Commission in cooperation with Member States to evaluate the implementation of EU policies in the area of freedom, security and justice by the authorities of the Member States. Such measures are non-legislative and are adopted by qualified majority voting (QMV) in the Council. This regulation is new to the Lisbon Treaty. All results emanating from such an evaluation should be made available to the European Parliament and national parliaments, Article 70 TFEU. The Article mentions in particular the application of the principle of mutual recognition and thereby underlines the importance of this particular principle and the issues of trust and reciprocity that it brings with it.

1. REGULATING POLICE COOPERATION IN THE EUROPEAN UNION

When dealing with EU police cooperation and its legislative process it is important to make a distinction between operational and non-operational police cooperation since different legislative procedures apply for these two different forms of police cooperation. However, determining what is operational cooperation and what is not is not necessarily as straightforward as it seems. More conventional forms of police cooperation such as the exchange of information and analysis, developing common investigation techniques and joint training are for the most part non-operational, even though the sharing of information could obviously form an important part of operational cooperation. Operational cooperation, on the other hand, is in all probability more focused on joint investigations and providing/receiving assistance in specific operations. The sensitive nature of the sharing of information related to inter alia data protection, the right to privacy, personal integrity, the right to a fair trial and the equality of arms makes it all the more important for the dividing line between operational and non-operational cooperation to be as clearly defined as possible. As will be discussed further below, neither the Treaties nor case law from the Court of Justice of the European Union (ECJ) offer any clear definition of operational and non-operational police cooperation. Some of the most important regulations concerning operational police cooperation, such as the Framework Decision on joint investigation teams[2] and the Prüm Decision,[3] which were processed pre-Lisbon and thus adopted by unanimity in the Council might provide a certain amount of guidance.

Let us start with non-operational police cooperation in order to describe how the legislative process has changed post-Lisbon. According to Article 87(1) TFEU, the EU shall establish joint cooperation between the law enforcement bodies of the Member States in order to prevent, detect and investigate criminal offences. In order to achieve this, the European Parliament and the Council can, in accordance with the ordinary legislative procedure, adopt certain measures, ie regulations, directives and decisions. Hence, as a result of the Lisbon Treaty, matters of non-operational police cooperation are as a rule decided by a qualitative majority vote (QMV).[4] Moreover, and to a certain extent as a result of QMV, the potential influence of national parliaments has increased. National parliaments have the right, and duty, to control that the principle of subsidiarity is applied correctly by EU institutions in the legislative process, Article 69 TFEU.[5]

[2] OJ 2002, L 162/1.

[3] OJ 2008, L 210/1.

[4] In addition, see Article 16 TFEU, which also provides for the ordinary legislative procedure. This Article could be used as a legal base for measures that involve data protection.

[5] See also Articles 5.3 and 12 TEU on the role of national parliaments and the control of the principle of subsidiarity. For an analysis on its impact on the Swedish national parliament see A Jonsson, 'EU:s lagstiftningsprocess och subsidiaritetsprövningen: Nya möjligheter till nationellt inflytande?' (2011) *SvJT* 413–429.

However, the legislative process differs when it concerns operational police cooperation. As stipulated in Article 87(3) TFEU, the Council can adopt regulations, directives and decisions in accordance with the special legislative procedure, which in this case means unanimously and after consulting the European Parliament. Should the Council fail to obtain unanimity, nine Member States can refer the draft measures to the European Council. If the European Council reaches a consensus on the measure it is referred back to the Council for adoption. If not, at least nine Member States can request to proceed by establishing an enhanced form of cooperation on the basis of the draft measure. Such a request should be addressed to the European Parliament, the Council and the Commission.[6] The enhanced cooperation mechanism and the possibility to refer a draft measure to the European Council do not apply to measures that are considered as being a part of the Schengen *acquis*. However, a second area where a special legislative procedure is to be applied concerns the regulation of conditions and limitations as to the activities of the law enforcement agencies of one Member State in the territory of another Member State, Article 89 TFEU. Here a unanimous vote by the Council after consulting the European Parliament is required and there is no enhanced cooperation mechanism tied to Article 89.

At the EU level this regulatory framework on police cooperation means that the difficulty of defining non-operational and operational cooperation may complicate the legislative procedure. Should there be any uncertainty as to the nature of the regulation it is preferable to apply a double legal basis.[7] However, this means that two different legislative processes will have to be applied, entailing in all probability considerable practical issues. Furthermore, the ECJ does not have the jurisdiction to assess the validity and proportionality of the operational measures of national law enforcement agencies when reviewing aspects related to Chapters 4 and 5.

This brings us back to the question of a definition of an operational and a non-operational measure. Of course all forms of cooperation must include a transnational aspect. In the absence of a tangible definition of operational measures in the treaties, and in any case law for that matter, Steve Peers argues in favour of an *a contrario* interpretation of Article 87(2) TFEU; that Article 87(3) should at least include coercive measures; and that it should be interpreted narrowly since it could be considered as an exception.[8] In this context, and from a national constitutional law perspective, it is also worth asking why a special procedure is seen as appropriate when it comes to operational police cooperation and whether that per se should have an impact on the definition. Clearly, operational police cooperation includes the exercising of state power in some shape or form with the potential of infringing the rights and freedoms of

[6] Until 2011 the enhanced cooperation mechanism had only been applied to family law and EU patents.

[7] In the end it is objective criteria such as the aim and content of the measure that will decide the correct legislative base. See for example C-269/97, C-376/98, C-303/05.

[8] S Peers, *EU Justice and Home Affairs Law* (Oxford, Oxford University Press, 2011) 876.

individuals as they are protected by European and national law. Moreover, the use of force and coercive measures are seen as one of the most important tasks of the state and one very important aspect of the relationship between the state and its individuals. Such measures are as a minimum considered legitimate if conducted according to the rule of law. Furthermore, exercising this form of state power is from a constitutional law perspective considered as a necessary intrusion on the rights and freedoms of individuals for the purpose of upholding national sovereignty and security on the one hand, and individual security and rights on the other. All such intrusions must be regulated by law and be proportional both as to content and implementation. Leaving the national sovereignty argument aside, it could also be argued that issues of accountability, democratic legitimacy and practicality make it an area less suitable for EU regulation. Taking all these factors into account, it makes sense that issues regarding operational EU police cooperation are subjected to a unanimous vote in the Council and that the very nature of operational police cooperation should lead to a broader interpretation of the concept for the purpose of Article 87(3), hence increasing the number of cases where unanimity is required. You could at least argue that that is a purposeful interpretation from the perspective of the Member States.

A further aspect of the new EU legislative procedure concerning police cooperation is the relationship between national parliaments and governments. As a result of the QMV procedure, as opposed to unanimity, the direct influence of national parliaments over the legislative process has been weakened. The scrutiny of the application of the principle of subsidiarity will only indirectly and in a limited way, particularly as concerns substance, allow influence for national parliaments. However, as concerns operational police cooperation, unanimity in the Council is still required which provides national parliaments with a greater possibility of exerting influence through a government representative, even if this must be considered a rather blunt tool.[9] In this context it is also worth noting that Member States have lost their right to initiate legislation individually and that such initiatives will now require the collaboration of a quarter of the Member States according to Article 76(b) TFEU. Thus, there are many circumstances and preconditions pointing at the need for enhanced transnational and inter-parliamentarian cooperation between Member States; the right to initiate legislative acts being one area and the scrutiny of the principle of subsidiarity being another. Clearly, for any Member State to be successful in reaching its goal it will need to find a group of Member States that is willing to work to achieve the same goal. One additional circumstance that requires effective transnational cooperation, not dealt with above, is the scrutiny of Europol, which is to be conducted by the European Parliament together with national parliaments, Article 88(2) 3rd paragraph TFEU.

[9] In Sweden, for example, the government representative is not legally bound by the guidelines provided by the parliament and the only way to claim accountability is through a vote of no confidence.

2. EU COMPETENCE ON POLICE COOPERATION

The competence of the European Union on police cooperation is defined by the reference to three different substantive areas laid down in Article 87(2)(a)–(c) TFEU. The first being the collection, storage, processing, analysis and exchange of relevant information; the second, support for the training of staff, and cooperation on the exchange of staff, equipment and research on crime detection; and third, common investigative techniques in relation to the detection of serious forms of organized crime. These substantive areas are not new to the Lisbon Treaty. However, there are certain limits to the competence of the EU in the area of freedom, security and justice, which have a potential impact on the EU's ability to regulate police cooperation, the responsibility for national security being one example.

2.1 National and Internal Security as a Limitation of EU Competence

Maintaining law and order, and internal security, are still mainly the responsibility of Member States and nothing in Title V affects the exercising of this responsibility, Article 72 TFEU. In Article 73, which is new to the Lisbon Treaty, it is underlined that Member States are free to organize relevant authorities responsible for national security and their coordination as well as cooperation as they please in order to uphold national security. Moreover, Article 4(2) TEU underlines that the sole responsibility for guaranteeing national security lies with the Member States. Article 4 TEU further states that the EU should respect the national identity of the Member States and their essential state functions, including inter alia maintaining law and order and safeguarding national security. Additionally, the ECJ does not, according to Article 276 TFEU have the jurisdiction to review the validity or proportionality of operations carried out by law enforcement agencies of Member States, when interpreting Chapters 4 and 5 of Title V in the TFEU. The same applies to national measures in order to maintain law and order or safeguard internal security. There are further restrictions to the Union's ability to dictate the actions of Member States when internal and national security is at stake. For example, according to Article 346(1)(a) TFEU, no Member State should be forced to supply information which if disclosed could be considered contrary to that state's security interests. Articles 346, 347 and 348 regulate additional circumstances when EU measures can be set aside in the interest of inter alia law and order, and national security, and the procedure to be applied if such measures are deemed necessary.

So, what does this mean with regard to EU competence, legislative procedures and operational measures? First, Article 72 together with Article 276 could be interpreted as stipulating that the use of all coercive measures needed to implement EU measures in the policy area of freedom, justice and security must be conducted by national law enforcement agencies.[10] Hence, all coercive measures required in order to enforce EU measures are left to the Member States. However, it is important to note that Article 72 does not restrict EU competence in the area of freedom, security and justice in terms of substance, according to Steve Peers.[11] The substantive limits to EU competence concerning police cooperation are dealt with in Article 87 TFEU. Thus, the EU can legislate but not execute when coercive measures are required.

The question is then whether Article 73 TFEU limits EU competence on police cooperation. According to Peers, this Article does not restrict EU competence to regulate security services when they take part in law enforcement operations that might be distinct from functions relating to the upholding of national security. He also argues that Article 73 does not rule out EU measures concerning the cooperation and coordination between authorities responsible for national security,[12] should a legal base exist elsewhere in the Treaty.

In conclusion, the main operational responsibility for upholding law and order lies with the Member States, although certain legislative measures may be adopted at the EU level. When such legislative measures concern operational cooperation, which is interpreted as including coercive measures, unanimity is required. Moreover, the EU may be able to legislate in fields relevant to internal and national security as long as it does not interfere with operational measures and as long as there is a legislative base in the Treaty. And finally, operational aspects of police cooperation can be regulated but not executed.

3. OPERATIONAL ASPECTS OF THE ACTIVITIES OF EUROPOL AND COSI

3.1 Europol

Europol's primary task is to reinforce, assist and coordinate Member States in their fight against serious crime.[13] Furthermore, Europol plays an important role when it comes to the collection and analysis of data from Member States. However, one of the main remaining challenges is that only a few Member States provide Europol's databases with data.[14] Over the years Europol has among other

[10] Europol, according to Article 88 TFEU, can only act together with national law enforcement officials. More detailed regulations can be found in the JIT Framework Decision, The Europol Council Decision, and in relevant national laws.

[11] Peers argument is that Art 72 is to general to be interpret to that end and that it will have to be read in context of the other articles in Title V; when the drafters of the Treaty wished to limit EU's competence as to substance they have done so explicitly, compare Art 79(5). Peers, *EU Justice and Home Affairs Law* (Oxford University Press, Oxford, 2006) 55. Art 72 has not yet been subjected to interpretation by the ECJ.

[12] Ibid.

[13] See A de Moaor and G Vermeulen, 'The Europol Council Decision: Transforming Europol into an Agency of the European Union' (2010) 47 *Common Market Law Review* 1089–1121.

[14] *Study on the status of information exchange amongst law enforcement authorities in the context of existing EU instruments*, JLS/2009/ISEC/PR/001-F3, December 2010, 9.

things been criticized for leaking information and has hence not been trusted enough for it to be able to realize its coordinating and analytical potential. Europol has no mandate of its own to engage in operational actions or take coercive measures. All coercive measures shall be the exclusive responsibility of the competent national authorities, Article 88(3) TFEU, and all operational actions shall be carried out jointly with the Member States or within the framework of a joint investigation, Article 88(2)(b).

Since Europol is the body most likely to have an overall perspective on transnational crime in general but also concerning specific objects of interest, it can urge national authorities to start a criminal investigation.[15] Thus, the information collected and analysed by Europol will have a significant impact on operational planning and decision-making in Member States, and, as will be discussed further below, in COSI as well. Before moving on to COSI and its mandate in relation to operational planning and coordination, let us conclude that although Europol does not have the competence to conduct any operations on its own, its tools and activities are of great importance for operational measures in Member States.[16] Not only can its staff take part in national and joint investigations, but, more importantly, if Europol does its job correctly, the information collected and analysed will set off operational measures in Member States. Should this not be the case, however, Europol can urge a national criminal investigation to be opened. Europol's strategic tools such as OCTA will play an increasingly important role in the policy planning process in the area of freedom, security and justice in that it will act as a starting point for the activities and priority-setting of COSI.[17]

3.2 COSI

The entry into force of the Lisbon Treaty brought with it institutional changes, such as the breakup of the DG JHA into DG Justice and DG Home, as well as changes with regard to strategic planning and implementation at the EU level. As has been mentioned above, the Council now has a legal base in the Treaty for its defining of strategic and operational guidelines in the area of freedom, security and justice. Clearly, effective, strategic and operational planning requires knowledge about ongoing operational activities and priorities at both the EU and the national level. Even if the Council has, at least since the Tampere Summit, been setting the guidelines for priorities in the area of freedom, security and justice the implementation and follow up of these have been hampered by the large number of players involved, the fragmentation of

[15] OJ 2009, L 121/37, art 7.

[16] For example, Analysis Work Files (AWF), Joint Investigation Teams (JIT), and Liaison officers just to mention a few operational tools.

[17] See also, *Europol Review 2011. General Report on Europol Activities* (Luxembourg, Publications Office of the EU, 2012) 21–22.

strategy documents and action plans, and by the fact that there is not just one body which is responsible for the holistic point of view.[18] It is not very far fetched to draw the conclusion that COSI was established to remedy several of these weaknesses.

According to the Council Decision establishing COSI, COSI's main responsibility is to promote operational cooperation on internal security, and to ensure cooperation and coordination between the law enforcement agencies of Member States and EU bodies and agencies in order to establish more coordinated, integrated and effective operations.[19] COSI does not have the competence to adopt legislation or to conduct operations,[20] and should not be confused with the Committee on Policing and Criminal Law, which assists Coreper in the legislative process, although it is expected to advise on operational needs and strategic aspects of cooperation in the process of drafting new legislation. Apart from representatives from the relevant ministries and law enforcement agencies of the Member States,[21] COSI is populated by representatives from inter alia Frontex, Europol and Eurojust. Since the EU's Internal Security Strategy (ISS) is increasingly connected to the EU's external security strategy, this development is likely to have an impact on COSI's focus and activities. COSI's main task is not only to ensure operational cooperation and coordination, but also to identify weaknesses in existing operational actions and to suggest improvements. One of the main challenges seems to be the multilateral cooperation between for example Europol, Eurojust, Frontex and Cepol and the very fact that most operational cooperation is still bilateral and determined by nationally defined needs and interests.

Even though the workings of COSI do not involve operational tasks and measures, the strategic guidelines and priorities set up by COSI are likely to have an influence over the operational cooperation between Member States. Moreover, even if COSI is not involved in the legislative process, it is very likely that the analytical conclusions drawn by COSI will not only contribute to the strategic and operational planning, but also the legislative procedures of the Council.

So what has COSI achieved since its first meeting in 2010? A full overview is not possible here. However, a study commissioned by the European Parliament shows how COSI initially has focused on organizational questions such as the EU policy cycle, ISS, coordination mechanisms for joint operations and financing for operational cooperation.[22] One of the main conclusions of this study is that all EU JHA agencies systematically report to COSI on their operational activities,[23]

[18] See *Developing an EU Internal Security Strategy, Fighting Terrorism and Organized Crime* (European Parliament DG for Internal Policies, 2011) 40–41.

[19] Art 71 TFEU and The Cosi Decision OJ 2010 L 52/50, Art 3.

[20] 2010 OJ L 52/50, the COSI Decision, Art 4.

[21] In the Swedish case it is the Ministry of Justice.

[22] *Developing an EU Internal Security Strategy, Fighting Terrorism and Organized Crime* European Parliament DG for Internal Policies, 2011, 41.

[23] Ibid, 42.

which means that COSI is collecting necessary information on operational activities and capacities of EU JHA agencies. The study also discusses the role of COSI in the suggested policy-planning circle, which will not only potentially widen COSI's mandate but also reinforce the position of Europol as one of the more important JHA agencies and enhance its impact on strategic decision-making with regard to operational police cooperation. According to this policy-planning circle, Europol will present a threat assessment to COSI upon which COSI will draft a policy advisory document to be presented to the Council.[24] Hence, both Europol and COSI will contribute to the political decision-making process of the Council. COSI will draft multiannual strategic plans[25] and annual operational action plans, secure implementation of the latter, and finally conduct annual evaluations on the implementation of the operational action plans. It is suggested that every fourth year an overall evaluation of the implementation of the main strategy will be conducted and forwarded to the Council.

Should this model determine the working pattern of COSI and thereby its potential influence over both policy and legislation, the authors of the study raise concerns over the limited insight of the European Parliament and national parliaments into the process, referring to Article 87 (3) TFEU and the special legislative procedure established therein.[26] Nota bene, the operational action plans are to be implemented by EU agencies and the relevant national law enforcement bodies. Moreover, COSI's activities, especially the evaluation process, are criticized for not including the perspective of fundamental rights and freedoms and the EU agencies designated to safeguard the very same.[27] Thus, should COSI's role develop as suggested above it would mean that EU measures on operational police cooperation will be prepared with limited insight and room for debate, despite the fact that COSI is supposed to inform the European Parliament of its activities.[28] Moreover, COSI and Europol – two expert bodies over which the European Parliament and national legislative assemblies have limited control, will heavily influence the preparatory work, including strategy and operational planning.

In conclusion, any future legislative measures on behalf of the EU in response to needs to improve operational police cooperation in general and the sharing of information in particular will most likely be heavily influenced by the assessment and priorities of agencies such as Europol and COSI. This leads us to the second part of this chapter that focuses on the existing EU legislative framework and challenges connected to its implementation.

[24] See also the Council's Communication *EU Policy Cycle process review: From OCTA to OAP*, 5751/1/12, 9 February 2012.

[25] See, for example, *Strategic goals related to the EU's priorities for the fight against organised crime between 2011 and 2013*, 15850/11, 21 October 2011.

[26] *Developing an EU Internal Security Strategy, Fighting Terrorism and Organized Crime*, European Parliament DG for Internal Policies, 2011, 43.

[27] Ibid, 45.

[28] See the letter from COSI to the Chairman of the Civil Liberties, Justice and Home Affairs Committee, European Parliament, 24 June 2011.

4. THE SHARING OF INFORMATION IN OPERATIONAL POLICE COOPERATION – CHALLENGES AND OPPORTUNITIES

The most important EU legal framework for operational police cooperation today includes the Data Retention Directive,[29] Framework Decision on joint investigation teams,[30] the Prüm Decision,[31] the Swedish Initiative,[32] and what is known as the Atlas Decision.[33] The overall purpose of the EU regulatory activities in this field has been to enable and facilitate the exchange of information between the law enforcement bodies of the Member States. The Commission Communication on the different channels for the exchange of information within the framework of the European Exchange Information Model (EIXM) summarizes and evaluates the different instruments available for sharing information.[34] Before accounting for the main conclusions in the communication let us turn to a study within this framework commissioned by DG Home Affairs and conducted by the International Centre for Migration Policy Development (ICMPD). This study concludes that the available EU framework for information sharing is adequate, that the main remaining challenges and difficulties can be explained, for example, by differences in national legislation as to data protection, technical IT capabilities, and a lack of common or commonly understood security classifications.[35] The study further concludes that the potential of the Swedish Initiative has not been fully realized and that the Prüm Decision is considered a more effective tool to identify criminals and solve crimes. It is therefore recommended that future developments should focus on HIT/NO HIT systems rather than the opening up of national databases allowing for an unconditional and direct exchange of information.[36] A further obstacle to the exchange of information is the differences regarding when rogatory letters are required and when not. The main problem is that in some Member States certain information is available through police channels while in others the same information is handled by the Ministry of Justice or they require judicial involvement. The study also points out that certain Member States consider the sharing of confidential information the most challenging legal problem. It is not only the differences in categories of classifications, but also how to exchange classified information. Apparently, information is sent by ordinary mail due to weaknesses in the security of electronic systems.[37] Several other issues are

[29] OJ 2006 L 105/57.
[30] OJ 2002 L 162/1.
[31] OJ 2008 L 210/1.
[32] OJ 2006 L 386/89.
[33] OJ 2008 L 210/73.
[34] COM(2012) 735 final. For an overview of the databases available in 2008 see, F Geyer, 'Taking Stock: Databases and Systems of Information Exchange in the Area of Freedom, Security and Justice' (2008) CEPS, Research Paper no 9.
[35] *Study on the Status of Information Exchange Amongst Law Enforcement Authorities in the Context of Existing EU Instruments*, JLS/2009/ISEC/PR/001-F3, December 2010, p 8.
[36] Ibid.
[37] Ibid, 94–95.

listed, but one in particular deserves extra attention, namely the use of police information in criminal proceedings before national courts. In the Netherlands, for example, the police cannot receive information or intelligence from another Member State if the sending State has not approved the information to be used before a court of law. Due to the Dutch principle of transparency, which means that courts must have access to the case history and police information, the police cannot restrict access to information.[38] Situations like these are likely to arise when there are ongoing parallel investigations in two or more Member States, when secret investigations take place and when infiltration is used as a means to gather intelligence and evidence. In such situations, the establishment of a joint investigation and the signing of an agreement laying down all the preconditions might be helpful.[39]

Still, depending on the national law of the states involved related to the exchange of information and the conduct of joint investigations, the rights of the suspect and potential defendant might be put at risk due to cooperation agreements between the states involved. To give a concrete example, an interesting case concerning drug trafficking has caused a stir in Sweden. The investigation seems to be a joint investigation between inter alia the Swedish Police and law enforcement agencies from at least one other country. As a result, the Swedish prosecutors have had difficulties providing the defence with a full insight into the methods used and persons involved in the pre-investigative phase.[40] Moreover, the court of first instance refused to hear a witness, in this case the Swedish Police Officer that acted as the contact between the Swedish National Bureau of Investigation and DEA. The Court of Appeal declared that the Court of first instance was wrong in rejecting the witness, but concludes that this error can be healed in the procedure before the Court of Appeal.[41] In cases like this one, a situation may arise where due to an agreement between the cooperating states, Swedish prosecutors are, by law, prevented from revealing certain information to the defence, which obviously stands in contrast to a defendant's right to a fair trial and the equality of arms as enshrined in Article 6 of the ECHR. Thus, there is an obvious conflict of norms.

We now return to the main conclusions in the Commission's communication which allow us to contrast them to the findings of the study accounted for above. The main conclusions are that no new EU-level databases or information exchange instruments are needed at this point, that the existing EU instruments both could and should be implemented more efficiently, and that exchanges should be better organized.[42] The Commission is particularly discontent with the

[38] Ibid, 97.

[39] See, for example, A Jonsson, 'Gemensamma utredningsgrupper i gränsöverskridande brottsutredningar' (2010) *ERT* 312–334.

[40] Ulrika Öster, 'Åklagarna har förbrukat allt förtroende', *Advokaten*, Nr. 8 2012, årgång 78, 'Rikskriminalen vägrar lämna ut "under-cover" – material till Tingsrätten – på grund av löfte till USA', *Dagens juridik*, 2012-06-19.

[41] Mål nr B 2856-13.

[42] COM(2012) 735 final, 2.

implementation of the Prüm decision, due to the fact that several Member States are not exchanging data under Prüm although the deadline for transposition expired August 26, 2011.[43] The Commission ascribes the low performance to the lack of political will to implement and threatens with infringement proceedings come December 2014.[44] The Commission also concludes that the Swedish Initiative has not reached its potential. The explanations put forward to this by the Member States are that the alternatives are considered good enough and that the request reform is burdensome.[45] One of the findings of the study referred to above was that future developments should focus on HIT/NO HIT systems. The Commission however maintains that the Swedish Initiative will be of importance for what it calls 'post-hit follow-up requests'[46] and that this is especially important when follow-up information is not going to be used as evidence before a court of law (since in that case a request for judicial cooperation would be required). Another challenge pointed out by the Commission is the fact that Member States use different channels for sharing of information to different extents. The Commission would like to see a coherent approach giving the Europol channel a central role. There is a divergence between some of the Member States and the Commission in this question. The Commission's arguments for making Europol a hub for sharing of information are the, according to the Commission, advantages of the Europol channel, inter alia the role to be played by Europol liaison officers, Europol's infrastructure for sharing information (SIENA) which is considered (again by the Commission) to be secure, effective, structured and a guarantor for data protection. Moreover, it would be in line with the Commission policy that Europol is to become the hub for all law enforcement cooperation within the EU.[47]

In this context I find it of outmost importance to view this proposal in context of the role played by Europol not only in operational cooperation, but also, in cooperation with COSI, in the legislative and strategy planning process at the EU level (described in section 3 above). Should the one channel approach be successful it would mean that Europol will strengthen its position in all these aspects, which could be problematic in terms of separation of powers and functions, control, and accountability. The European Data Protection Supervisor (EDPS) gave an opinion on the Commission's Communication. Overall the EDPS did not put forward serious criticism towards the communication, except for the one channel approach and the use of the Europol channel by default. The EDPS did not highlight the constitutional law aspects as I did above, but rather and in line with its task focused on the risk that such an approach would pose to data protection in general and the principle of purpose limitation in particular. The EDPS warns that a one channel approach might lead to a '...gradual widening

[43] See also COM(2012) 732 final.
[44] COM(2012) 735 final, 8.
[45] Ibid.
[46] Ibid.
[47] Ibid, 10.

of the use of a system or database beyond the purpose for which it was originally intended'[48] and encourages the Commission to justify more clearly the use of Europol channel as default and assess whether this choice is in compliance with the principle of privacy by design.

5. THE SHARING OF INFORMATION – A LEGAL RIGHTS PERSPECTIVE

The legal base for the exchange of information in EU police cooperation is inter alia the above-mentioned EU legal instruments, bilateral and multilateral agreements, and national legislation. Conny Rijken provides a definition of law enforcement information as being 'all the information that might serve as a basis for criminal investigations and criminal intelligence operations in the pre-evidence phase. This information is always linked to a specific crime, person, or group.'[49] This broad understanding of the concept combined with the fragmented and array of databases and ways to access them clearly poses a challenge both to data protection and the protection of the legal rights of individuals. Information and data can be stored at several levels (MS of residence, other MS and at the EU level). This in itself may be enough to cause insecurity and confusion. Add to that the many ways in which the information can be accessed and shared between law enforcement agencies in different Member States.[50] It is not possible to elaborate on the issue of data protection here. This question and other relevant areas for the protection of rights in police cooperation are dealt with in Iain Cameron's contribution to this book. Suffice it to say that a direct and unconditional exchange of information, for example the sharing of intelligence, causes a real problem as this kind of exchange of information entails that the sending State loses control over how the information is used in the receiving State and to whom it is forwarded. Therefore Rijken draws the conclusion that from a data protection point of view, an unconditional direct exchange is not recommended, at the same time he also concludes that this form of exchange is not widely used.[51] Moreover, as the example above shows, even if information is conditional, national laws can make it difficult to protect and hence to use the information provided. This very aspect is of course connected to the right to a fair trial and the equality of arms. This particular issue is not likely to diminish in importance as operational police cooperation continues to grow. Additionally, and as pointed out by the EDPS, when criminal intelligence is

[48] *Opinion of the EDPS on the Communication from the Commission to the European Parliament and the Council on EIXM*, 8, 11.

[49] C Rijken, 'Re-Balancing Security and Justice: Protection of Fundamental Rights in Police and Judicial Cooperation in Criminal Matters', (2010) *Common Market Law Review* 1455–1492, 1457, footnote 7.

[50] For a review of the different ways in which information can be shared see, ibid, 1458–1466.

[51] Ibid, 1467. The study on *Study on the Status of Information Exchange Amongst Law Enforcement Authorities in the Context of Existing EU Instruments*, JLS/2009/ISEC/PR/001-F3, December 2010 also supports the conclusion that this kind of exchange is not widely used.

gathered outside of a concrete criminal case, the context of fundamental rights protection changes. The question is when the right to a fair trial is activated, and what protection should and must be guaranteed in the meanwhile. The EDPS also highlights the need to make a distinction between processing data on suspects and non suspects.[52]

6. CONCLUSIONS

An overview of the legislative process and strategy planning on police cooperation leads to the conclusion that operational police cooperation is still in many ways being dealt with as an intergovernmental issue and the Member States are the main players through both the Council and COSI. Moreover, all operational measures are to be taken by national authorities in accordance with national law and rights derived from EU law should be enforced at the national level. Moreover, EU agencies designated to protect fundamental rights are not part of COSI, which forms the basis of the criticism being put forward against the current policy planning process and legislative procedure concerning operational police cooperation. However, since there is no clear definition of operational police cooperation it is too early to say what implications the divide between operational and non-operational police cooperation will have on the understanding of the decision-making procedure, public debate, accountability and control.

[52] *Opinion of the EDPS on the Communication from the Commission to the European Parliament and the Council on EIXM*, 6, 7. See also COM(2012) 10 final, proposal for a Directive on the protection of individuals with the regard to processing of personal data by competent authorities for the purpose of prevention, investigation, detection or prosecution of criminal offences or the execution of criminal penalties, and the free movement of such data.

9

Council of Europe Standards on Police Data Storage and Sharing

IAIN CAMERON*

1. INTRODUCTION

The need for effective police cooperation between EU states requires a degree of EU regulation of these national systems for storing and sharing intelligence. The existing, and future, EU regulation involves both an application of the mutual recognition principle and also a degree of harmonization. This takes into account, and builds upon, the variety of 'soft' standards of data protection produced within the Council of Europe, particularly the standards emerging as a result of the case law of the European Court of Human Rights (ECtHR). The ECtHR is part of the general principles of EU law, as well as being binding on the EU as a result of Article 6 of the Treaty on European Union. The ECtHR case law is thus particularly important in the EU legislative process, and for the Court of Justice of the EU (CJEU).

This article aims to give an overview of the Council of Europe standards. Data transfer is (obviously) characterized by a sender and a recipient. Previously, transfer of police data was for a given purpose; a specific criminal investigation, a specific intelligence gathering exercise, etc. However, at least in the future, transfer of data between police forces in EU states is expected to be much more extensive and more 'routine', even automated. When actors act together in a network, securing accountability for each actor's individual actions can become much more difficult. I look at this particular issue from the perspective of the case law of the ECtHR. I will begin by mentioning some of the problems involved in sharing of police data, before, very briefly, sketching out the EU legal framework regarding police data storage and sharing.

* Professor of Public International Law, Faculty of Law, Uppsala University

2. SOMETHING ABOUT THE CONTEXT OF POLICE DATA TRANSFER WITHIN THE EU AND THE DANGERS THIS CAN INVOLVE FOR HUMAN RIGHTS

To begin with, the argument is often made that the need for better transnational exchange of police data is a reaction to increased international organized crime. The legislative competence of the EU over substantive criminal law is confined to 'particularly serious crime with a cross-border dimension' (Article 83, Treaty on the Functioning of the European Union, TFEU).[1] This argument is thus a justification for using this EU competence. One should not accept uncritically the argument that transboundary organized crime now amounts for a large part of crime in European states – it does not.[2] Most crime is still local. But, where there are people, there is crime. The creation of the internet and the massive growth in internet usage mean a growth in computer facilitated crime (child pornography, hate speech, frauds, etc). The creation of the EU internal market means that there has a large increase in movement of people and goods between EU states (particularly within Schengen states), and it is a reasonable supposition that there has been a growth in transboundary frauds, etc. And when all the evidence for a fraud or other transnational crime is in another state, or several other states, then without effective police cooperation between these states, the crimes will go unpunished. Still, it is important to bear in mind that the developments we have seen facilitating transfer of data between police in EU states are not simply a *response* to the increase in transboundary crime. There are other drivers involved.[3]

I should also add that, accepting that there has been a growth in transboundary crime does not mean that the solution to this is more police powers and more EU level regulation of these. A repressive approach to transboundary EU is not the only, or even primary, way forward. A structural approach to EU transboundary fraud, for example, would mean limiting the amount of subsidies (primarily within the Common Agricultural Policy) which provide the incentive to defraud the EU in the first place.

It is a truism that the police power has, until relatively recently, been inherently national (which in most cases is synonymous with the territory of the state). The state monopoly on legitimate violence is, according to Weber, the criterion for defining the state.[4] The control of, and oversight over, this police power has

[1] It is further specified in the article that 'These areas of crime are the following: terrorism, trafficking in human beings and sexual exploitation of women and children, illicit drug trafficking, illicit arms trafficking, money laundering, corruption, counterfeiting of means of payment, computer crime and organised crime'.

[2] K von Lampe, 'Organized Crime in Europe', (2008) 2 *Policing* 7–17.

[3] B Bowling, 'Transnational Policing: The Globalization Thesis, a Typology and a Research Agenda', (2009) 3 *Policing* 149–160 and C Harfield, 'Transnational Criminal Investigation and Modes of Governance' (2011) 5 *Policing* 3–14.

[4] M Weber, 'Politics as a Vocation' 1919, http://www.sscnet.ucla.edu/polisci/ethos/Weber-vocation.pdf.

also been national. If one created a supranational police power at the EU level, then one could create a supranational accountability structure, in the same way as a federal state has both federal and local/state accountability mechanisms.[5] This would involve EU level centralized data banks and centralized oversight of these. There are certain embryonic tendencies towards transnational policing within the EU, in particular, cooperation involving exercise of hot pursuit and joint investigation teams[6] and the 'Atlas decision' cooperation within the EU, ie cooperation for policing major public events and emergencies. But genuine transnational policing it is a long way off, and probably moving further away, rather than closer, as a result of the present financial crisis. Instead, the police power is to remain national, and police forces in EU states are expected to cooperate with each other effectively, primarily by exchanging information. Transfer of police data by the old 'letters rogatory' system was hugely time-consuming and ineffective (which is why police forces with frequently recurring transnational contacts tended to cooperate more informally). A request from police force in state A might have to go through a prosecutor, to a court, to the Justice Ministry, then to the Foreign Ministry and then the reverse in State B. Requests for clarifications, and for more information had to go through the same process. The room for misunderstandings was great. Above all, there was no duty to reply. Moving away from this hierarchical system to a decentralized data flow is a huge step forward. However, it means that there will be a much larger number of people involved in transfer of data, with corresponding greater room for errors committed by non-specialists, for data leakage through incompetence, for corruption etc. Previously discretionary transfer will instead become an obligation subject to certain exceptions, meaning that the default position will be transfer (the so-called 'principle of availability').[7] The room for refusal will diminish.

This is mainly positive. But there can be good grounds for refusing transfer of data, eg the feared inadequacy of the data protection mechanisms or practices in the recipient state. It is well known that corruption is much more prevalent in some EU states than others. And, of course, while the ostensible goal is that data should be transferred as easily between the police in Naples and the police in Stockholm, as it is between the police in Naples and the police in Rome,

[5] For a discussion, see eg I Loader and N Walker, 'Locating the Public Interest in Transnational Policing' in A Goldsmith and J Sheptycki (eds), *Crafting Transnational Policing* (Hart, 2006).

[6] C Rijken, G Vermeulen, (eds), *Joint Investigation Teams in the European Union: From Theory to Practice* (TMC Asser Press, The Hague, 2006), and in the Swedish context, A Jonsson, 'Gemensamma utredningsgrupper i gränsöverskridande brottsutredningar' (2010) 2 *Europarättslig tidskrift* 312–334.

[7] The Commission proposal on the Stockholm programme refers inter alia to 'criteria for gathering, sharing and processing information obtained for security purposes, while complying with data protection principles, [creation of] a follow-up mechanism for assessing how the exchange of information operates; [and] guiding principles for a policy on the international transfer of data for security purposes (applying demanding data-protection criteria'. Communication from the Commission to the European Parliament and the Council COM (2009) 262 final 10.6.2009, http://eur-lex.europa.eu/LexUriServ/LexUriServ.do?uri=COM:2009:0262:FIN:EN:PDF.

this is not to say that *intra*-state police data transfers always go smoothly and effectively. There are only a few EU states where there is a national police force, such as Finland and Denmark. Other EU states split the policing function territorially (federal/länder, national/local). Sweden has at present 21 county police forces, although it is intended that these are to be amalgamated into a national police force by 2015.[8] Functional divisions are also common (judicial police, financial police, security police, etc). Policing in a state can also be split between a civilian police force and a paramilitary force (eg the Carabinieri in Italy or the Guardia Civil in Spain). In internal security, the police may have to share the responsibility with (and even be the junior partner of) a civilian security agency (as is the case in, eg the UK and the Netherlands). There can be rivalries, incompetence, inefficiencies, etc which apply between all of these 'intra-police' data transfers.

In dealing with data protection in general, two of the standard rules are individual access to the data and the right to demand correction or completion of inaccurate or incomplete data (see below). Both of these rules are backed up by access to an independent data protection authority with powers to require compliance from the data holder. While both of these rules can be made applicable to certain forms of data held and processed by the police (eg criminal records), neither can be applicable to police data which must be kept secret for operational or other reasons: criminal and police intelligence data.

Here one can point to the forward-looking (preventive) nature of intelligence gathering as well as the growing together of criminal intelligence and security intelligence. Organized crime and security threats are diffuse and fragmented. While there have historically been differences in approach between datamining states (such as the UK) and states applying the paradigm of investigation of given individuals for given criminal activity, even in states following the latter paradigm such as Sweden we are seeing developments linking the use of signals intelligence (SIGINT) (and so datamining) to security, and organized crime, investigations.[9]

For the police, purely factual information, and analysis of it, such is insufficient. It also needs to gather *speculative* intelligence in order to determine which people are, or are probably or possibly, engaged in crime. Once it has established who the suspects are, it must gather intelligence on their activities, movements and contacts. This information can be obtained from, inter alia, secret electronic surveillance, other public data banks, analysis of crime statistics and patterns ('hot spots' etc.), forensic material (fingerprint and DNA registers), foreign police forces and, above all, informants. The reliability of information from informers will obviously vary but the risk is always present that the informant's motives (a desire for revenge, for personal or ideological reasons or

[8] In accordance with the proposal made by a Commission of Inquiry, SOU 2012: 13 En sammanhållen svensk polis.

[9] Prop. [legislative bill] 2011/12:179, Polisens tillgång till signalspaning i försvarsunderrättelse-verksamhet.

a simple wish to be seen as important) will cause him or her to colour, selectively omit or fabricate information.[10] Moreover, a proportion of this information will inevitably be of a speculative nature, or even pure invention.

Like factual information, such 'soft criminal intelligence' can, and must if the police agency is to do its job properly, be collated to produce a personality profile of a suspect or an analysis of a suspected activity. Seemingly unrelated bits of information can be pieced together to add up to a criminal purpose. This means that the filing system must be constructed in such a way as to facilitate linking of information on the same subject matter filed after considerable elapses of time, as well as allowing synthesis of (apparently) unrelated information, eg to discern patterns of activity. It should be noted here that files are obviously not simply person files, but can be a file on a particular phenomenon, event or place (eg a suspected meeting place for terrorists or organized crime). The data system must also allow all operators to obtain quick overviews of large quantities of data. A standard system would rather be a computerised central register, searchable on a large number of different variables, which in turn refers to paper files containing more details.

The above shows clearly that there are dangers to human rights in cases of mistaken identity.[11] Moreover, the more information is kept, and the more sensitive this is, the more the risk of leaking of information for political reasons, leaking of information to newspapers, leaking to organized crime as a result of corruption. The process of analyzing the information may be tainted by filing inaccurate/biased information, or mixing it with information from private data banks which has been gathered for other than law enforcement purposes, and over which there is low quality control. Other dangers are caused by inaccurate risk assessments – that a person, a group or a phenomenon is a threat. These can be caused in a variety of ways, eg, incompetence, bias, or badly constructed proactive search profiles.

Dangers can also be caused to human rights when two or more police intelligence cultures meet.[12] As regards data storage and transfer one should draw a distinction between formal safeguards in rules and legal-cultural safeguards which come to expression in training, recruitment of staff and their actual filing practices. There can be differing levels of compliance with the applicable norms. For example, there can be differences in practice (even if the rules are identical on paper) regarding thresholds for initiating personal files, on transfer between ad hoc phenomenon files and personal files long term and short term. Different police forces may have a satisfactory overall control but place the bulk of their safeguards at different stages in the intelligence cycle. For example, the police force of state A may make it relatively easy to start collecting criminal intelligence

[10] There are many other problems involved in the use of informers, particularly the direct and indirect corrupting effect on the police or security agency themselves. I will not go into these issues here. See eg G Marx, *Undercover* (University of Berkley Press, 1980) 152–158.

[11] For an ECHR case, see, eg, *Andre v France*, No 26932/95, 89 DR 71 (1997).

[12] See generally B Loftus, *Police Culture in a Changing World* (OUP, 2010).

on a person, group or phenomenon, but place tough restrictions on release of that intelligence outside a very small group of investigating officers. The police force of state B may have much tougher limits on initiation of files, but taking into account a more holistic and integrated approach to crime investigation, may be more liberal in permitting access to this data by officers involved in related criminal investigations, or even permit the transfer of data to other administrative authorities (eg welfare authorities, to investigate benefit fraud).

While I am focusing on human rights problems, I should stress that I do not consider the police power to gather and exchange data to be part of a sinister conspiracy. The police must keep and exchange criminal intelligence data. The police must also have access to other state data systems – when they have shown they need this for their work in preventing and investigating crime. And as Lyon pointed out long ago, the exercise of state rights (to vote etc) and the disbursement of state benefits is linked to accurate means of determining identity, marital status, health, work capacity etc.[13] By emphasising the dangers, one can easily forget the other dimensions to the question.

3. SOMETHING ON THE LEGAL FRAMEWORK UNDER EU LAW

I will not go into detail on the complicated EU legal framework. Part of the reason for the the complicated picture is the pillar structure of the EU which existed prior to the Lisbon treaty. After the Amsterdam treaty amendments, police cooperation fell to some extent within the 'first pillar' (EC law), as this pillar partially incorporated the so-called Schengen acquis, a detailed body of norms dealing largely with immigration matters, but also certain forms of police cooperation.[14] Exchanges of immigration data, and police data connected to this, thus fell within the first pillar.[15] Remaining elements of police cooperation, including the rest of the Schengen acquis fell within the third pillar (police and judicial cooperation in criminal matters). In both cases, simply put, the EU had competence only to regulate 'transborder' police cooperation. This is still the case today, after the entry into force of the Lisbon treaty. The present legal basis for data exchange generally can be found in Article 16 TFEU,[16] and

[13] D Lyon, *The Electronic Eye: The Rise of the Surveillance Society* (University of Minnesota Press, 1994) 33.

[14] The Schengen treaty was not, originally, an EU treaty. However, the EU states later agreed to incorporate it into the acquis.

[15] See inter alia Regulation 767/2008 9 July 2008 on information systems for visas.

[16] Article 16 provides in relevant part that

1. Everyone has the right to the protection of personal data concerning them.
2. The European Parliament and the Council, acting in accordance with the ordinary legislative procedure, shall lay down the rules relating to the protection of individuals with regard to the processing of personal data by Union institutions, bodies, offices and agencies, and by the Member States when carrying out activities which fall within the scope of Union law, and the rules relating to the free movement of such data. Compliance with these rules shall be subject to the control of independent authorities.

for data exchange as regards the police in Article 87 TFEU.[17] Data exchange within the CFSP is to be found in Article 39 TEU. The Charter of Fundamental Rights should also be borne in mind, particularly Article 8[18] (privacy) read in conjunction with the general limitation clause (Article 52).

The secondary instruments have grown organically, and contain inter alia three treaty-based systems, the Schengen acquis, EUROPOL (the constitutive document of EUROPOL was later transformed into a EC Council decision)[19] and the Prüm treaty. Still other standards can be found in Directive 95/46/EC on the protection of individuals with regard to the processing of personal data and on the free movement of such data.[20] This directive was adopted under the first pillar dealing with personal data protection generally. Supervision of data requires an independent authority.[21] However, the directive does not cover the areas of public security, national defence and national security. Transfers of police data within JHA were as regulated much later, in the so-called 'Swedish initiative' (setting out the form of information, and routines for exchange)[22] and in Framework Decision 2008/977 on the protection of personal data in the framework of police and judicial cooperation. Although the latter framework decision has only recently entered into force, it is already planned to replace it as part of the Commission's fundamental revision of data protection (also for a new General Data Protection Regulation) announced on 25 January 2012.[23] Data protection by EU institutions is monitored by the European Data Protection Supervisor.[24]

[17] Article 87 provides in relevant part that

1. The Union shall establish police cooperation involving all the Member States' competent authorities, including police, customs and other specialised law enforcement services in relation to the prevention, detection and investigation of criminal offences.

2. For the purposes of paragraph 1, the European Parliament and the Council, acting in accordance with the ordinary legislative procedure, may establish measures concerning: (a) the collection, storage, processing, analysis and exchange of relevant information…

[18] This provides that

1. Everyone has the right to the protection of personal data concerning him or her.

2. Such data must be processed fairly for specified purposes and on the basis of the consent of the person concerned or some other legitimate basis laid down by law. Everyone has the right of access to data which has been collected concerning him or her, and the right to have it rectified.

3. Compliance with these rules shall be subject to control by an independent authority.'

[19] Council decision 2009/371/JHA, 6 April 2009 on establishment of Europol.

[20] OJ L 281/31, 23.11.1995.

[21] See further *European Commission v Federal Republic of Germany* 2010 ECR I-01885 where the CJEU ruled that the mere risk of political influence through state scrutiny is sufficient to hinder the independent performance of the supervisory authority's task.

[22] Council Framework Decision 2006/960/JHA of 18 December 2006 on simplifying the exchange of information and intelligence between law enforcement authorities of the Member States of the European Union OJ L 386/89 29.12.2006.

[23] 'Safeguarding Privacy in a Connected World: A European Data Protection Framework for the 21st Century' (COM(2012) 9 final).

[24] I will not go into the supervisory system. The mandate of the Data Protection Supervisor (http://www.edps.europa.eu/EDPSWEB/edps/cache/off/EDPS/Membersmission) is set out in Regulation (EC) No 45/2001.

The draft directive makes a number of important changes.[25] Firstly, the scope of the directive will be wider than Framework Decision 2008/977/JHA which was not applicable to purely domestic data processing. Additional principles have now been explicitly included in the rules on data protection: the transparency principle, the data minimisation principle, and the accountability of the data controller. Moreover, the draft directive provides for different degrees of accuracy and reliability of data as well as the distinction between different categories of data subject (accused, victim, and witness).[26] The European Parliament is at present considering the directive and has adopted a draft report on it.[27]

I should note, in conclusion in this short section, that the 2008 framework decision[28] and the proposed directive do not, and will not, cover all exchanges of police data between EU states. First, EU member states can agree amongst themselves more intensified cooperation arrangements. The Nordic states, for example, have a simplified system of cooperation, including data transfer.[29] Second, data relating to internal security is likely to be excluded. In accordance with the exception to EU competence under Article 4(2) TEU national security remains the sole responsibility of each Member State.

4. APPLICABLE COUNCIL OF EUROPE DATA PROTECTION NORMS

The applicable Council of Europe norms for police databanks can be found in a variety of sources, some binding, some 'soft law' standards (guidelines, best practices etc). The main standards are to be found in the European Convention on Human Rights and the case law of the European Court of Human Rights (ECtHR) (considered in the next section). Another important Council of Europe treaty is the Convention for the Protection of Individuals with regard to Automatic Processing of Personal Data 1981 and its Additional Protocol regarding Supervisory Authorities and Transborder Dataflows (2001).[30] This Convention is also in the process of being revised to take into account new technology and new practices.

[25] For more detail, see EuCrim 2012 (1), 13.

[26] This follows CoE Recommendation (R (87)15) below. However, the draft directive does not set out standards for transfer of data from private companies to police.

[27] Committee on Civil Liberties, Justice and Home Affairs Draft Report on the proposal for a directive of the European Parliament and of the Council on the protection of individuals with regard to the processing of personal data by competent authorities for the purposes of prevention, investigation, detection or prosecution of criminal offences or the execution of criminal penalties, and the free movement of such data (COM(2012)0010 – C7-0024/2012 – 2012/0010(COD)), 20.12.2012.

[28] Article 1.4 provides that the framework decision is 'without prejudice to essential security interests and specific intelligence activities in the field of national security'.

[29] See J Boucht, 'Cross-border Use of Police Powers within the EU – A Finnish, Norwegian and Swedish perspective' (2012) 3 *European Criminal Law Review* 203.

[30] ETS no 108. The OECD has also adopted guidelines on protection of personal integrity regarding transborder data flows. To a large extent these are equivalent to the 1981 Data Protection Convention.

The 1981 Data Protection Convention can be said to be the 'foundational document' on data processing. It sets out minimum standards aimed at protecting individuals against abuses which may accompany the collection and processing of personal data. It also seeks to regulate the transborder flow of personal data. The basic rule is that personal data should not be processed at all, except when certain conditions are met. These conditions fall into three categories: transparency, legitimate purpose and proportionality. Under Article 7, processing is permissible inter alia when it is necessary for the performance of a task carried out in the public interest or in the exercise of official authority vested in the controller or in a third party to whom the data are disclosed and for the purposes of the legitimate interests pursued by the controller or by the third party or parties to whom the data are disclosed, except where such interests are overridden by the interests for fundamental rights and freedoms of the data subject.

The data subject generally speaking has the right to access all data processed about him or her. The data subject also has the right to demand the rectification, deletion or blocking of data that is incomplete, inaccurate or is not being processed in compliance with the data protection rules (Article 12).

Personal data may be processed only insofar as it is adequate, relevant and not excessive in relation to the purposes for which they are collected and/or further processed. The data must be accurate and, where necessary, kept up to date. Every reasonable step must be taken to ensure that data which are inaccurate or incomplete, having regard to the purposes for which they were collected or for which they are further processed, are erased or rectified. The data should not be kept in a form which permits identification of data subjects for longer than is necessary for the purposes for which the data were collected or for which they are further processed. Member States shall lay down appropriate safeguards for personal data stored for longer periods for historical, statistical or scientific use (Article 6)

When sensitive personal data (religious beliefs, political opinions, health, sexual orientation, race, membership of past organisations) are being processed, extra restrictions apply. (Article 8).

The most specific Council of Europe standards on police data protection are to be found in Recommendation N° R (87) 15 regulating the use of personal data in the police sector and the periodic evaluations which have been made of member states' practices in implementing this recommendation.[31]

[31] See in particular Report on the Impact of Data Protection Principles on Judicial Data in Criminal Matters including in the framework of Judicial Co-operation in Criminal Matters (2002) Third evaluation of Recommendation N° R (87) 15 regulating the use of personal data in the police sector (2002) http://www.coe.int/t/e/legal_affairs/legal_cooperation/data_protection/documents/reports_and_studies_of_data_protection_committees/2Report%203%20evaluation_R_87_15_2002.pdf and the study on the recommendation in 2010 http://www.coe.int/t/dghl/standardsetting/dataprotection/J%20A%20Cannataci%20Report%20to%20Council%20of%20Europe%20complete%20with%20Appendices%2031%20Oct%202010.pdf.

Other relevant soft law standards can be found in some of the opinions of the constitutional advisory body of the Council of Europe, the Venice Commission. In the course of its work on internal security services, and in the knowledge of the abuses which had come to light during the former US adminstration's 'war on terror', the Venice Commission made a number of recommendations intended to deal with the particularly troublesome problem of transfer of police or security data which could result in, or contribute to, torture.[32]

The Venice Commission advised that transfer of data should be regulated in statutory or other rules to avoid a vacuum of responsibility. Both the supply and receipt of data must be regulated by agreements in writing made by the proper authorities.[33] These should be submitted to parliamentary or expert oversight bodies.[34] Conditions should be attached to intelligence transferred. Limits must be placed both on the type of intelligence which can be transferred[35] and requirements must exist to check the reliability and accuracy of the intelligence, before it is transferred and also, for a receiving agency, to check reliability and accuracy when information is received from another State.[36]

5 THE CASE LAW OF THE ECTHR ON POLICE DATA SYSTEMS

The main Convention article which is relevant is Article 8 (privacy). However, data collection and transfer issues can arise even under other articles,[37] in particular, Article 13. Much of the relevant case law has concerned security data banks, rather than police/criminal intelligence data. This is paradoxical in one sense, bearing in mind the greater secrecy which surrounds the former, and consequent greater difficulties in proving one has suffered a violation of one's Convention rights. But the Court has made it easier to prove victim status

[32] See in particular Venice Commission, Report on the democratic oversight of the security services, 71st Plenary Session (Venice, 1–2 June 2007) CDL-AD(2007)016 http://www.venice.coe.int/docs/2007/CDL-AD(2007)016-e.pdf.

[33] See, eg, the Dutch Intelligence and Security Services Act 2002 (De Wet op de inlichtingen- en veiligheidsdiensten) Article 36(1)(d), 40(1) and 42.

[34] See eg, Canadian CSIS Act, Section 17(2) which requires that the oversight body, the Security Intelligence Review Committee (SIRC) be given copies of all CSIS agreements with foreign governments and international organizations.

[35] See, eg, Article 9 (conditions and limits on supply of data) of the Agreement on Co-operation Between the Republic of Bulgaria and the European Police Office http://www.europol.europa.eu/legal/agreements/-Agreements/15977.pdf which specifies inter alia that 'Personal data revealing racial origin, political opinions or religious or other beliefs, or concerning health and sexual life as referred to in Article 6 of the Council of Europe Convention of 28 January 1981 for the protection of individuals with regard to automatic processing of personal data shall only be supplied in absolutely necessary cases and in addition to other information'.

[36] See Article 10 of the Europol-Bulgaria Agreement, ibid. (assessment of the source and of the information). An example of a supply rule can be found in the German statute governing the BundesVerfassungsschutz Bundesverfassungsschutzgesetz (BVErfSchG), Germany, 2002, Art 19

[37] See, eg, *Al-Nashif v Bulgaria* No 50963/99, 20 June 2002 and *Ramzy v Netherlands* No 25424/05, 27 May 2008 (expulsion on security grounds).

by allowing people who can show, on reasonable grounds that they may be a victim, to claim victim status. And the violation in question has often been of the 'accordance with the law' requirement, regarding the quality of the law (foreseeability, precision of regulation etc.) which does not usually involve the Court in having to have access to secret, and difficult to evaluate, information regarding the working of safeguards.

The Court's case law on security data is, however, applicable mutatis mutandis to criminal intelligence data. To begin with, the scope of Article 8 in this respect is wide. It covers the collection of 'any information relating to an identified or identifiable individual'.[38] Even publicly available information can fall within the scope of private life where it is systematically collected and stored in files held by the authorities.[39] It covers fingerprints and DNA.[40]

When such information is collected, it is necessary to provide adequately accessible and foreseeable legal authority to do so.[41] It is necessary to 'specify the conditions in which [files] may be created, the procedures that have to be followed, the information which may be stored or comments which might be forbidden'.[42] The age of the information and the length of time for which information may be kept must also be regulated and there must be effective independent supervision of the files.[43] Certain types of particularly sensitive data must be 'flagged' so that they can be traced in computerized systems, allowing special limitation of access to this data, special rules on destruction, etc.[44] Disproportionate collection of data is not permissible.[45] Where there is a right of individual access to the data (eg it concerns objective 'hard' intelligence such as criminal records), access must not be unduly delayed or made difficult in practice.[46] There must also be effective remedies in practice against disproportionate acts, possible abuse or misuse, including erroneous or insufficiently substantiated risk-assessments.[47] The Court has increasingly emphasized that remedies must exist not only on paper but in

[38] See *Amann v Switzerland* [GC], No 27798/95, ECHR 2000-II para 65.

[39] *Rotaru v Romania*, [GC], No 28341/95, ECHR 2000-V at para 43.

[40] *S and Marper v UK*, [GC] Nos 30562/04 and 30566/04, 4 December 2008.

[41] *Shimovolos v Russia*, No 30194/09 21 June 2011 (A security database created on the basis of a ministerial order which had not been published and was not accessible to the public meant that concerned individuals could not ascertain who was registered in it, what type of information was included and for how long, how it was stored and used or who had control over it – violation of Article 8).

[42] *Amman v Switzerland*, at para 76.

[43] *Rotaru v Romania*, above.

[44] *Weber and Saravia v Germany*, No 54934/00, 29 June 2006.

[45] *S and Marper v UK*, above.

[46] *Haralambie v Romania*, No 21737/03, 27 October 2009

[47] See *Khelili v Switzerland*, No 16188/07, 18 October 2011. The case concerned the classification of a French woman as a 'prostitute' in the computer database of the Geneva police for five years. The Court found that this, and the difficulties she had in practice of having this – insufficiently substantiated – value judgment removed from the files constituted a violation of Article 8. See also *Dimitrov-Kazakov v Bulgaria*, No 11379/03, 10 February 2011. The applicant's name was entered in the police registers, with reference to a rape, as an 'offender', after being questioned about a rape, even though he had never been indicted for the offence. He was unable to obtain the removal of the entry. Violation of Articles 8 and 13.

practice. In *Segerstedt-Wiberg v Sweden,*[48] the then existing oversight body, the Register Board, could look at the security files, indeed, was the only body with sufficient competence to evaluate these files. However, it could not order the deletion of inaccurate data or data which it considered no longer should be retained. The Swedish Data Inspectorate could do this, but in practice it lacked the competence to evaluate the files in question. The Court accordingly found a violation of the Convention.

6. THE ECTHR AND THE ISSUE OF TRANSNATIONAL DATA TRANSFER

As noted above, transfer of data between police forces in EU states will be increasingly extensive and more 'routine'. The question posed at the beginning of this article was how to ensure legal accountability for this type of network activity, where inaccurate, or insufficiently substantiated, information given by state A, and relied upon by state B, can have serious implications for an individual in state B. The case-law of the ECtHR is still developing in the area of the extent to which a state can, and should, bear responsibility for acts with an extraterritorial dimension. It is, however, already evident that a vacuum of accountability is not acceptable.[49] For example, removing a person from the territory to another territory where he will be tortured clearly grounds responsibility[50] as does kidnapping a person in the territory of another state (not a party to the ECHR).[51] More recently the Court has held that it is a violation of Article 6 to transfer a person to a state where s/he will not receive a fair trial, because the evidence against him/her has partially been obtained by torture.[52]

There is case law under the ECHR relating to the issue of responsibility in relation to mutual assistance in criminal matters.[53] There is also case law in which a state was found responsible for issuing a defective arrest warrant which resulted in a person being arrested and held in another state.[54] The Court found here that it was the issuing state which bore responsibility for the unlawful deprivation of liberty, not the state where the deprivation of liberty actually occurred. These cases concerned Article 5, not Article 8 and the question is

[48] No 62332/00, 6 June 2006.

[49] See, in particular *Bankovic and Others v Belgium* and 16 other Contracting States decision of 12 December 2001; *Assanidze v Georgia* judgment of 8 April 2004; *Issa and Others v Turkey* judgment of 16 November 2004; *Ilascu v Moldova and the Russian Federation* judgment of 8 July 2004.

[50] *Soering v UK* Series A No 161, 7 July 1989. See also El-Masri, below.

[51] See, eg, *Stockè v Germany*, 12 October 1989, A/199, *Öcalan v Turkey*, No 46222/99 14 December 2000.

[52] *Othman (Abu Qatada) v UK*, No 8139/09, 17 January 2012. See further *El Haski v Belgium*, No 649/08, 25 September 2012.

[53] *Szabó v Sweden*, No 28578/03, 27 June 2006. The last of these concerned the transfer of a prisoner to serve sentence in his native country which resulted in a longer de facto term of imprisonment.

[54] *Stephens v Malta* No 11956/07, 21 April 2009.

whether one go so far as to find responsibility under the ECHR where state A simply transfers intelligence material concerning person X to another state.[55]

To begin with, there will usually be very large problems of proof. The Court does, admittedly, weigh in all relevant material, and can take into account circumstantial evidence. In the Grand Chamber judgment in *El-Masri v The Former Yugoslav Republic of Macedonia,*[56] the Court came to the conclusion, despite denials by the respondent government, that the applicant had been secretly detained, 'rendited' into the custody of US officials and then subjected to torture in Afghanistan. The Court found the respondent state responsible even for the subsequent torture.

However, the situation is rather different as regards data transfer. It is one thing to transfer a person outside of one's jurisdiction. The series of events involved may be able to be reconstructed, albeit painstakingly. But without cooperation from either the sending or receiving state, it will be very much more difficult for the ECtHR to find out if information was transferred, and, if so what this information was.

Secondly, intelligence which is transferred on person X by police force in state A will presumably only seldom be *decisive* for action taken in state B which might be in violation of X's Convention rights. Thus, in most cases, B's discretion to act – and thus its responsibility for its actions under the Convention, if it is bound by it – will continue to exist. The situation can be different in the cases of transnational EU policing mentioned – hot pursuit, joint investigative teams and 'Atlas' decision cooperation. But all of these are governed by special rules transferring (or retaining) the responsibility of the host state. It can also conceivably be different in situations of urgency where intelligence is transferred concerning an impending and serious threat to public order and safety, such as a terrorist attack. In such cases, it might, in exceptional cases, be reasonable to let the state transferring the intelligence bear responsibility for acts taken by the police force in the receiving state which bear a direct causal connection to the intelligence in question. But even here, it would only be reasonable for such a transfer of responsibility to occur where the intelligence was manifestly incorrect but the transferring state claimed that it was accurate, a sort of 'reckless' transfer of intelligence. Otherwise, states will not be inclined to transfer intelligence at all – which will undermine the whole purpose of the system.

7. CONCLUDING REMARKS

The soft law standards of the Council of Europe, and the case law of the ECtHR, might seem to some to be too vague to provide for meaningful safeguards on

[55] The Venice Commission, in its opinions on rendition (Venice Commission Opinion No 363/2005, on the international legal obligations of Council of Europe member States in respect of secret detention facilities and inter-State transport of prisoners, 66th Plenary Session, Venice, 17–18 March 2006) and democratic control over internal security services (above) indicates that state responsibility may arise under the ECHR under certain circumstances.

[56] No 39630/09, 13 December 2012.

police data collection, retention and exchange. Certainly, much more detailed and structured rules are necessary in this area, inter alia to provide clear lines of accountability. Once the EU has legislated in an area, there is the possibility of supervision by the Commission and the CJEU. However, there are gaps in the EU competence as regards police data – inter alia the internal security exception. Moreover, the recent serious problems with human rights protection in Hungary show the relative weakness of EU mechanisms of supervision for compliance with human rights standards. In reality, much of the safeguards in this area are provided not by the legislation but by police culture. Thus, the – hopefully – persuasive standards of the Council of Europe will, for want of anything better, continue to play a role in improving efficiency and human rights compliance in this area.

Part IV
New Configuration and Dynamic Evolution

10
*In Search of a New Lens!**

BO WENNSTRÖM**

By way of introduction, I would like to start with a quotation. We have today, according to Neil Walker, a tendency to 'view and interpret the new configurations ... through an old lens'.[1] What Walker is referring to here is global law. However, the same can be said to apply to the police, policing, etc in today's world. This article goes in search of this new 'lens'.

Let us start with some common sense statements and relate them to the above-mentioned 'new configurations':

I. 'Nation states are modelled around vertical thinking'.

However, here there have been changes, 'new configurations'.

II. 'For the states, this is reflected internally by a diffusion of power caused by phenomena such as privatization and deregulation; externally by phenomena such as globalization.'

III. 'For this and many other reasons, fighting crime is a matter of concern for many actors today, from the local to the international level. Locally, we even incorporate private actors, such as private security firms, and subnational actors, such as NGOs.' 'Fighting crime is something we do together today', as Jenny Fleming and Jennifer Wood express it.[2]

Now I would like to introduce a symbol for the old way of thinking, the 'old configuration'. It is a simple one, which I will call Hobbes' Pyramid.[3] Society was, in this idealization, a hierarchy with a sovereign at the top. The organization was, strictly speaking, 'top down'. I would say that we still live with the image of Hobbes' Pyramid deep down in our subconscious view of society. However, it is an image that does not fit in with the contemporary 'new configurations' at all, which is a problem.

* This chapter is based on a speech held at the Interests and Actors in European Police and Criminal Justice Cooperation – Legal and Practical Challenges conference in Uppsala in April 18–19, 2011.

** Professor of Jurisprudence, Faculty of Law, Uppsala University.

[1] N Walker, 'Beyond boundary disputes and basic grids: Mapping the global disorder of normative Orders' (2008) 6 *International Journal of Constitutional Law* nr 3–4.

[2] J Fleming and J Wood, *Fighting Crime Together: The Challenges of Policing and Security Networks* (Sydney, UNSW Press, 2006). The shift can also be described as a shift from a police-centric to a multi-agency or nodal approach.

[3] T Hobbes, Leviathan, www.forgottenbooks.org.

Fighting crime today, as said before, involves many actors. Hence, 'top down' is not the only direction within this organization. If we include the subnational level in the fight against crime, and take it seriously, with 'real' community policing, crime victim groups, volunteers, etc, then we have to add a 'bottom up' direction to the 'top down'. Internally, within nations, we also have a great deal of cooperation between agencies, so it is necessary to also add a 'horizontal' axis. However, the picture becomes even more complicated if we include regional and international cooperation. The horizontal axis subsequently becomes tiered. States are embedded in, constrained by and participate in other activities than the solely national ones, together with other actors at level from the regional to the international. States are members of international organizations and bound by treaties taking them in many directions.

Particularly in Europe it has been possible to discern a movement away from national central control. From the 1980s onwards, this movement has gone in three distinct directions: upwards, to institutions such as the United Nations (UN) and the European Union (EU); sideways, in connection with, for example, the creation of new government institutions; and downwards, in the form of decentralised power to regional, municipal/local and other levels. In addition, as mentioned above, privatisation and deregulation have created a new landscape and have contributed to a diffusion of power.

Another problem with the old configuration is the current shift in emphasis from 'who' to 'what'. This shift can be seen in healthcare, the care of the elderly, education, etc. 'Who' does things is no longer as important as before, instead 'what' is done is more important.

Regarding security management we see the same tendency. Take an airport, a residential area, or a commercial mall as an example, a variety of public and private bodies can be found collaborating with each other to manage 'security'. The 'network society' is a fact today in the Western world.[4]

A way to grasp these new situations, which allows Hobbes' Pyramid to be replaced, so to speak, will be discussed later on. I will call this modularity.[5] At this stage, I only wish to bring your attention to it. Later, I will return to how we intellectually can deal with 'top down', 'bottom up', and 'horizontal' in a tiered system,[6] without losing control of our thoughts.

If we look at the new configurations, we see that they create complex hierarchies. Not the simple Hobbes' Pyramid. Not the straightforward systems of checks and balances, chains of responsibility, matrix organizations, etc. The EU can be used to illustrate the situation. Here there has been an ongoing battle over how to describe the organization and how to set the agenda.[7] At one extreme

[4] Cf B Hoggenboom, 'Bring the police back in', *Stichting Maatschappij, Veilighet en Politie* Dordrech, 2009.

[5] B Wennström, *När summan är mer än delarna* (Uppsala, Iustus, 2007).

[6] Cf L Hooge and G Marks 'Unraveling the Central State, but How? Types of Multi-level Governance' (2003) 97:2 *American Political Science Review* 233.

[7] Cf M Kumm, 'Who is the Final Arbiter of Constitutionality in Europe?: Three Conceptions of the Relationship Between the German Federal Constitutional Court and the European Court of Justice' (1999) 36:2 *CML Rev* 351.

there is, for example, European statism, where the EU is viewed as a hierarchal system formed nearly as a Hobbesian Pyramid, with the Member States at the bottom and the EU at the top. At the opposite extreme, there is democratic statism, which can be illustrated by the German constitutional court. We do not need to go further into this matter here, but only keep the illustration at the back of our minds.

Into this world of new configurations, have come the Treaty of Lisbon and the new area of Justice, Freedom and Security. The latter has been accompanied by a quest not only for police cooperation, but also for coordination. You might say that partly through the Treaty, one side of the new institution is in place, the formal side. However, all those who are familiar with institutional theory are aware of the fact that also another side has to be in place for an institution to be formed.[8] This is the informal side, in other words the way we do, act, and think. For example, in the area of Justice, Freedom and Security, the Stockholm Programme can be regarded as the beginning of an answer: a good starting point, but not the whole answer.

There are two simple reasons as to why we should bother with theoretical perspectives on the new configurations. The first is for our own sake as lawyers, jurists, police men and prosecutors. The other is for the sake of the general public, the citizens. Let us start with ourselves.

New configurations create, as mentioned before, complex hierarchies. How complex hierarchies function is discussed at length throughout the sciences: in physics, chemistry, medicine.[9] The focus is on complex hierarchies in natural systems. I think that we can learn a great deal from these discussions where the main question is: How can complex hierarchies function and perform, when you in these tiered systems at the same time have 'top down', 'bottom up' and 'horizontal' processes? The answer is modularity. Complex hierarchies are tiered and modular.

A system may be complex in many different ways. We usually think of a system as complicated in one way or another. But the complexity may also lie in the fact that layers of order are, so to speak, stacked on top of each other. These layers may also be modular, ie, with each layer having its own special structure, separate from other 'layers' in the hierarchy.[10]

Therefore, that a hierarchy in a structure is modular means that the parts in the system display a high degree of independence, but also that influence over

[8] North defines an Institution as: 'the rules of the game of a society composed of the formal rules (constitutions, statute and common law, regulations) the informal constraints (norms, conventions and internally devised codes of conduct) and the enforcement characteristics of each. Together they define the way the game is played'. D North, The Process of Economic Change (1997) *UNU/WIDER Working papers* No 128 Helsingfors, cf E Ostrom, *Understanding Institutional Diversity* (Princeton 2005) and E Ostrom & A Hess, *Framework for Analyzing the Knowledge Commons in Understanding Knowledge as a Commons* (Cambridge MA, 2007).

[9] G Ellis 2005 *Physics and the Real World*, www.physicstoday.org/vol-58/iss-7/p49.shtml.

[10] B Wennström, *The Horizontal State – States and Agencies in a World Without Boundaries* (forthcoming Brill 2012), cf G Ellis, *Physics and the Real World*, www.physicstoday.org/resource/1/phtoad/v58/i7/p49_s1, visited on 27 May 2012.

one 'module' in a hierarchy may occur in different ways, in other words not only 'from the top to the bottom'. Independence in a modular system reveals itself in at least two directions, vertically and horizontally. So also does dependence. Modules in a complex hierarchy are semi-autonomous.[11]

How can we apply this to, for example, law, governance, and the police? If we take the European Union and ask the same question as earlier about natural complex hierarchies, the answer will be similar. How can a governance system like the EU actually function and perform? It consists of a multileveled, complex hierarchy where each of the 'modules' shows a high degree of independence. All three directions are present at the same time: 'top down', 'bottom up' and 'horizontal'. This bumblebee, the EU, should not actually be able to fly!

The reason here is the same as earlier: it is not despite, but because of, the independence of the 'modules' in the system that the EU functions and performs well. Neil MacCormick touched upon this at the beginning of the 1990s, when he spoke about 'interlocking systems' which recognize each other, but have different grounds for recognition. His view was that this perspective posed a profound challenge to our present understanding of how things function.[12]

This is also very important when we discuss police assistance, cooperation and coordination, which involve coordination in modular systems. In relation to coordination, the view in the international debate expressed by, for example Brooks and Grint, places an emphasis on the importance of 'shared vision based on shared aims and values' as opposed to old-fashioned command and control.[13] Rhodes, who discusses the difference between the bureaucratic state, contract state and the network state, stresses the importance of diplomacy and mutual adjustment in the latter, instead of, for example, rules and commands.[14]

But if we adopt such a new 'modular' view of networking and apply it to police cooperation in the EU, many new problems will also become visible. The problems exist today, but will become even more visible with, for example, the strategy of the Stockholm Programme. This will require that we rethink many things: responsibility, for example. Who is actually responsible and who should be held accountable in a complex hierarchal system when things go wrong? Other questions too, such as, are our legal systems capable of adequately handling the respect for privacy, or fundamental questions regarding the rule of law in the new forms of network structure which a 'modular' system creates?

The Treaty of Lisbon and the Stockholm Programme are therefore, as was mentioned before, a good start for the EU, but much has yet to be done on the

[11] Ibid.

[12] N MacCormick, *Questioning Sovereignty* (Press Oxford, Oxford University, 1999) 102. He says: 'This interlocking of legal systems, with mutual recognition of each other's validity, but with different grounds for that recognition, poses a profound challenge to our understanding of law and legal system'.

[13] S Brookes and K Grint, *The New Public Leadership Challenge* (Basingstoke Hampshire, Palgrave MacMillan, 2001).

[14] Rhodes, 'The Sour Laws of Network Governance' in J Fleming and J Wood (eds), *Fighting Crime Together* (Sydney, UNSW Press, 2006).

formal side of building a new institutional framework. On the more 'informal side' of institution-building there is even more to do.

Now, let us turn to the citizen perspective on the questions. Ian Loader, among others, has discussed the relationship between the police and the citizens in a new way.[15] He emphasizes the symbolic role of police and policing, the police as representing public good,[16] and the fragile relationship between the police, the state, and the nation, and how the police in many ways symbolize not only the state, with focus on repression, but also the nation. As mentioned earlier with regard to 'new configurations' and to changes, it is possible to speak of a fragmentation and pluralisation of policing. The police constitute, beside the repressive side,[17] an institution deeply associated with feelings of protection and security. There are powerful symbols for this in Britain, for example, there is the 'bobby on the beat'. In Sweden we love to joke about the old-fashioned 'fjärdingsman' and in Italy you have the endless tales about the 'carabinieri', and at the same time as we love to joke about them these 'icons' are part of our cultural heritage, not only symbols of the repression of states but also as strong symbols of security and safety in society.

However, many do not agree with Loader. Some say that we should not tone down the repressive side of the police. Others say we should not worry too much, that what we see today is the emergence of multiple authorities in society on a broad front, and that a great deal of good can come of replacing rigid hierarchies with mobility and freedom. After all the EU stands for 'mobility and freedom'. The major challenge, they say, is to communicate this in the right way within a broader sphere.

In spite of these arguments, I think that Loader is right in many ways, but also that communicating 'the new configurations' within a broader sphere is crucial. Police and policing are not only instrumental entities; they have symbolic functions connected with the nation's image and are associated with security. This is especially important given that today's society faces new threats originating from new criminal behaviour including riots in suburbs, new forms of threatening behaviour, cyber crimes, and the abuse of children in new, transnational ways for criminal purposes, etc. All of these may create a sense of increased public harm. One of the most important objectives for the European Union is to guarantee the security and safety of its citizens. If for example the new area of Justice, Freedom and Security do not live up to people's expectations and instead give an impression of pour performance, it will pose a danger for the whole of society.

[15] I Loader, 'Policing and the social: Questions of Symbolic Power' 48(1) *British Journal of Sociology* and I Loader & N Walker, 'Policing as a Public Good' (2001) 5 *Theoretical Criminology* 9, I Loader & N Walker, *Civilizing Security* (Cambridge, Cambridge University Press, 2007).

[16] Cf Geuss R, *Public Goods, Private Goods* (Princeton, 2001).

[17] The classical formulation of 'repression' comes from Weber, he states that the state is what it is in that it 'claims monopoly of the legitimate use of physical force'. M Weber, *From Max Weber: Essays in Sociology* (London, Routledge and Kegan Paul, 1948) 78. See also P Manning, *The Technology of Policing: Crime Mapping, Information Technology, and the Rationality of Crime Control* (New York, University Press, 2008).

To summarize, we need a 'new lens' to see the 'new configurations' mentioned here and to address the problems we discussed about police cooperation and coordination in the EU in the right way. We should also do it for the general public, and not jeopardize a project like the new area of Justice, Freedom and Security by ignoring, for example, the symbolic function of the police and policing and only strictly stick to the instrumental ones.

11
The Dynamic Evolution of EU Criminal Law

MARIA BERGSTRÖM

1. INTRODUCTION – THREE PERSPECTIVES FOR ANALYSIS

The aim of this chapter is to illustrate the dynamic evolution of EU law in the specific field of EU criminal law. By doing so, the chapter uses three examples, all typical for the evolution of EU law in general, but which have had significant impact upon the development of EU criminal law in particular. These examples are, first, the evolution of EU law as a set of compensatory measures, second, the choice of legal basis and creeping EU law competence, and third, exportation and legalisation of practices between pillars[1] and dimensions. Since these examples have implications on the transfer of powers, they might have specific implications on the wider European constitutional law perspective analysed in this volume. This chapter thus reconnects to the main theme of this volume, i.e. the broader European constitutional law implications on the rapid evolution of EU criminal law.

2. COMPENSATORY MEASURES – ADMINISTRATIVE AND CRIMINAL SANCTIONS IN EU AML REGULATIONS MOVING TOWARDS A LEGAL BASIS IN ARTICLE 83(1) TFEU

The emergence of the European Single Market required European rules on financial transactions. On 1 January 1993, a number of rules were adopted such as rules on the free movement of capital, and the liberalisation of the banking,

[1] This notion refers to the three pillar structure of the European Union introduced by the Maastricht Treaty, including the European Communities (first pillar), the Common Foreign and Security Policy (second pillar), and Police and Judicial Co-operation in Criminal Matters (third pillar). Although never specifically mentioned as pillars in the treaties, this structure was formally abandoned when the Lisbon Treaty entered into force on 1 December 2009. This development had started already before the Lisbon Treaty, while at the same time some distinguishing features still remain in the former pillars. For the purposes of this Chapter, the notion will therefore still be used.

insurance and investment services.[2] Preventive measures to ensure that an open and liberal financial market was not abused by criminal elements, such as the first Anti-money Laundering (AML) Directive (91/308/EEC), were also adopted. The elimination of national borders demanded compensatory measures to delimit financial cross-border crimes. Hence, the rationale for adopting the first AML Directive was clearly to compensate for the development of the internal market.

Hence, although the EU's fight against money laundering represents a new area of competence with an explicit legal basis in Article 83(1) TFEU introduced by the Lisbon Treaty, rules against money laundering have been on the EU agenda since 1991. The purpose of the first Directive was to prevent the freedom of capital movement and freedom to provide financial services to be used for money laundering purposes. That objective has since been expanded to also prevent organised crime and terrorist financing.

Accordingly, the second and third recital of the third AML Directive (2005/60/EC) states that:[3]

> The soundness, integrity and stability of credit and financial institutions and confidence in the financial system as a whole could be seriously jeopardised by the efforts of criminals and their associates either to disguise the origin of criminal proceeds or to channel lawful or unlawful money for terrorist purposes. In order to avoid Member States' adopting measures to protect their financial systems which could be inconsistent with the functioning of the internal market and with the prescriptions of the rule of law and Community public policy, Community action in this area is necessary.
>
> In order to facilitate their criminal activities, money launderers and terrorist financers could try to take advantage of the freedom of capital movements and the freedom to supply financial services which the integrated financial area entails, if certain coordinating measures are not adopted at Community level.

The first and second Directives were introduced to protect the financial system and other vulnerable activities as well as service providers from being exploited for money laundering and terrorism financing purposes. The rules cover, in other words, not only the proceeds of crime but also the collection of funds that can be used for terrorism purposes. Against this background it is perhaps less surprising that the third EU AML Directive is based on the legal bases for establishment and the internal market. Still, this choice of legal bases can be put into question.

The third AML Directive, as well as its predecessor, outlines a long list of actions to be considered an offence when committed intentionally (Article 1). The Directive applies to a large number of private players whose participation is no longer voluntary.[4] Recital 41 of the Directive states that the importance of

[2] S M Seyad, 'Legal Instruments to Combat Money Laundering in the EU Financial Market' (2002) 6(1) *Journal of Money Laundering Control* 66; S M Seyad, *European Community Law on the Free Movement of Capital and the EMU* (Stockholm, Norstedts, 1999).

[3] Directive 2005/60/EC of 26 October 2005 on the prevention of the use of the financial system for the purpose of money laundering and terrorist financing, OJ 2005, L 309/15.

[4] M Bergström, K Svedberg Helgesson, U Mörth, 'A New Role for For-profit Actors? The Case of Anti-Money Laundering and Risk Management' (2011) 5 *Journal of Common Market Studies* 1043.

combating money laundering and terrorist financing should lead Member States to establish effective, proportionate and dissuasive sanctions in national law for failure to respect the national provisions adopted pursuant to the Directive. Article 39(1) provides that Member States shall ensure that natural and legal persons covered by the Directive can be held liable for infringements of the national provisions adopted pursuant to the Directive. Again, the Directive states that sanctions must be effective, proportionate and dissuasive, which resembles, for instance, the wording of the environmental crime case further discussed in the next section.[5] The Directive further provides that sanctions should be provided for natural and legal persons. Hence, there are rules on liability also for legal persons (Articles 39(3) and 39(4)) and the Directive states that sanctions should be tailored to the operations of legal persons as they are often involved in complex money laundering or terrorist financing operations.

The use of administrative sanctions is governed by Article 39(2) which states:

> Without prejudice to the right of Member States to impose criminal penalties, Member States shall ensure, in conformity with their national law, that the appropriate administrative measures can be taken or administrative sanctions can be imposed against credit and financial institutions for infringements of the national provisions adopted pursuant to this Directive. Member States shall ensure that these measures or sanctions are effective, proportionate and dissuasive.

In sum, the requirements imposed in the form of customer due diligence, the reporting and record-keeping of statistics are extensive and cover a wide range of private players.[6] The sanctions required, however, are largely of an administrative rather than a criminal nature. A comparison between Articles 39(1) and 39(2) does not preclude Article 39(1) from including criminal sanctions should this be required in order to be effective, proportionate and dissuasive. Nevertheless, after Lisbon, this is no longer a problem, should the EU legislator decide to adopt minimum rules on criminal sanctions relying on the new legal basis for criminal law in Article 83(1) TFEU. Having said this, the proposal for the fourth AML Directive that like its predecessors closely follow the FATF update of the 40 recommendations,[7] at the same time as it adds a few

[5] The third AML Directive was published one and a half months after the ECJ's judgement in the environmental crimes case. Compare ground 48 of the European Court of Justice's judgement on 13 September 2005 in case C-176/03 Commission v Council, [2005] ECR I-7879: '... the last-mentioned finding does not prevent the Community legislature, when the application of effective, proportionate and dissuasive criminal penalties by the competent national authorities is an essential measure for combating serious environmental offences, from taking measures which relate to the criminal law of the Member States which it considers necessary in order to ensure that the rules which it lays down on environmental protection are fully effective.'

[6] See further E Herlin-Karnell, 'The EU's Anti-Money Laundering Agenda: Built on Risks? in C Eckes and T Konstadinides (eds) *Crime within the Area of Freedom, Security and Justice: A European Public Order* (Cambridge, Cambridge University Press, 2011) 76.

[7] For a more extensive analysis, see M Bergström, 'EU Anti-Money Laundering Regulation: Multilevel Cooperation of Public and Private Actors' in C Eckes and T Konstadinides (eds) *Crime within the Area of Freedom, Security and Justice: A European Public Order* (Cambridge, Cambridge University Press, 2011) 97.

EU-specific matters, is based on the main legal basis for the internal market, ie Article 114 TFEU.[8] The so far rather hypothetical question, which legal basis the first, second and third AML Directives respectively would have been based on had Article 83(1) TFEU been in place already at the time of their adoption, thus seems to have been answered. The proposal is expected to be adopted at the very earliest during 2013.

3. THE CHOICE OF LEGAL BASIS AND CREEPING EU COMPETENCE – TOWARDS INSERTION IN ARTICLE 83(2) TFEU?

The case law concerning the choice of legal basis represents an important constitutional development in EU law. The Court of Justice of the European Union (CJEU) has through its case law shaped and defined the boundaries between the European Union and its Member States and between the players involved in the law-making process of the European Union.[9]

Over time there have been relatively few legal battles over competencies most of which have concerned internal Union competence. Legal battles have been fought by the EU institutions over the right legal basis – and the right level of involvement in the legislative process by the various institutions. In the early 1990s environmental measures clearly fell within Union competence,[10] and prominent legal battles, including the challenging of two waste directives in the *Titanium Dioxide* and *Waste* cases, turned in particular around the competence of the European Parliament in relation to the internal market and the environmental legal basis respectively.[11]

A broad competence to regulate traditional spillover competencies such as environmental issues with reference to the internal market was not curtailed until 2000 when the CJEU in the *Tobacco Advertising* case ruled to the benefit of Germany in a competence battle concerning EU *vis-à-vis* Member State competence. A far-reaching Union-wide ban on tobacco advertising and sponsorship was annulled and implicitly held to be *ultra vires*.[12] Only limited health protection measures

[8] Proposal for a Directive of the European Parliament and of the Council on the prevention of the use of the financial system for the purpose of money laundering and terrorist financing, COM(2013)45 final.

[9] This subsection is developed from M Bergström, 'Spillover or Activist Leapfrogging? Criminal Competence and the Sensitiveness of the European Court of Justice', (2007) 2 *Sieps European Policy Analysis* (EPA 2007:2) at www.sieps.se. For a contribution on EU law competence in general see eg T Konstadinides, *Division of Powers in European Union Law: The Delimitation of Internal Competence between the EU and the Member States* (Kluwer Law International, 2009), and on EU Criminal Law competence in particular, see eg P Asp, *The Substantive Criminal Law Competence of the EU: Towards an Area of Freedom, Security & Justice*, Part 1 (Stockholm, Skrifter utgivna av Stockholms Universitet, 2012).

[10] Environmental issues were formally incorporated into the Treaty structure by the Single European Act 1987.

[11] Case C-300/89 *Commission v Council* [1991] ECR I-2867 *(Titanium Dioxide)*, and case C-155/91 *Commission v Council* [1993] ECR I-939 *(Waste)*. This analysis is developed in M Bergström (EPA 2007:2).

[12] Case C-376/98 *Germany v European Parliament and Council*, [2000] ECR I-8419 (*Tobacco*

could be approximated within the framework of the internal market legal basis. Measures taken under this provision had at least the potential to improve the functioning of the internal market. For the first time, an entire legislative measure was annulled *probably* due to a lack of competence. The court did not explicitly say so, but this is the most feasible reading of the case.

Although the CJEU did not clearly state that the Union lacked competence altogether to adopt the Directive, but simply that it could not validly be adopted on the chosen legal bases, this was an attempt to establish clear constitutional limits to Union competence as set out in the Treaty. As such, it was more about the scope of Union competence and less about the preference of a specific treaty article and a particular degree of institutional participation in the legislative process. Although the residual powers clause in Article 308 EC Treaty (now Article 352 TFEU) was not even mentioned there should be little doubt that this provision could not have been used as an alternative legal basis for the Advertising Directive. This is particularly so since the public health legal basis in Article 152 EC Treaty (now Article 168 TFEU) explicitly excluded harmonising measures on public health. In short, if this ruling implicitly limited the scope of Article 308 EC Treaty, it gave no further room for creeping competence, or *Kompetenz Kompetenz*, in this context.

Five years later, in another high profile judgement, the *Environmental Crimes* case,[13] the CJEU again annulled a legislative measure but this time since it *should have* been based on the first-pillar environmental competence, and not the third-pillar criminal competence. In stark contrast to the *Tobacco Advertising* case, this ruling broadened the scope of first-pillar competence. This was yet again a power struggle between institutions, but at the same time a competence case between the EU and its Member States. The *Environmental Crimes* case is framed in the terminology of ensuring the effectiveness of EU law, and thereby referring to the doctrine of *implied powers*. This is nothing new,[14] but since the result shapes the distribution of power in the Union, the case had far reaching consequences.

Although this case was reasoned as criminal competence being necessary to achieve effective environmental protection, the case ought not to be explained as a simple result of spillover[15] between sectors. Seemingly activist, a sensitiveness

Advertising). For some interesting developments concerning the scope of Article 95 EC Treaty and the Community discretion in relation to the words 'measures for the approximation', see Case C-66/04 *UK v European Parliament and Council* [2005] ECR I-10553, paragraph 45; Case C-217/04 *UK v European Parliament and Council* [2006] ECR I-3771, paragraph 43-44; and Case C-380/03 *Germany v European Parliament and Council* [2006] ECR I-11573, paragraphs 42-43.

[13] Case C-176/03 *Commission v Council* [2005] ECR I-7879 (*Environmental Crimes*).

[14] See for example Case 22/70 *Commission v Council* [1971] ECR 263.

[15] In political science literature, functional spillover refers to when integration in one industry/sector necessitates further integration in the same, as well as in other industries/sectors. Cultivated spillover assumes that the Commission will propel European integration. Finally, institutional or political spillover describes a phenomenon where changing demands and expectations on the part of interest groups, political parties and bureaucracies lead to an increase of new powers and tasks in a

reading of the case offers an alternative explanation to activist leapfrogging[16] between pillars.[17]

3.1 Background to the Case

According to the CJEU, a framework decision on the protection of the environment through the harmonisation of Member State criminal laws could not validly be made with reference to a legal basis in the third pillar. While this decision was being prepared, there was a similar proposal for a directive under the first pillar. Yet, the Commission was not able to obtain the necessary support for its adoption in the Council although the adoption of an environmental measure after the Maastricht Treaty only required a qualified majority. Instead, the then fifteen Member States adopted a framework decision with reference to police and judicial cooperation in criminal matters. Third-pillar measures are mainly intergovernmental in nature and the Framework Decision was adopted unanimously.

Hence, it was not very surprising that as many as 11 of the Member States supported the Council in the proceedings before the CJEU. The most obvious reason why a framework decision was chosen over a directive concerns the legal effects. Both measures need implementation by the Member States but a framework decision cannot yet have direct effect and cannot, before 1 December 2014, be invoked by individuals before national courts. Likewise, before 1 December 2014, the Commission or another Member State, do not have the power to bring infringement proceedings against a misbehaving Member State.[18] The two most effective tools to make EU law effective therefore previously only existed within the first pillar. According to the CJEU the measure in question was mainly about making EU environmental law effective and should therefore have been based on the environmental provision in Article 175 EC Treaty (now Article 192 TFEU). In accordance with a narrow legal analysis,[19] both the aim and the content of the relevant articles of the Framework Decision had the protection of the environment as their main purpose. Accordingly, the CJEU yet

central institutional structure. For a brief overview see eg K Howell, Developing Conceptualizations of Europeanization and European Integration: Mixing Methodologies. ESRC Seminar 1, 2002, at http://aei.pitt.edu/1720/01/Howell.pdf.

[16] This term has been borrowed from the English legal system when a certain (infrequently used) type of appeal from the High Courts directly to the House of Lords (instead of to the Court of Appeal) is commonly referred to as 'leapfrogging'. 'This (infrequently used) procedure exists because a trial judge's decision may be bound by previous Court of Appeal or House of Lords decisions and a point of law of general public importance may be involved.' P Nathanail, *Introduction to the Legal System in England* at http://www.lqm.co.uk/free/2002%20uk%20law.pdf. In this context, the term refers to a kind of leapfrogging between pillars in the three-pillar structure of the European Union.

[17] Argument put forward by M Bergström (EPA 2007: 2).

[18] Article 10, Protocol (No 36) on Transitional Provisions, TFEU.

[19] See further EPA 2007:2, 2 ff.

again annulled a legislative measure but this time since it *should have* been based on the first-pillar environmental competence, and not the third-pillar criminal competence. This was the first major case on the division of competence between the pillars. In this respect, it has been argued that it adopted a one-sided logic since it suggested that first-pillar action always took precedence over second or third-pillar action.[20]

Yet, instead of changing the balance between the principles of attributed and implied powers,[21] this and previous high profile cases can be explained using one guiding principle, namely the rule of 'sensitive interpretation', thus referring to the CJEU's sensitiveness towards the unison will of the Member States as pronounced in a treaty amendment, not necessarily yet in force.[22]

3.2 The Rule of Sensitive Interpretation

In 1986, environmental issues were formally incorporated into the treaty structure through the Single European Act, SEA. Already before then, environmental measures had been adopted with reference to the dual legal basis of the common market and the residual powers clause, what were then Articles 94 and 308 EC Treaty (now Articles 115 and 352 TFEU). To give an example, while the 1975 Directive on the quality of bathing water was adopted with reference to this dual legal basis, subsequent measures were based on the environmental provision in Article 175(1) EC Treaty (now Article 192(1) TFEU).[23] Clearly, this Directive was more about environmental concern than about the functioning of the common market.

In 1991, the CJEU ruled that the *Titanium Dioxide* Directive should have been based on the general internal market provision.[24] In March 1993, the court ruled in the *Waste* case that another waste directive could validly be based on the environmental provision.[25] Whereas the Maastricht Treaty, signed in February 1992, only entered into force on 1 November 1993, it might have had a decisive impact on the outcome of the second *Waste* case. In a sensitiveness reading, the concern about the importance of a representative assembly in *Titanium Dioxide* towards the preference of the general internal market provision was not equally acute in March 1993, although the Maastricht Treaty had not yet entered into force.[26]

[20] D Chalmers et al, *European Union Law*, (Cambridge Cambridge University Press, 2006), 141. Cf. also Case C-170/96 *Commission v Council* [1998] ECR I-2763 (*Airport Transport Visas*) in which case the Community did not have a certain competence vested outside the Community pillar.

[21] On this subject see H Goeters, 'New Criminal Law Developments in the Community Legal Order' (2007) 1u *Sieps working paper* (2007:1u), at www.sieps.se.

[22] Argument put forward by M Bergström in EPA 2007:2.

[23] Council Directive 76/160/EEC of 8 December 1975 concerning the quality of bathing water, OJ 1976, L 31/1.

[24] Case C-300/89 *Commission v Council* [1991] ECR I-2867 *(Titanium Dioxide)*.

[25] Case C-155/91 *Commission v Council* [1993] ECR I-939 *(Waste)*.

[26] M Bergström (EPA 2007:2).

By the Maastricht Treaty, the Public Health Title X was introduced. What might at a first glance have looked like an extension of Union competence into a new area was in fact quite the contrary. Limits to the Union's competence within this policy field were inserted directly in the Treaty excluding any harmonisation of the laws and regulations of the Member States.

In light of a *rule of sensitive interpretation*, the *Tobacco Advertising* case took due account of the treaty changes limiting the Union competence in the field of public health. As the court stated, harmonising measures with a high level of health protection can be adopted on other treaty provisions. Still, despite the CJEU's focus on the appropriateness of Article 95 EC Treaty (now Article 114 TFEU) as a legal basis, it is possible to argue that the outcome might have been different in the absence of the restrictive public health provision. This is particularly important given the number of equivalent provisions covering a number of other policy areas.[27]

If you read the *Tobacco Advertising* case from October 2000 in this new light, you might find an explanation for this unusually restrictive case. Seen as sensitiveness by the CJEU towards the unison will of the Member States, which was undoubtedly to restrict Union competence within the field of public health, the case seems less ambiguous. Further, whereas the 2001 Treaty of Nice did not offer solutions to the problem of the division of competencies, the 2004 Constitutional Treaty and the Lisbon Treaty had more to offer. It is highly relevant that they departed from the three-pillar structure and introduced qualified majority voting in the Council for acts on police and judicial cooperation.

The resemblance between the wording of the *Environmental Crimes* case and what was Article III-270(2) of the Constitutional Treaty and became Article 83(2) TFEU is striking. While the CJEU states:

> As a general rule, neither criminal law nor the rules of criminal procedure fall within the Community's competence…[this] does not prevent the Community legislature, when the application of effective, proportionate and dissuasive criminal penalties by the competent national authorities is an essential measure for combating serious environmental offences, from taking measures which relate to the criminal law of the Member States which it considers necessary in order to ensure that the rules which it lays down on environmental protection are fully effective.[28]

Article III-270(2) reads as follows:[29]

> If the approximation of criminal laws and regulations of the Member States proves essential to ensure the effective implementation of a Union policy in an area which has been subject to harmonisation measures, European framework laws [now in Article

[27] Identical or similar limits were introduced elsewhere in the EC Treaty: Article 13 on non-discrimination based on sex, racial or ethnic origin, religion or belief, disability, age or sexual orientation; Article 137 on social policy; Article 149 on education, Article 150 on vocational training policy; Article 151 on culture; and Article 129 on employment.

[28] Case C-176/03 *Environmental Crimes*, in footnote 9, paras 47-48.

[29] According to Article III-270(3) the Member States might follow a particular procedure if a proposed measure would affect fundamental aspects of its criminal justice system, cf Article 83(3) TFEU.

> 83(2) TFEU 'directives'] may establish minimum rules with regard to the definition of criminal offences and sanctions in the area concerned. …'

This comparison might further indicate the importance of the CJEU's ruling in relation to other policies besides environmental protection. According to the Constitutional Treaty, the approximation of Member State criminal laws would be possible for all Union policies that have been subject to harmonisation measures, and which embrace a whole series of policies besides environmental protection (cf. Article 83(2) TFEU). Further, whereas a third-pillar framework decision had previously been granted indirect effect by the CJEU,[30] this time, the content of a framework decision should validly have been adopted within the first pillar. Clearly, the long criticised three-pillar structure, which should have disappeared with the entry into force of the Constitutional Treaty, but which formally disappeared with the Lisbon Treaty, had already started to dissolve.

Arguably, since the CJEU did not determine the appropriate legal basis by reference to provisions not yet in force, but rather seems to have *interpreted* the current treaty provisions against the background of changes yet to enter into force, this analysis is neither contrary to the principle of legal certainty in general, nor the *Bovine Animals* case in particular.[31] In this case the CJEU ruled that:

> …Community measures must be adopted in accordance with the Treaty rules in force at the time of their adoption. It would be contrary to the principle of legal certainty if, in determining the legal basis of such a measure, account were to be taken of an alleged development in relations between institutions which does not yet find confirmation in any provisions of the Treaty currently in force or in the provisions of a treaty which has not yet entered into force.[32]

Likewise, the CJEU stated that whether or not the contested measure was correctly adopted: '… must be determined by reference to the EC Treaty as it was in force at the date on which the contested regulation was adopted.'[33] Clearly, this is nothing less than what is required by the principle of legal certainty.

If using a *rule of sensitive interpretation* of the relevant treaties, guidance could be found in treaty changes not necessarily yet in force. Firstly, in comparing *Titanium Dioxide* and *Waste*, the Maastricht Treaty played a role even before it entered into force. Secondly, in *Tobacco Advertising*, the CJEU took due notice of treaty changes limiting the competence of the Union legislature. Thirdly, in *Environmental Crimes*, the CJEU have been inspired by the Constitutional Treaty in spite of the constitutional crisis and its uncertain status.

Certainly, it could be argued that there are limits to the *rule of sensitive interpretation*. In particular the *Environmental Crimes* case raises doubts about the legitimacy of cases which seem to take into consideration changes not yet in force, and which perhaps never will enter into force. In this case the CJEU

[30] Case C-105/03 *Criminal Proceedings against Maria Pupino* [2005] ECR I-5285.
[31] Case C-269/97 *Commission v Council* [2000] ECR I-2257 (*Bovine Animals*).
[32] Ibid, para 45.
[33] Ibid, para 46.

was well aware of the distinct French and Dutch no-votes to the Constitutional Treaty. Still, the resemblance between the outcome of the *Environmental Crimes* case and Article III-270(2) of the Constitutional Treaty that later became Article 83(2) TFEU is too noticeable to ignore. Put in a different way, falling within the possible limits of interpretation of the current treaties a diverse outcome of the case would have been less likely in the absence of the Constitutional Treaty provision.

As a result, a different explanation of the case might be needed. Does it mean that the *Environmental Crimes* case lacks in legitimacy? Certainly, there is always a risk of loss of legitimacy were the court to transgress the vague and fluctuate line of possible interpretation in a Union based on the rule of law. Yet, indisputably important, such arguments go far beyond the assessment of this chapter. For the purposes of this section it is enough to identify some associated problems without necessarily presenting comprehensive solutions.

Yet, according to the author, the *Environmental Crimes* case can possibly be explained without legitimacy losses for the CJEU. It is possible to argue that the case stands firm within the possible interpretation of the relevant treaties with or without the entry into force of the Constitutional Treaty. As such, the case is simply codifying what was already valid law. As mentioned above, this explanation is not complete given the resemblance between the reasoning of the CJEU and Article III-270(2) of the Constitutional Treaty. Instead, in rephrasing harmonisation of criminal matters in the terms of making Community policy effective and thus further blurring the boundaries between the supranational and the intergovernmental features of the European Union, the case gave a hint of reasonable as well as possible future developments. Not surprisingly, harmonisation of criminal matters and the departure from the three pillar structure have been presented as key concerns irrespective of the fate of the Constitutional Treaty. Awaiting political clarification, the CJEU dealt with the extent of criminal law competence under the former Treaty in the *Ship Source Pollution* case. [34] Meanwhile, a legislative proposal on the approximation of sanctions in the field of intellectual property rights was delayed;[35] the proposed legal basis was changed to Article 83(2) TFEU, via a change to Article 118 TFEU, before the proposal was finally withdrawn by the Commission in September 2010.[36] Additional examples where the choice of legal basis has come under attack although perhaps so far to a lesser extent, is the proposed Directive on the fight against fraud to the Union's financial interest, where Article 325 TFEU has

[34] Case C-440/05 *Commission v Council* [2007] ECR-I 9097.

[35] Amended proposal for a Directive of the European Parliament and of the Council on criminal measures aimed at ensuring the enforcement of intellectual property rights. COM(2006)168 final (IPRED 2). See further House of Lords European Union Committee, The Criminal Law Competence of the EC: Follow-Up Report: Report with evidence, 11th Report of Session 2006–07, (13 March 2007), HL Paper 63, at pp 6–7. This is a follow-up report to, House of Lords European Union Committee, The Criminal Law Competence of the European Community: Report with evidence, 42nd Report of Session 2005-06, (28 July 2006), HL Paper 227.

[36] OJ 2010, C 252/7.

been proposed rather than Article 83 TFEU. Besides providing fewer safeguards, this legal basis hinders Denmark, Ireland and the United Kingdom from opting out, an option open under Article 83 TFEU.[37]

Still, to concentrate on provisions currently in force which are open for interpretation, while at the same time seeking data for interpretation in treaty provisions not necessarily yet in force, is something different to either spillover or activist leapfrogging between pillars. The rulings are more than a general spillover between sectors, but less than *ad hoc* activist rulings of the CJEU which in the long term would undermine the legitimacy of its precedents. Conclusively, such a *rule of sensitive interpretation* could help explain high profile cases on Union competencies including the notorious *Environmental Crimes* case from 2005, and possibly also offer guidance in predicting the outcome of future cases. With the entry into force of the Lisbon Treaty and Article 83(2) TFEU all remaining doubts are overruled concerning the EU having criminal law competence to ensure the effective implementation of a union policy in areas which have been subject to harmonising measures. This will, however, not stop the legal battles over the proper legal basis or the exact limits to its field of application. Whether the use of Article 83(2) TFEU for various reasons is a good development or not is an entirely different issue which is further discussed by Petter Asp and Anna Wetter in this volume.

4. THE EXPORTATION AND LEGALISATION OF PRACTICES BETWEEN PILLARS AND DIMENSIONS – AN EXAMPLE FROM THE EXTERNAL DIMENSION

In the Pupino case,[38] where the application of the loyalty principle, previously inserted in the EC Treaty and as such a first-pillar principle, was extended to a third-pillar framework decision is a good example of the exportation of practices between pillars. In this case the Framework Decision was granted indirect effect irrespective of the explicit prohibition in former Article 34 TEU to grant direct effect to such measures. Another example is the gradual exportation of the mutual recognition principle from internal market purposes to third-pillar situations where it is now the guiding principle for both criminal and civil law cooperation explicitly spelled out in the TFEU (Articles 82 and 81 respectively).[39]

Similarly, the need to respect fundamental rights implies, in particular, that proper attention is given to the protection and observance of the due process rights extending beyond the first pillar where they first appeared on the EU scene,

[37] Protocol (No 20) on the Position of Denmark, and Protocol (No 21) on the Position of the United Kingdom and Ireland in Respect of the Area of Freedom, Security and Justice, TFEU. See also P Asp, in footnote 9, 148.

[38] Case C-105/03 *Criminal Proceedings against Maria Pupino* [2005] ECR I-5285.

[39] See in particular V Mitsilegas, 'The Constitutional Implications of Mutual Recognition in Criminal Matters in the EU' (2006) 43 *Common Market Law Review* 1277.

towards EU criminal law, and now even to the area of internal and external security and more specifically to persons listed as suspected terrorists. Within the EU system, this has been given considerable attention with the rulings of the CJEU.[40] According to the Council, listing and de-listing procedures pursuant to Regulation 2580/2001 and Common Position 2001/931/CFSP have been improved in accordance with these rulings.[41] Accordingly, the EU judicature 'has carefully and respectfully motivated the Council to improve the legal rights of targeted parties by enforcing customary standard of human rights and the rule of law.'[42] Many academics have, however, generally remained more critical.[43] Nevertheless, after the changes by the Lisbon Treaty, fundamental rights protection has been improved by the now legally-binding effect of the Charter of Fundamental Rights and by allowing for judicial review even of lists of terrorist suspects 'adopted with a view to imposing economic sanctions.'[44]

The Lisbon Treaty introduced two new legal bases within this field. Article 75 TFEU permits the adoption of counter-terrorist sanctions on the freezing of all financial assets of natural or legal persons, groups or non-State entities that are suspected of supporting terrorism (cf. UNSC Resolution 1373), and Article 215(2) TFEU permits the adoption of restrictive measures against natural or legal persons, and groups or non-State entities, following the adoption of a decision in accordance with Chapter 2 of Title V TEU on specific provisions on the common and security policy (cf. UNSC Resolution 1267).[45]

These provisions thereby end the discussion on the legality of EU 'smart sanctions', since the adoption of restrictive measures against individuals is now permitted.[46] For the choice of legal basis after the entry into force of the Lisbon Treaty, see Case C-130/10 *European Parliament v Council*. In this judgement the Court held that:

> While admittedly the combating of terrorism and its financing may well be among the objectives of the area of freedom, security and justice, as they appear in Article 3(2)

[40] The CJEU thereby including its General Court. Considerable attention has been paid to this case law where almost every EU Law scholar, International Law scholars and many Penal Law and Procedural Law scholars have published at least one article on this subject, in particular following Joined Cases C-402/05 P & C-415/05 *P Kadi and Al Barakaat* [2008] ECR I-6351.

[41] Council of the European Union, Revised Strategy on Terrorist Financing, 17 July 2008, p 8.

[42] J Vestergaard, 'Terror Financing – Asset Freezing, Human Rights and the European Legal Order' (2011) 2 *New Journal of European Criminal Law* 175, 198.

[43] C C Murphy, *EU Counter-Terrorism Law: Pre-Emption and the Rule of Law* (Oxford, Hart Publishing, 2012). See also I Cameron, T Andersson, and K Norback, 'EU Blacklisting: The Renaissance of Imperial Power, but on a Global Scale' (2003) 14(2) *European Business Law Review* 111; I Cameron, *The European Convention of European Rights, Due Process and United Nations Security Council Counter-Terrorism Sanctions* (Strasbourg, Council of Europe, 2006); and P Eeckhout, 'Community Terrorism Listings, Fundamental Rights, and UN Security Council Resolutions. In Search of a New Fit' (2007) 3(2) *European Constitutional Law Review* 183.

[44] C Eckes, 'The Legal Framework of the European Union's Counter Terrorism Policies' in C Eckes and T Konstadinides (eds), *Crime within the Area of Freedom, Security and Justice: A European Public Order* (Cambridge, Cambridge University Press, 2011) 127, 158.

[45] For the choice of legal basis after the entry into force of the Lisbon Treaty, see Case C-130/10 *European Parliament v Council*, judgment of 19 July 2012, not yet reported.

[46] Cf eg Joined Cases C-402/05 P & C-415/05 P Kadi and Al Barakaat, [2008] ECR I-6351.

> TEU, the objective of combating international terrorism and its financing in order to preserve international peace and security corresponds, nevertheless, to the objectives of the Treaty provisions on external action by the Union.[47]

Accordingly, the Court dismissed the European Parliament's claim that the Al Qa'eda Regulation 1286/2009[48] should have been based on Article 75 TFEU instead of Article 215 TFEU.[49] As a result, Article 75 TFEU is the legal basis for a framework of legal methods, the objective being to include an internal EU dimension, whereas Article 215 is being used as the legal basis for EU external action. This distinction may well have important implications on the division of competencies within the Union.

5. CONCLUSIONS

This chapter illustrates the dynamic evolution of EU law in the specific field of EU criminal law. In this respect, the chapter has used three examples, all typical for the evolution of EU law in general, but which have had significant impact on the development of EU criminal law in particular. First, the evolution of EU law as a form of compensatory measures was discussed with examples taken from the AML regulatory regime. Here, it was established that the first AML Directives were introduced as preventive measures to ensure that an open and liberal financial market was not abused by criminal elements. Such a spillover competence is now codified and even extended where Article 83(1) TFEU provides the Union with a clear legal mandate to establish minimum rules concerning the definition of criminal offences and sanctions in the area of particular serious crime with a cross-border dimension. When carefully read, Article 83(1) may, however, have a limiting effect, since all the requirements stipulated in this Article need to be fulfilled when the Union legislature wishes to have recourse to this legal basis. It is still unclear, whether a subsequent AML Directive would best be based on the former or on the new legal basis, depending of course on the specific content of such a measure. The proposed fourth AML Directive based on the Internal Market legal basis in Article 114 is in this respect only one measure amongst many other within this broader field of financial crime.

Second, despite the introduction of the competence catalogue and the embracing of even more policy fields, most notably EU criminal law, under the ordinary legislative procedure, the legal basis battles and creeping EU law competence do not seem to have ended, but rather seem to have shifted focus towards the involvement of different legal bases such as the choice between

[47] Joined Cases C-402 and 415/05 *P Kadi & Al Barakaat*, para 61.

[48] Council Regulation (EU) 1286/2009 of 22 December 2009 amending Regulation (EC) 881/2002 imposing certain specific restrictive measures directed against certain persons and entities associated with Usama bin Laden, the Al-Qaida network and the Taliban, OJ 2009, L 346/42.

[49] See also C Eckes, 'EU Counter-Terrorist Sanctions against Individuals: Problems and Perils' (2012) 17(1) *European Foreign Affairs Review* 113, 120–22.

Article 83 TFEU and Article 325 TFEU, and in particular the embracing of EU external competence and the division of competence between the EU and its Member States concerning these issues, This is not surprising given the remaining special standing of this field in the Treaty. Here again, any legal analysis must embrace a reading of the Treaty in context, taking into account all the relevant provisions in the Treaty thus even going beyond the most obvious interpretation if read in isolation. The CJEU hereby seems to protect the limitation of the specific powers granted under the still existing second pillar.

Thirdly, some examples are provided concerning the exportation and legalisation of practices between pillars and dimensions. In this respect, it must be added that the previous explicit limit to the direct effect of third-pillar measures has now been removed from the Treaty and any remaining third-pillar measure will probably be able to have direct effect when the transition period in Article 10 of Protocol 36 will cease to have effect on 1 December 2014.[50] On that date, the Commission will have powers under Article 258 TFEU also concerning any remaining acts in the field of police and judicial cooperation in criminal measures and the CJEU will have full jurisdiction concerning such measures. Needless to say, any established limits to the principles of direct and indirect effect will of course remain in relation to specific EU criminal law measures adopted within this fast-evolving policy area. The exact extent of these principles to such measures along with the applicability and extent of fundamental rights under the ECHR and the Charter will continue to puzzle us until a clear legal authority has been granted by the CJEU,[51] probably in continuous dialogue with the Constitutional courts and Supreme Courts of the Member States,[52] within our without the procedural boundaries of the preliminary reference procedure. To conclude, this chapter provides some evidence of a limiting of EU law principles along with the more traditional view of EU law propelled by integrationist goals and rationale as emphasised initially in this chapter. Not surprisingly, the CJEU will be a powerful force in setting exact limits for all these issues as well as the future development of this field, procedural safeguards, and other important principles necessary to uphold the rule of law.

[50] The views on this issue abound and are doubting, but see K Lenaerts, 'The Contribution of the European Court of Justice to the Area of Freedom, Security and Justice' (2010) 59 *ECLQ* 255.

[51] For an illustration of the inherent problems and challenges, see e.g. S Iglesias Sánchez, 'The Court and the Charter; The Impact of the Entry into Force of the Lisbon Treaty on the ECJ's Approach to Fundamental Rights' (2012) 49 *CML Rev* 1565.

[52] See for example Case C-617/10, *Åklagaren v Hans Åkerberg Fransson*, Judgement of 26 Feb 2013, unpubl, available at curia.europa.eu; Case BVerfG, 1 BvR 1215/07, judgement of 24 April 2013, where the Bundesverfassungsgericht gave a judgement concerning the establishment of a Counter-Terrorism Database in Germany. In this case, the German Constitutional Court took the opportunity to comment upon the *Åkerberg Fransson* case. Another recent example is the judgement by the Swedish Supreme court of 11 June 2013 in case B 4946-12, where the Supreme Court dealt with another case concerning the ne bis in idem principle that dramatically changed the legal situation in Sweden.

Index

www.ingramcontent.com/pod-product-compliance
Ingram Content Group UK Ltd.
Pitfield, Milton Keynes, MK11 3LW, UK
UKHW020844290926
15470UKWH00004B/1539

9 781849 463508